ALSO BY FRANCES MCCULLOUGH AND BARBARA WITT

Great Food Without Fuss

Great Feasts Without Fuss

Great Feasts Without Fuss

Frances McCullough and Barbara Witt

VILLARD
New York

Library of Congress Cataloging-in-Publication Data

McCullough, Frances M.
Great feasts without fuss / Frances McCullough and Barbara Witt.
p.   cm.
Includes index.
ISBN 0-679-43139-X
I. Entertaining.   2. Cookery, International.   3. Menus.   I. Witt, Barbara.   II. Title.
TX731.M393   1995
642'.4—dc20   95-11615

Manufactured in the United States of America on acid-free paper
2   4   6   8   9   7   5   3
First Edition

Book design by Deborah Kerner

Contents

Introduction • *xiii*

Drew Allen • *3*

Radishes, Pickled Chiles, and Fresh Creamy Cheese with a Sweet
and Spicy Sauce • Shrimp Sautéed in Hoja Santa Sauce •
Rice with Corn Kernels • Warm Tortillas • Sliced Tomatoes with Lime •
Sweet Potato and Fresh Pineapple Pudding

Paul Bartolotta • *8*

Pinzimonio • Baked Fish Fillets with Clams, Leeks, and Yukon Gold Potatoes •
Mixed Green Salad • Baked Peaches Stuffed with Almonds, Chocolate, and
Brandied Raisins

Paul Bertolli • *12*

Picholine Olives and Toasted Almonds • Baked Lingcod with Leeks, Fennel,
and Peppers • Grilled Lamb Chops • Slow-Cooked Tomatoes • Buttermilk
Mashed Potatoes • Red Leaf and Butter Lettuce Salad Served
with Aged Goat Cheese • Raspberry Tart

Jo Bettoja • *19*

Toti's Pennette with Zucchini • Roast Pork with Lemons and Grapes •
Watercress Salad with Chilled Gorgonzola • Oranges with Grand Marnier •
Dark Chocolate Brownies

Jennifer Brennan • *26*

Ginger Shrimp Salad • Pork Avarua • Hot Sesame Green Beans with Sweet
Red Pepper • Bulgur Pilaf with Cashews and Golden Raisins •
Midori Melon Sorbet and Cookies

Jeffrey Buben · 35

Chilled Cucumber Soup · Grilled Salmon Steaks au Poivre · Red Swiss Chard and Dilled New Potatoes · Field Greens Salad with Vidalia Onion Vinaigrette · Lemon Chess Pie with Fresh Berries and Raspberry Sauce

Bright Ideas: Hors d'Oeuvres · 43

Hugh Carpenter · 45

Southwest Caesar Salad with Chile Croutons · Grilled Chinois Rack of Lamb · Thai Rice Pilaf · Kahlúa Chocolate Decadence

Susan Feniger and Mary Sue Milliken · 53

Susan's Menu

Edamame (Boiled Soybeans) · Red Cabbage and Sprouts with Sesame Dressing · Spaghetti with Feta, Fresh Tomato, Spinach, and Kalamata Olives · Steamed Artichokes with Lime and Cracked Pepper Mayonnaise · Date Bars or Chocolate Chip Cookies with Yogi Tea

Mary Sue's Menu

Lime and Chile Roasted Pepitas and Cashews · Crispy-Bottomed Basmati Rice with Lamb and Tomato · Yellow Split Pea Puree with Garlic and Basil · Red and Green Romaine Salad with Lemon Vinaigrette · Orange Pistachio Cake

Carol Field · 64

Antipasto · Penne with Bitter Greens, Mozzarella, and Toasted Walnuts · Salad of Mixed Lettuces · Vanilla Ice Cream with Crumbled Panforte

Edmond Foltzenlogel · 70

Cervelat and Provençal Olives · Herbed Fresh Cheese with Radishes · Romaine Lettuce with Sherry Vinaigrette, Mint, and Garlic Croustades · Couscous Chez Edmond · Strawberries and Oranges with Red Wine Sauce

Bright Ideas: Starters · 78

Suzanne Hamlin · 80

Cold Sesame Noodles · Baked Chicken in a Salt Crust with Soy-Ginger Dipping Sauce · Perfect Chinese Rice · Stir-Fried Broccoli · The Frozen Mango and Fortune Cookies · Green Tea

Reed Hearon · 87

Mixtec Guacamole with Tortilla Chips · Spicy Grilled Yucatán Chicken with Caramelized Onions · Grilled Corn with Lime and Chiles · Mexican Sundaes with Cajeta or Tropical Fruit Salsa

Jean-Marie Josselin · 93

Sesame Soba Noodles with Tempura Vegetables · Seared Swordfish with a Tomato and Kalamata Vinaigrette · Ginger Curried Muffins · Sliced Peaches with Fruited Red Wine

Diana Kennedy · 100

Fish Shehadi with Tahini and Pecans · Brown and Wild Rice Pilaf · Sautéed Spinach with Chiles · Asian Watercress Salad · Sliced Oranges with Almond Brittle

Johanne Killeen and George Germon · 107

White Peaches in White Wine · Red Creamer Potatoes with Anchovies · Spaghettini with Littleneck Clams *Macchiato* · Spicy Braised Lobster · Corn on the Cob · Soused Peaches with Mascarpone Amaretti

Deborah Madison · 114

Baked Ricotta and Goat Cheese with Thyme · Olives with Roasted Cumin and Paprika · Fennel Crudités with Sea Salt · Saffron Noodle Cake · Herb Salad with Roasted Walnuts · Caramelized Pineapple with Vanilla Ice Cream

CONTENTS

Carlo Middione · 121

Veal Carpaccio on Crostini with Lemon Mascarpone · Salmon with Red Cabbage Sautéed with Orange and Capers · Poached Pears Filled with Apricots and Hazelnuts on Raspberry Sauce

Bright Ideas: Pick Up a Chicken · 128

Michael Min Khin · 129

Spicy Fish Steamed in Lettuce Parcels · Burmese Chicken Curry with Noodles · Tropical Fruit and Ginger Crisps

Nancy Oakes and Bruce Aidells · 135

Southwest Turkey and Sausage Pie · Jícama, Red Onion, and Orange Salad · Nancy's Coconut Pudding with Lime

Patrick O'Connell · 141

Soft-Shell Crabs with Toasted Hazelnuts · Garden Tomato Salad · Grilled Cornish Hens with Blueberries and Wild Mushrooms · Ginger Ice Cream with Rhubarb Sauce

Michael Roberts · 151

Provençal Roasted Eggplant Vinaigrette · Bow Tie Pasta with Scallops, Bacon, and Peas · Mixed Green Salad · Blueberries with Cajeta

Hubert Sandot · 156

Sautéed Oysters with Cumin and Mushrooms · Beef Tenderloin Aiguillette · Grilled Potatoes with Thyme · Soft Lettuce Salad with Balsamic Vinaigrette · Chocolate Hazelnut Mousse

Norma Shirley · 163

Red Pea Bisque Flambé · Johnnycakes · Shrimp Jamaica · Fluffy Mashed Sweet Potatoes · Sugar Snap Peas and Green Beans · Green Salad with Cucumber Ribbons · Piña Colada Mousse · Jamaican Blue Mountain Coffee

Martha Rose Shulman · *170*

Olives, Tapenade on Red Pepper Squares, Radishes, and Parmesan Curls ·
Fusilli with Red and Yellow Tomato Vinaigrette · Arugula and Mushroom Salad
with Parmesan · Sourdough Baguettes · Baked Pears with
Ginger Preserves and Biscotti

David Tanis · *175*

Tapas · Vegetable Paella · Assorted Sweets

John Taylor · *181*

Cuban Roast Pork with Lime · Black Beans and Rice · Mango Relish ·
Warm Tortillas · Minted Strawberry and Champagne Sorbet

Jan Weimer · *187*

Chilled Tomato and Red Pepper Soup with Basil and Shrimp · Baked Salmon
with Spinach and Leeks · Lemon Rice with Dill · Fig Kebabs with
Raspberry Cabernet Sundaes

Eileen Weinberg · *194*

Haricots Verts on Baby Greens with Shaved Goat Cheese · Smoked Duck with
Lavender and Lime Honey Glaze · Roasted Sweet Potatoes with Red Onion ·
Raspberry Shortcake

Patricia Wells · *200*

Mixed French Olives, Country Sourdough Bread, and Salami · Grilled Quail with
Sherry-Shallot Vinaigrette · Provençal Couscous Salad · Mixed Green Salad ·
French Cheese Board: Fresh and Aged Chèvre, Roquefort, and Gruyère ·
Modeste: A Modest Berry Dessert

Faith Heller Willinger · 207

Fettunta with Caviar · Spaghetti alla Carrettiera · Tonno di Pollo · White Beans with Garlic, Oregano, and Tomato · Minimalist Cheesecake

Paula Wolfert · 214

Pulled Parsley Salad with Black Olives and Pecorino · Fillet of White Fish with Mixed Nuts and Raisins · Fried Rice with Nutmeg · Mixed Green Salad · Sicilian Ricotta Ice Cream

Diane Rossen Worthington · 221

Smoked Trout Mousse · Beef Stew with Sun-Dried Tomatoes and Butternut Squash · Salad of Winter Greens · Corn Muffins · Apple Crisp with Dried Fruit
Bright Ideas: Desserts · 228

Some Great Single Dishes · 231

Lemon Chicken Black Bean Salad with Corn (Bruce Aidells)
Lentil Soup with Prosciutto (Michel Richard)
Butternut Squash Soup with Crayfish (Charles Dale)
Warm Bird Salad with Wild Mushrooms and Crisp Potatoes (Catherine Brandel)
Fresh Mint Chutney (Michelle Mutrux)
Roasted Habañero Salsa (Reed Hearon)
New Orleans Shrimp Rémoulade on Fried Green Tomatoes (JoAnn Clevenger)
Pickapeppa Chicken (Norma Shirley)
Tuna and Fennel Seeds (Carlo Middione)
Potatoes Baked in Sea Salt (Paula Wolfert)
Gingerbread (Diana Kennedy)
Syrian Nutmeg Cake (Laurie Colwin)
Giant Almond Cookie (Jo Bettoja)
Simple Wines for Simple Meals · 247

Index · 251

INTRODUCTION

We feel a little sheepish about offering a no-fuss cookbook for company since fussing over friends is a large part of what having company is all about. Beyond the conviviality that comes with spending an evening with friends is the gift of treating them at your table and pleasuring them in other ambient ways like setting an appealing table and selecting a good wine. Sure there's a little fuss involved—but it measures up to the kind of thoughtfulness we care about.

What we all seem to need—and the reason we decided to put this book together—is a fresh look at entertaining. We hear over and over from our own friends and readers that they just can't seem to find the time to put together a dinner party. And, of course, we're not immune ourselves. So we've thought a lot about the problem and come up with some solutions that work for us.

Our first step was to ask some chefs and food writers we particularly admire—the culinary chroniclers of our times—how they themselves entertain within the same time constraints. Their answers were interesting. Understandably, some chefs never want to cook at home. Some chef-proprietors just pack up dinner from their restaurants. Others love to lavish the same treatment on their friends as they do on their clientele and have trouble *not* fussing. Food writers are interminably testing and experimenting, and sometimes their friends are the eager guinea pigs. Since many of them are now writing about lighter fare, they're creating naturally easier menus. But within each cook's frame of reference, they've figured out ways to do it more simply. Here are their menus, which exemplify their personal entertaining styles.

Almost without exception, the menus in this book are very simple, sometimes practically instant. *Simple* means easy to prepare as well as partially or totally do-ahead. It also means using the best-quality ingredients. There are a few menus or dishes that are a bit more complex to prepare, but they were so delicious and interesting we thought some readers might find them worth the extra time. All of the menus are coded to denote which dishes can be done ahead—which means earlier in the day. If whole recipes or parts of recipes can be done even earlier, the recipe will tell you.

Simplifying the food doesn't mean it can't be special. The menus of Michael Roberts, Carol Field, and Diana Kennedy, among others, typify the kind of imagination and invention you can use to override the fuss. Or you can rely on the freshest of ingredients to carry a simple meal such as those from Drew Allen or Paul Bertolli. No side dish is more gorgeous and delicious than a platter of red and yellow garden tomatoes topped with thin red onion rings, ribbons of basil, and a drizzle of olive oil. You could choose something exotic like Michael Min Khin's menu or Jennifer Brennan's—or rely on something that's a treat in itself like caviar or truffles on pasta, foie gras on a grilled veal chop, the braised lobster in Killeen and Germon's menu, or the beef filet with shallots of Hubert Sandot.

Of course, anything homemade is a real treat as fewer of us have time to cook up a storm. Try Laurie Colwin's Syrian Nutmeg Cake or Jeffrey Buben's Lemon Chess Pie or Jean-Marie Josselin's Ginger Curried Muffins or Norma Shirley's Johnnycakes. Think about justifiable cheating with dishes that are half-homemade, like sundaes with a homemade sauce (Reed Hearon's Tropical Fruit Salsa, Patrick O'Connell's Rhubarb Sauce, or Jan Weimer's Raspberry Cabernet Sauce) or take-out food that's dressed up, like rotisserie chicken supplemented with something you made yourself such as an herb pesto, fresh salsa, chutney, or wild mushroom ragout.

There are vegetarian meals—from Carol Field, Deborah Madison, and Susan Feniger—low-fat meals by Suzanne Hamlin and Jan Weimer, meals that can be made almost entirely ahead (John Taylor, Patricia Wells, Faith Willinger, and Martha Rose Shulman) or entirely ahead (Nancy Oakes and Bruce Aidells, Diane Worthington), and homey reach-across-the-table meals like Paul Bartolotta's Italian family-style menu. They come from Jamaica, Hawaii, Asia, Mexico, the American South, the Southwest, and the heartland, Polynesia, Provence, and the home of no-fuss food: Italy.

Of course you can mix and match, and we encourage you to do that; there are boxes of these menus scattered through the book. Also be sure to see the chapter of single dishes for alternatives. With all the resources in this book you can put together interesting hybrids to solve particular problems: spur-of-the-moment, make-ahead, buffet, room-temperature, special occasions, etc.

Casual and informal works particularly well when there's a plenitude of do-ahead elements on the table. We very much like the style of David Tanis's spread of tapas before an easy paella and Paula Wolfert's Mediterranean way of serving many tasty side dishes *(meze)* as appetizers and then adding in the main dish when the time comes. The same concept works for dessert: a lot of little purchased or instantly prepared tidbits with a good dessert wine provide a feast of treats (see "Bright Ideas" box on dessert, page 228, and "Simple Wines for Simple Meals" on page 247). And of course you can ransack the "Bright Ideas" boxes to make up a whole menu of quick dishes.

Once you've decided on the menu, what about organizing the rest? Obviously the only solution is to get a jump on it and do as much as you can ahead. Part of that is bringing to consciousness all the little elements you're going to have to deal with. In case you hate making lists, we've done one for you.

• When you invite your guests, ask them if there's anything they can't eat or drink. Recipes in this book are calculated for six, which is an ideal number for the cooking, seating, and serving of dinner and perfect for conversation. But think about food critic James Villas's contention that an odd number can be more interesting.

• Plan the menu—think about what's in season and at its peak of flavor. Check the index to see where those elements appear in menus. Read through the recipes to see what you can do ahead; in some cases there are parts of menus and recipes that can be done days beforehand. Do-ahead dishes are starred on the menus.

• Get the housecleaning out of the way the weekend before. Sort out and consolidate things in your refrigerator so you can find room for the groceries. Clean the outdoor grill if you're going to use it. Sharpen the knives. Wash the wineglasses; plan on two glasses per person.

• Make the shopping lists: one for perishables, one for nonperishables, one for other items like candles, cocktail napkins, flowers, liquor, setups, and nonalcoholic drinks. Start shopping for the nonperishables so you don't have to haul everything in at once.

• Read through the recipes again and walk yourself through the preparation and serving—it's a great way to remember to dig out the necessary equipment and shelf ingredients. Make a cooking schedule.

• A day ahead:

        If there will be flowers, arrange them.

        Start stockpiling ice.

        Set up the bar.

        Refrigerate the white wine and other beverages.

        Set the table.

        Set out the serving dishes and implements.

        Buy the perishables.

        Clean and dry the salad greens if you're serving salad.

        Set up the coffee-serving elements.

• On the day itself: get out your prep schedule and do as much as you can as early as you can—allowing yourself a good hour off before the guests arrive. No doubt something will get screwed up at the last minute, but if it does, forget about it and remember that the whole point of all this is for everyone to relax and enjoy the evening—including you.

Please note:

- Unless otherwise specified, all menus serve 6.
- Do-ahead dishes are starred on the menus.

Great Feasts Without Fuss

Drew Allen

San Antonio, Texas
and Mexico City

*Radishes, Pickled Chiles, and Fresh Creamy
Cheese with a Sweet and Spicy Sauce

Shrimp Sautéed in Hoja Santa Sauce

Rice with Corn Kernels

Warm Tortillas

Sliced Tomatoes with Lime

*Sweet Potato and Fresh Pineapple Pudding

Wine:
White Rhône

*D*rew Allen seems much more like a mild-mannered scholar than the co-owner of the mellow, slightly funky Liberty Bar, a nineteenth-century San Antonio establishment where the walls lean and the floor slopes off at an alarming angle and the patrons are definitely expecting a good time. The eclectic menu is a mix of classic Mexican food, Mediterranean ideas, and impeccable versions of good old American cooking, dishes like pot roast and lime chess pie. Of course sometimes the lines cross and you can find some very interesting things on the Liberty Bar menus, such as fettuccine with goat cheese and tomatillo sauce. And we can't remember seeing fried salsify on anyone else's menu. Or geranium cream with blackberry sauce for that matter.

In fact Drew *is* something of a scholar, at least of traditional Mexican cuisine. That food is of course very complicated, but when he's cooking at home, which is upstairs at The Liberty, or at his Mexico City apartment, Drew is always drawn to the simplest possible dishes, things like chicken breast grilled inside a hoja santa leaf (a giant Mexican herb with a strongly anisey tarragon taste that's sometimes available in the Southwest). And you can't get much simpler than perfect ripe tomatoes, sliced and sprinkled with fresh lime juice for a bright new taste.

This menu is one he served friends on his apartment terrace in the center of Mexico City. The rarely available hoja santa is a key ingredient here, but Drew has figured out a way of substituting that works very well. The shrimps are absolutely delicious, with a fresh zesty sauce that's just a little hot. Serve warm tortillas with this meal.

With drinks, Drew recommends Tio Pepe sherry and Hornitos Tequila, Sauza. With dinner he serves a white Rhône wine or Mexican beer or fresh limeade for those who prefer it.

Fresh Creamy Cheese with a Sweet and Spicy Sauce

½ pound fresh cream cheese at room temperature
½ pound soft fresh goat cheese at room temperature
1 garlic clove, pressed
½ cup dark brown sugar (Mexican piloncillo, if available)

1 tablespoon minced chipotle chiles (canned are fine—puree them in a food processor)
about 1 tablespoon heavy cream

whole wheat toast points

Mix the cheeses together and combine with the garlic. In a large nonstick skillet over low heat, melt the brown sugar slowly and add the pureed chiles. Cook about 10 minutes and add just enough cream to keep it from caramelizing. Mound the cheese on a serving plate and surround it with the toast points. Pour the warm sauce over the cheese and serve.

- *By fresh cream cheese, Drew means the kind you get at a cheese shop or a bagel store, not the preservative-enhanced guar-gum-thickened product at the supermarket.*

Shrimp Sautéed in Hoja Santa Sauce

*M*ake the sauce just before you start the shrimp since this dish is ready in just a few minutes and you don't want the shrimp to wait.

Sauce:

½ cup chopped hoja santa leaves or
    equal parts fresh basil and tarragon

¼ cup cilantro leaves

2 serrano chiles

2 garlic cloves

1 tablespoon chopped white onion

¼ cup fresh lime juice, about 2 limes

¼ cup olive oil

1 teaspoon salt

¼ cup water

Shrimp:

2 pounds large shrimps, peeled and
    deveined

1 tablespoon olive oil

Blend the sauce ingredients in a food processor. Sauté the shrimp in the oil in 1 or 2 large skillets over medium-high heat until barely done, no more than 5 minutes. Pour the sauce over the shrimp and cook until the sauce is hot.

Rice with Corn Kernels

1 tablespoon olive oil

2 cups white rice

1 cup fresh or defrosted frozen corn
    kernels

1 quart boiling water

1 teaspoon salt

In a large saucepan, heat the olive oil over medium heat, add the rice and corn, and cook until the rice is almost translucent. Pour the boiling water over, add the salt, reduce the heat to low, cover, and cook for 20 minutes. Fluff the mixture with a fork before serving.

- *If you'd like the corn a little crunchier, sauté it. When the rice is cooked, fold in the corn.*

∞

Sweet Potato and Fresh Pineapple Pudding

*T*his is an old Mexican home-cooking dish, one you won't see in contemporary Mexican cookbooks. In Mexico it's made with *camote,* a tuberous starchy root that's a cousin to our sweet potato. This dessert is unusual, at least to our taste, and interesting. It's also incredibly easy to make. If you think your guests have unadventurous palates, serve a tropical fruit salad for dessert instead, with a plate of macaroons.

3 cups mashed baked sweet potato, about 3 large

3 cups finely chopped fresh ripe pineapple with the juice

2 teaspoons ground cinnamon

¼ cup dark rum

raw (turbinado) or light brown sugar to taste

Mix everything together and put it in a serving bowl. Allow at least several hours for the flavors to develop. Serve at room temperature.

PAUL BARTOLOTTA

Chicago

Illinois

*Pinzimonio

The classic Italian crudité with seasoned olive oil for dipping

Baked Fish Fillets with Clams, Leeks, and Yukon Gold Potatoes

Mixed Green Salad

*Baked Peaches Stuffed with Almonds, Chocolate, and Brandied Raisins

Wine:

1991 Cervaro della Sala (Antinori)

At thirty-one Paul Bartolotta seems too young to have done all the things he's done in his life to date: spent seven years learning how to cook in Italy, been the founding chef at New York's San Domenico (his cooking earned the restaurant three stars), and established a whole new highly praised restaurant in Chicago, Spiaggia. To top it all off, in 1994 he won the James Beard Award for Best Midwest Chef.

When he first went to Italy, which was supposed to be for a six-month apprenticeship, Paul knew only two words in Italian: cappuccino and ciao. But somehow this Italian-American couldn't say ciao to Italy, and his initial venture turned out to be just the beginning of a passionate study of Italian cooking that has taken him all over the country. What he learned is the heart and soul of Italian food, the simple essence of it—from famous chefs, from home cooks, from fishermen bringing in the catch.

Not for Paul the crisp vegetables presented on virtually every American restaurant plate; he wants his vegetables overcooked in the classical Italian style. And he won't have just one olive oil in the kitchen; there are at least six and sometimes as many as thirteen. Although he's fanatic about the details, his food is almost without exception simple. This menu is a good example—it's a rustic, deeply satisfying meal meant to be shared around a convivial table. The first course isn't cooked at all, and the main dish goes like the wind once the garlic is cooked, so be sure to have everything ready to go, as though you were stir-frying. Dessert can be made a day ahead.

Pinzimonio

*T*his traditional beginning to an Italian meal requires only perfect vegetables and fine olive oil. Choose all or some of the following: scallions, fennel, radishes with their leaves, chunks of Belgian endive, chunks of radicchio, sweet red pepper pieces, little sweet carrots, raw artichoke heart pieces brushed with lemon juice, and baby turnips. Clean and trim the vegetables and just before serving arrange them on top of cracked ice in a wide bowl. For dipping them, have either individual bowls or one large bowl of very good olive oil—Paul likes Trevi from Tuscany or Monini from Umbria. Add salt and pepper to taste and possibly a little vinegar.

Baked Fish Fillets with Clams, Leeks, and Yukon Gold Potatoes

*P*aul makes this dish with John Dory, which isn't readily available outside restaurants. Use it if you can find it, but grouper makes a good substitute.

salt

6 small fillets of John Dory or grouper

6 tablespoons olive oil

3 large garlic cloves, sliced

pinch of hot red pepper flakes

36 littleneck clams, scrubbed

3 medium leeks, center yellow part only, cut into strips

3 bay leaves

3 large yellow potatoes, such as Yukon Gold, cooked and cubed

1½ cups dry white wine

additional olive oil to drizzle over the soup plates

minced parsley for garnish

country bread toasts rubbed with a garlic clove

Preheat the oven to 400°F. Salt the fish fillets and set aside. In 2 large ovenproof skillets or 1 large roasting pan over 2 burners, heat the olive oil over low heat and add the garlic and red pepper. Cook slowly for about 10 minutes, until the garlic is softened but not brown. Add the clams, leeks, and bay leaves and cook over medium-high heat until the leeks soften. Add the potatoes. Splash the wine all over the pan and turn the heat up to high to deglaze the juices. Add the fillets to the pan and cook them for 2 minutes.

Transfer the skillets to the oven and bake for 6 minutes, until the fish is done, the clams are opened, and the wine is evaporated.

To serve, put a fish fillet in each wide soup plate, then add 6 clams, the vegetables, and a portion of the broth. Taste for salt, drizzle with olive oil, and garnish with the parsley. Serve with garlic toasts.

• *You can use canned clams instead of fresh if that would make life easier—two 7½-ounce cans—but it's the gorgeous clamshells that make this dish so appealing.*

ॐ

Baked Peaches Stuffed with Almonds, Chocolate, and Brandied Raisins

6 large ripe peaches, unpeeled
½ cup chopped almonds, toasted (see footnote, page 217)
12 amaretti cookies, coarsely chopped
3 ounces bittersweet imported chocolate, coarsely chopped

1 tablespoon unsweetened Dutch cocoa
¼ cup raisins, soaked for 20 minutes in brandy and drained
¼ cup sugar

Preheat the oven to 425°F. Cut the peaches in half and remove the pits. Cut a little slice off the bottom of each peach so it will sit flat. Put the peaches in a glass baking dish large enough to hold them. Scoop out a little of the peach flesh and combine it with the remaining ingredients in a bowl to make a pulpy paste. Divide the paste evenly among the peaches. Bake for 15 minutes. Cool and serve either warm, at room temperature, or cold—we like them best at room temperature.

Paul Bertolli

Berkeley
California

Picholine Olives and Toasted Almonds

Baked Lingcod with Leeks, Fennel, and Peppers

Grilled Lamb Chops

Slow-Cooked Tomatoes

Buttermilk Mashed Potatoes

Red Leaf and Butter Lettuce Salad Served with
Aged Goat Cheese

Raspberry Tart

Wine:
Domaine Tempier Rouge, *served cool*

*P*aul Bertolli made a name for himself in his ten years as chef at Chez Panisse, which has launched so many extraordinary cooks. He's an extremely thoughtful cook, as his *Chez Panisse Cooking* demonstrates—that's where we learned, for instance, that taking brussels sprouts apart into individual leaves before cooking them produces a subtle and delectable vegetable. Since Bertolli left Chez Panisse in 1992 he has been active as a teacher, food writer, and restaurant consultant and now is executive chef at Oliveto in Oakland. Whatever he does, Paul's signature is his ability to coax an amazing depth of flavor from the simplest dishes.

When he entertains, Paul wants most of all to free himself from the kitchen so he doesn't have to be both cook and host at once. For this dinner almost every dish has elements that can be prepared ahead and needs only last-minute attention in the kitchen. In fact, Paul didn't have time to make an hors d'oeuvre, so he just toasted some almonds and tossed them in oil and kosher salt while they were still warm. What could be better? With the almonds he put out the inevitable dish of olives, the lovely little ones called *picholine*.

For drinks he likes to tempt people out of their usual bar habits with an intriguing aperitif. Sometimes it's white wine with a little sugar syrup, eau-de-vie, and orange peel, served cold. Or another time it might be red wine with peach leaves (be sure they're unsprayed) infused in it for a couple of hours. In summer it tends to be a long tall

Campari and soda. On the bar are single-malt scotch, Bombay Sapphire gin, and white wine. After dessert he serves an old Armagnac (Château Monluc 1939) to his lucky guests.

This is a late-summer menu, one that takes full advantage of the peak of the tomato season. But cooking tomatoes slowly in the oven improves almost any tomato, even lackluster ones. For a less bountiful spread, serve the lingcod as a main course, adding a side dish of steamed little new potatoes.

Those of us who don't live in California may not have tomatoes of colors beyond red and yellow, but of course the usual tomatoes work perfectly here.

☙

Baked Lingcod with Leeks, Fennel, and Peppers

*T*his Provençal dish is full of light, clean, sweet flavors, punched up with garlic mayonnaise (see below). The lingcod is a so-called false cod, a West Coast fish. If you can't find it, try grouper or snapper—we've even made this with eastern baby cod, but Paul wouldn't. Gypsy peppers are thin-walled and mild; you probably won't see them outside a farmer's market, but you can substitute Italian frying peppers or red and green bells or a combination.

6 gypsy peppers
1 tablespoon olive oil or more if needed
3 fennel bulbs, branches removed, sliced
3 leeks, thoroughly cleaned and cut into
*   rings*
a handful of fresh basil and parsley
*   leaves*

1 pound lingcod or grouper fillets
salt and freshly ground pepper
3 tomatoes, mixed red and yellow if
*   possible, peeled*
chopped parsley for garnish

Preheat the oven to 375°F. Cut the peppers into rings and remove the seeds. Heat the olive oil in a large nonstick skillet, add the pepper rings, and cook over medium-high heat until the peppers have softened a bit, about 10 minutes. Add the fennel and leeks and continue to sauté until the vegetables are soft, about 5 more minutes.

Rub an oval gratin dish with olive oil and spread the cooked vegetables evenly over the bottom. Strew the vegetables with the basil and parsley leaves. Lay the fish on top and season with salt and pepper to taste. Thinly slice the tomatoes and place them on top of the fish. Put the dish in the oven for 10 to 15 minutes, until the fish is cooked through. If there's a lot of liquid when the fish is done, save it to whisk into the mayonnaise. Scatter the parsley over the tomatoes before serving.

⁓

Garlic Mayonnaise

Of course Paul makes his own mayonnaise, and if you make a quick blender mayonnaise you'll be glad you did. But if you can't take the extra time, just use Hellmann's and whisk 1 cup into a beaten egg yolk with either a head of roasted garlic* or 1 to 4 fat cloves of fresh garlic, minced and mashed to a paste with a little salt (use a mortar and pestle or the flat side of a cleaver). Taste and see if some fresh lemon juice would be a good idea. If cooking juices are left from the fish, reduce over high heat to 2 tablespoons and whisk them in too.

⁓

Grilled Lamb Chops

It's easy to forget what a treat lamb chops are and how easy they are to cook. Here the chops are marinated in a subtle herb dressing for two days, so all you have to do at the last minute is grill them. Paul uses a rack of lamb cut into chops, but ordinary loin lamb chops—one per person—or rib chops, two per person, will do fine. They're best cooked over a wood fire, but of course charcoal-grilled chops will be delicious too.

*To roast a head of garlic, slice off just enough from the top to expose the cloves, drizzle a little olive oil on top, and bake inside heavy foil for 1 hour at 325°F.

15

12 rib lamb chops or 6 loin lamb chops,
  trimmed
¼ cup olive oil
2 tablespoons dry white wine
1 teaspoon minced fresh rosemary
3 teaspoons minced fresh thyme

¼ cup minced parsley
3 large garlic cloves, slivered
2 shallots, minced
pinch of dried lavender if available
salt and freshly ground pepper

Put the chops in a large glass dish. Mix the remaining ingredients and coat the chops well with the marinade, brushing it over all the surfaces. Cover the dish and refrigerate for 2 days.

Prepare the grill. When the fire is ready and the coals are covered with white ash, add the chops. If your grill has a lid, raise and lower it every few minutes to intensify the smoky flavor. Don't overcook the chops—they should still be juicy inside.

- *If you forget the marinating 2 days ahead, an overnight marinade will still give you good flavor.*

Slow-Cooked Tomatoes

12 ripe medium tomatoes
2 tablespoons olive oil

1 tablespoon sugar
salt and freshly ground pepper

Preheat the oven to 250°F. Don't core the tomatoes, but cut them in half horizontally. Brush a baking sheet with the olive oil. Put the tomatoes on the pan cut side up.

Sprinkle the tomatoes with sugar and salt and pepper to taste. Put the pan in the oven and bake for 3½ to 4 hours, until the skins are shriveled and the pulp appears somewhat dry. The tomatoes should have a jamlike consistency. Serve warm with the lamb chops.

Buttermilk Mashed Potatoes

*T*hese are great—light, fluffy, with an interesting tang. Figuring one big potato per person, cook the potatoes as usual (the microwave works perfectly), put them through a ricer or mash them with a potato masher, and thin them out with gently warmed buttermilk. Add salt and pepper. Be careful not to overheat the buttermilk, or it will curdle and separate.

Raspberry Tart

*T*here are a couple of ways to make this dessert. Either way the essential ingredients are a crust of some sort, a jar of seedless raspberry jam, and 2 pints of raspberries. If you don't mind rustling up a piecrust, you can make this tart the way Paul does and fully bake a pâte sucrée shell. When it's cooled, spread the bottom with a thin layer of seedless raspberry jam. Fill it with raspberries, both red and gold if available, with the colors in concentric circles. Paint a little more jam on the berries for a glaze—easier if the jam is warmed to thin it.

Or do this: Preheat the oven to 350°F. On a lightly floured board, roll out some defrosted Saucier frozen puff pastry (or any brand made with butter) into a large circle (put a 10-inch pie plate over the dough to give you an idea and cut the largest possible circle). Move the pastry circle onto a baking sheet and make a free-form piecrust by crimping up the edges—the more rustic and imperfect it looks, the better. Put in a layer of aluminum foil and cover the foil with beans to weight the crust. Bake the weighted crust for 30 minutes. When it's cool, add the jam and the berries and glaze with more jam.

• *Melt the jam in the microwave right in the jar, adding a jigger of framboise. Brush the warm jam over the berries.*

- *To make individual tarts, don't roll the pastry but cut it into 6 little tart shapes and bake as the package directs. When the pastry has cooled, fill it with the berries gently tossed with the framboise-and-jam mixture.*

Mix-and-Match Menus

A SICILIAN FEAST—ALMOST

Ask the butcher to tie up racks of lamb into a crown roast so that you can fill the center, after roasting, with Jo Bettoja's Toti's Pennette with Zucchini. Ring the base of the roast with the remaining pasta. Start the meal with a room-temperature mix of vari-colored roasted sweet peppers and thin white onion rings soft-fried (not browned) in garlic oil. Toss the onions with the peppers, salt, and pepper and drizzle lightly with balsamic vinegar. You can fix the peppers a day or two ahead and store in the refrigerator. Accompany the peppers with crisp crostini or thin bread sticks. For each guest, stem two fresh figs and open them into four-pointed stars by cutting from the stem end down, leaving them attached at the bottom. Put a fig on each dessert plate and drizzle with Marsala, a little sugar, and a puff of mascarpone or whipped cream—or mix them together. Put the second fig on top and twist it so the points make a star, then repeat the garnish.

Jo Bettoja

Rome / Italy

*Toti's Pennette with Zucchini
Small tubular pasta tossed with sautéed zucchini, mint, pistachios, and pine nuts

*Roast Pork with Lemons and Grapes
Boneless pork braised with lemon slices and seedless grapes

Watercress Salad with Chilled Gorgonzola
Dressed with extra-virgin olive oil and fresh lemon juice

*Oranges with Grand Marnier

*Dark Chocolate Brownies

Wine:
Marino Colle Picchioni Oro, *chilled*

*A*lthough Jo Bettoja grew up in rural Georgia surrounded by great cooks, she didn't really learn to cook until her Italian husband, Angelo, taught her. The student ran away with the spoon, however, and soon she had her own cooking school in Rome, teaching Italians how to cook Italian food—that's how good a cook she is. Her fame has spread back home, where she's published two much-admired cookbooks full of recipes collected painstakingly from Italian cooks reluctant to part with their family treasures: *Italian Cooking in the Grand Tradition* and *Southern Italian Cooking*. Jo is particularly fascinated with Sicilian cooking, a fantastic blend of Arab, Greek, Norman, Byzantine, and even Swedish influences. She's one of the few foreigners who've managed to gain access to the secrets of the Sicilian kitchen—though tradition prevails even now, and she's not yet been invited into the kitchen itself.

An invitation to dinner with the Bettojas at their Roman rooftop apartment behind the Trevi fountain is greatly prized. Dinner usually includes some of Jo's trademark heirloom Italian family recipes—these are from Sicily. But of course the brownies are pure Georgia.

On a hot summer evening this dinner might be served on the terrace, where four different jasmines trail up into the arbor. You'd be offered anything to drink you'd like, but the wine cellar here is irresistible. The Bettojas are as passionate about wine as they are about food. Angelo feels strongly that wine needs to be served at exactly the right temperature to be at its best, which could be anything from cold room temperature to slightly chilled to chilled to cold. These are subtle distinctions, but if you follow his advice here you'll be well rewarded.

This is a terrific do-ahead summer menu—everything can be prepared ahead in the cool of the morning, even the watercress, and served at room temperature or cold. In fact, unless you make the pasta ahead, this isn't really a no-fuss dinner, since it has to be made at the last minute if served hot. This menu has a wonderfully refreshing quality—the mint, the lemons, the grapes, and the oranges all have a cleansing zest that would be particularly welcome on a hot day.

Toti's Pennette with Zucchini

*T*his gorgeously green dish comes from Jo's friend Toti, one of the great cooks in Palermo. His recipe has a fresh, intriguing taste and a little crunch from the al dente zucchini and nuts. Serve hot or room temperature or cold.

⅔ cup olive oil

4 garlic cloves, peeled

1 dried hot red pepper or 1 teaspoon hot red pepper flakes (optional)

2 pounds zucchini, cut into thin rounds

⅔ cup packed fresh mint leaves

salt and freshly ground black pepper

1 pound pennette rigate or similar short stubby pasta

heaped ¾ cup coarsely chopped shelled pistachios

¼ cup coarsely chopped pine nuts

In a 12-inch skillet, heat the oil over medium heat, add the garlic and red pepper, reduce the heat to low, and cook slowly until the garlic is golden, about 5 minutes. Discard both the garlic and the pepper. Drizzle the seasoned oil over the zucchini and toss to coat.

Add the zucchini and a third of the mint to the pan (if the leaves are large, chop them coarsely). Stir-fry over brisk heat until the zucchini are tender but al dente, about 15 to 20 minutes. Season with salt and pepper to taste.

Transfer half the zucchini to a food processor and add another third of the mint leaves. Process until the zucchini are finely chopped but not pureed. Return to the pan with the remaining zucchini.

Cook the pasta in a large pot of boiling salted water until al dente, taking care not to overcook it. Drain the pasta, reserving ½ cup of the pasta water, and mix the pasta with the hot zucchini, adding the reserved pasta water slowly if the pasta seems too dry. Add half of the pistachios and all of the pine nuts, tossing well.

Sprinkle half the remaining mint and 1 tablespoon of the remaining pistachios into a serving dish. Pour in the pasta and sprinkle on the rest of the mint and pistachios.

- *If only salted pistachios are available, you may want to rinse them quickly under cold water and dry them in the oven to take off the salt. But taste them first; if they're not overly salty, use them and just cut back a little on the salt in the recipe.*
- *You may be tempted to toast the pine nuts, but Jo doesn't.*
- *You may also be tempted to leave out the hot pepper, but try it; it adds another dimension to the dish.*

Roast Pork with Lemons and Grapes

*T*his delicate pork roast is a little sweet, a little sour, altogether delicious and distinctive. The lemons, onions, and grapes melt together into a lovely jam. This is one of the rare roasts that's even better the next day—if you want to serve it at room temperature.

2½-pound boneless pork roast, rib or loin, rolled and tied	1 medium onion, thinly sliced
salt and pepper	½ cup dry white wine
2 teaspoons light brown sugar	1 bouillon cube, beef or chicken
2 teaspoons olive oil	2 lemons, sectioned, all peel and pith removed
2 tablespoons butter	1 pound seedless grapes

Have the butcher, if there is one, leave a thin layer of fat on your roast for flavor. Mix salt and pepper to taste with the brown sugar in a saucer and rub the roast all over with the seasonings.

In a heavy sauté pan or Dutch oven large enough to hold the roast, heat the oil and butter over medium heat and add the onions. Reduce the heat to low and cook the onions, stirring occasionally, until transparent, about 10 minutes.

Turn the heat to medium, add the meat, and brown lightly on all sides, stirring the onions constantly so they don't burn. This should take about 10 minutes. Add the wine and allow to evaporate for 30 seconds. Crumble the bouillon cube into the pan and add the lemon sections and two thirds of the grapes.

Cover the pan, lower the heat, and cook the roast for about 1½ hours, until an instant-read meat thermometer registers 140°F, turning every 15 minutes to cook it evenly.

Allow the meat to rest for about 10 minutes before slicing and serve in its sauce, hot or at room temperature. Decorate the serving dish with the remaining grapes.

- *Italian cooks are fond of using bouillon cubes—as are many American chefs, for that matter, though most food critics are snobbish on this point. Try the oblong ones offered by Knorr; they're a great convenience, and they work well in this recipe.*
- *Sectioning lemons is a little fuss, and you can get away with just peeling the lemons and cutting away all the white pith, then slicing them crosswise. Check for seeds and you're done. But sectioning isn't as complicated as it sounds. With a very sharp paring knife, cut a slice off the top and a slice off the bottom. Stand the lemon on a cutting board and cut away a strip of peel and pith in one fell swoop, following the shape of the fruit all the way down. Be sure there's no white pith left; it's very bitter. Continue all around the lemon. Now rest the lemon on its back on the cutting board and cut down along both sides of the membrane, separating each section to release it.*

JO BETTOJA

Oranges with Grand Marnier

*T*his lovely dessert is simplicity itself, but it has an unusual quality—the currants add a very special note.

3 tablespoons dried currants
¼ cup Grand Marnier

8 large navel oranges, sectioned, all peel and pith removed

Put the currants in a small bowl and pour on the Grand Marnier. Let the flavors blend for at least 30 minutes.

Drop the orange sections into a pretty glass bowl. Spoon the currants and Grand Marnier over the oranges and refrigerate until ready to serve.

Dark Chocolate Brownies

*T*hese intense fudgy brownies are superlative—the perfect ending to almost any meal.

Brownies:
4 ounces bittersweet chocolate
½ cup (1 stick) butter
1 scant cup sugar
3 eggs at room temperature
¼ cup flour
2 tablespoons unsweetened cocoa powder
1 teaspoon vanilla extract

¼ pound pecans or walnuts, broken into pieces with your hands, about 1 heaped cup

Icing:
2 ounces bittersweet chocolate
1 tablespoon butter
1 cup confectioners' sugar, sifted
2 or 3 tablespoons warm milk

Preheat the oven to 350°F.

Make the brownies: Flour and butter an 8-inch square pan. Put the chocolate, butter, and sugar in the top of a double boiler and bring the water to a boil. Turn off the heat, cover the pan, and allow to melt. Stir the chocolate until smooth. Remove the top part of the double boiler and allow the chocolate to cool slightly.

In a bowl, beat the eggs thoroughly. Sift the flour and cocoa over the eggs, then mix and add the vanilla. Stir in the chocolate mixture and, when blended, fold in the nuts.

Pour into the prepared pan and bake for 30 minutes. Put on a cake rack while you make the icing.

Make the icing: In the same double boiler, melt the chocolate and butter for the icing. When melted and smooth, add the confectioners' sugar. Stir to mix, adding 2 or 3 tablespoons milk to make a spreadable icing. When the brownies are still a little warm, spread icing over them. Refrigerate, covered, until 1 hour before serving to make cutting easier. Cut into 1-inch squares (these are very rich) and remove with a small spatula.

- *You can simplify this recipe by melting the chocolate and butter in the microwave. Do this in incremental zaps, taking care not to burn the chocolate—it goes fast once it begins to melt. Add the sugar when the chocolate and butter are completely melted.*
- *Make the brownies far ahead and freeze them, securely wrapped. Remove them from the freezer several hours before serving and cut before they reach room temperature.*

JENNIFER BRENNAN

Yokohama

Japan

*Ginger Shrimp Salad

Shrimp steamed in fresh ginger and sweet rice wine, served over mesclun, cucumber, and orange with onion dressing

*Pork Avarua

Smoky Polynesian-style pork loin wrapped and baked in vegetable leaves

Hot Sesame Green Beans with Sweet Red Pepper

*Bulgur Pilaf with Cashews and Golden Raisins

*Midori Melon Sorbet and Cookies

Wine:

With the first course: Sake, *seasonally chilled or warmed*

With the main course: Gewürztraminer or Sauternes

*J*ennifer Brennan is a third-generation child of the British Raj brought up in the Punjab and Mysore regions of India. Her earliest culinary memories are of elaborate meals prepared and served by imperial standards. All of those delicious sensory impressions were revisited in her fourth cookbook, *Curries & Bugles*, a charming blend of memoir and recipes punctuated with her own evocative illustrations.

Jennifer continues to travel, immersing herself in the cuisine of the country she's exploring and then coming home to cook and write about it. This intensity of style is reflected not only in the meals she cooks each day but also in her dinner party menus. She uses those occasions to experiment with ingredients and to translate unfamiliar techniques for American cooks. Her recent adventures have introduced her to the fascinating cuisines of the South Pacific, and because she lives in Japan we also can see the subtle influence of that country's cooking in her menu.

This exotic dinner may seem complex at first glance, but it's actually quite easy to assemble. Once you've managed the specialty shopping the rest is a snap. Superb and unusual flavors aside, here's a wonderful opportunity for drop-dead presentation. The pork, green beans, and pilaf look stunning together on a single large platter—the long leaf-wrapped meat package is a bit charred, as if lifted from an earthen pit. It nestles appealingly between the bright green beans flecked with red pepper and the golden pilaf. There's still room for a tropical floral accent in the Polynesian style—a spray of tiny orchids to crown one edge of the platter or a single white anthurium anywhere but the predictable center.

This meal is also the ideal patio buffet. In that case, grill the shrimp, tails on, and add them to the salad straight from the fire. After a head start in the oven, the pork could cook and smoke over low coals for its final hour.

◌

Ginger Shrimp Salad

*T*his refreshing starter has the clear flavors of Japan and sets a high visual standard for the rest of the meal.

1¼ pounds medium (25 to 30 count) shrimp, shelled and butterflied

mesclun or other tender mixed salad greens

Marinade:

2 tablespoons grated fresh ginger with the juice

½ teaspoon salt

2 tablespoons mirin (Japanese sweet rice wine)

Onion Dressing:

¼ cup light soy sauce (low-sodium is fine)

2 tablespoons mirin

2½ tablespoons rice wine vinegar

2 tablespoons safflower or canola oil

2 teaspoons hot Asian sesame oil or regular Asian sesame oil plus a dash of hot chile sauce

¼ cup grated white onion with its juice

Salad:

½ English cucumber, peeled and thinly sliced

3 navel oranges or 4 tangerines in 18 sections, all peel and pith removed

Place the shrimp and marinade ingredients in a plastic bag and shake, kneading well to distribute the seasonings. Refrigerate for at least an hour or up to four.

Place the shrimp and marinade in a shallow glass or ceramic container, cover, and steam in the microwave on high for 2 to 3 minutes, stirring the shrimp around halfway through. Cook only until they feel slightly springy to the touch, not firm. You can also cook the shrimp in a conventional steamer basket or insert. Rinse the cooked shrimp under cool water to stop the cooking and to clean off excess marinade. Refrigerate until ready to serve.

Cut the cucumber slices into half-rounds if the disks are large. Set aside along with the oranges until you're ready to assemble the salad.

Combine all the dressing ingredients in a screw-top jar. Shake well. Taste and adjust the seasonings. You can make this dressing up to four hours ahead.

Cover each salad plate with the mixed greens, then arrange the orange sections and cucumber slices in an alternating stripe down the center. Place 3 shrimp on either side. Shake the dressing again and drizzle it lightly over all.

- *To butterfly shrimp: Hold the head end of the peeled shrimp between your thumb and forefinger at the 10 o'clock position, with the underside (where the legs were) down against the cutting board. With the tip of a very sharp paring knife, cut through the center back, splaying the shrimp but not cutting all the way through.*
- *If you don't have a little china ginger grater, use the finest holes on your hand grater. You don't have to peel the ginger, but grate it on a small plate to save the juice.*
  If you have any dressing left over, use it to marinate fish fillets or chops or add it to a stir-fry for an all-in-one seasoning. Or plan ahead and cook extra shrimp to enjoy for lunch a day or two later. Just dip them in the leftover onion dressing.
- *The shrimp will look a lot prettier if you leave their tails on as Jennifer suggests, but provide a plate for the tail shells otherwise your guests will end up mixing them back into the tangle of greens.*

ᕙ

Pork Avarua

Avarua is the capital of Rarotonga in the Cook Islands and also denotes the Polynesian style of food preparation. In this instance the pristine little pork loin is metamorphosed into a smoky and voluptuous centerpiece straight from Gauguin's table. Expect a chorus of *ohs* and *ahs* from your guests when you serve this sensual main course.

3 to 4 pounds boneless pork loin or
Boston butt in 1 or two pieces

Marinade:

2 teaspoons coarse salt
¼ cup light soy sauce (low-sodium is
fine)
1½ teaspoons liquid smoke, a natural
hickory seasoning
⅓ cup unsweetened pineapple juice,
canned or frozen
1 tablespoon minced fresh ginger

To Assemble the Dish:

6 large collard leaves or Swiss chard
leaves—whichever is larger, washed
and drained
1½ bunches of spinach or 2 bunches of
red Swiss chard, stems removed
1 tablespoon canola or safflower oil

Place the pork in a 1-gallon resealable plastic bag. Pour in the marinade ingredients and massage into the meat. Set aside at room temperature for at least an hour or in the refrigerator overnight.

Preheat the oven to 325°F.

Excise the thick sections of stem from the collard and/or chard leaves by cutting up through the leaf on either side of the stem and knifing it out at a thin and tender point. Blanch the collard and/or chard wrapping leaves by spreading them out flat on a rimmed baking sheet and barely covering them with boiling water. A minute later, pour off the water and blot the leaves with paper towels. The interior spinach or chard leaves can be blanched quickly in the microwave since they don't need to remain flat for wrapping.

Tear off a rectangle of heavy-duty foil about 6 inches longer than the meat (end to end if there are 2 pieces). Lay the foil out on the counter lengthwise in front of you. Spread the oil over the surface with your fingers. Cover the foil with the flat wrapping leaves, leaving about a 3-inch margin all around, overlapping them as needed. Layer the interior spinach or chard leaves over the wrapping leaves.

Remove the pork from the marinade and place it on the leaf bed to your side of center. Bend the edges of the foil up on all sides to form a tray. Pour the remaining marinade over the pork. Lift the leaf wrapper and the interior leaves up over the top of the pork and press down with your hands. Now carefully roll up the meat in the leaves just as tightly as you can without tearing the wrapping. The meat will shrink, so you want the package as tight as possible. Fold and crimp-seal the foil to form a compact package and to prevent the juices from leaking out.

Place the package in a roasting pan and bake for 3 hours. Remove the package from the oven and carefully unwrap the foil. The meat will be almost falling apart. Gently transfer the pork to a serving dish with a couple of spatulas or carefully roll it out of the foil onto the platter. Slice the meat thickly with a very sharp blade while it's on the platter, but keep the slices together in their original attractive shape. Serve hot or warm.

- *To blanch greens in the microwave: Wash them, leaving some water on the leaves. Pile them loosely in a glass or ceramic bowl. Do not cover. One or 2 minutes on high should wilt the leaves perfectly.*
- *You may precook this dish as much as a day before. After bringing it to room temperature, reheat in a moderate oven (350°F) for about 30 minutes, or until warmed all the way through. It doesn't need to be served piping hot.*
- *You might want to serve a condiment to enhance the subtle flavors of the meat and emphasize its origin. Try a chunky tropical relish of minced fresh pineapple with its juice, grated ginger, slivered scallions, minced cilantro and/or mint, a sprinkle of sugar if the pineapple is immature, and a squirt of hot chile sauce. This will keep for 3 or 4 days in the refrigerator.*
- *You don't have to wait for company to enjoy this pork if you're willing to finesse the drama. Dispense with the wrapping leaves, marinate the pork, set it on the chopped blanched chard or spinach, and just seal it up in the foil as instructed. Stick a couple of sweet potatoes in the oven during the last hour and open up a jar of chutney.*

JENNIFER BRENNAN

Hot Sesame Green Beans with Sweet Red Pepper

1½ pounds tender young green beans, haricots verts, or frozen petite green beans if available

1 tablespoon safflower or canola oil

1 small red bell pepper, cored, seeded, and diced into confetti-size pieces

6 scallions, slivered on the diagonal

2 teaspoons hot Asian sesame oil or regular Asian sesame oil plus a dash of hot chile sauce

grated zest of 1 small lime or a couple of drops of pure lime oil*

salt

Blanch the beans in boiling salted water for 2 minutes—or in the microwave, with very little water, for 2 to 3 minutes, stirring them once. Drain the beans and quickly empty them into a bowl of ice water to halt the cooking and retain the bright color. Blot them dry with a paper towel when they're cool.

Heat 2 teaspoons of the safflower oil in a large skillet or sauté pan over medium heat and rotate the pan to distribute the oil. Add the beans, red pepper, and scallions and stir and toss the vegetables, cooking them for about 1 minute. Mix the hot sesame oil, remaining safflower oil, and lime zest or lime oil and stir the mixture into the vegetables, stirring and tossing to season. Add salt to taste and serve immediately.

Bulgur Pilaf with Cashews and Golden Raisins

2 tablespoons butter or vegetable oil

1½ cups quick-cooking bulgur

3 large garlic cloves, minced

3 quarter-size coins of fresh ginger, peeled and minced

1 teaspoon ground turmeric

*The Boyajian label is available at Williams-Sonoma stores.

1 teaspoon garam masala (Indian spice
    mix available in specialty shops,
    often labeled sweet curry powder)
small pinch of cayenne pepper
¼ cup golden raisins

3 cups chicken stock or canned broth,
    boiling
salt
½ cup unsalted roasted cashews

Melt the butter in a 2- or 3-quart saucepan. Add the bulgur, garlic, and ginger and stir to combine, sautéing over medium heat for 30 seconds. Lower the heat a bit, sprinkle the spices over the mixture, and add the raisins. When the mixture becomes aromatic, raise the heat back to medium and pour in two thirds of the boiling broth. Stir with a fork and cook for 2 or 3 minutes. Keep the broth simmering in case you need to add more (taste the grains before doing so). Add salt to taste. Cover the pilaf and set it aside with the lid slightly ajar to let the grains absorb the liquid. The pilaf should be fluffy, with the grains separate. Sprinkle the cashews over the top just before serving.

- *Pilaf can be prepared up to 4 hours ahead. Do not refrigerate. Reheat, uncovered, in moderate (350°F) oven for 20 minutes.*

◦

Midori Melon Sorbet and Cookies

*J*ennifer makes this recipe with *umeshu*—a green plum liqueur made from macerating this puckery relative of the apricot in a vodkalike spirit with rock sugar for several months. This delicious liqueur is prized as a digestive. Alas, we can't find *umeshu*, and if you can't either, substitute the Japanese melon liqueur Midori.

juice of 1 large lemon
¾ cup Midori (melon liqueur)
1½ cups ginger ale

1 egg white
fresh mint sprigs for garnish
crisp almond or ginger cookies

Squeeze the lemon juice into a mixing bowl. Pour in the liqueur and ginger ale and stir briefly. Pour the mixture into an ice cream freezer and freeze until it's the consistency of thick mush. Meanwhile, beat the egg white until it forms stiff peaks. Beat it into the semifirm sorbet a spoonful at a time. The mixture will be very foamy. Pour it back into the ice cream maker and continue freezing until it has the consistency of firmly packed snow.

If you don't have an ice cream maker, you can make this in 1 or 2 empty metal ice cube trays or in a stainless-steel bowl you can set in the freezer. Be sure to set the freezer compartment to the lowest temperature and follow the same procedure as above—stirring the sorbet every 30 minutes and scraping the ice from the sides of the metal trays with a fork.

Spoon the sorbet into dessert glasses, decorate with a sprig of mint, and serve with crispy almond cookies.

Mix-and-Match Menus

A TASTE OF INDIA

Make Jennifer Brennan's Bulgur Pilaf with Cashews and Golden Raisins, even a day or two ahead. While it's reheating, sauté plump patties of ground lamb mixed with minced mint leaves, a little grated lemon zest, and salt and pepper. Be sure to cook the lamb like a beef burger—medium-rare—so it stays nice and juicy. A big bowl of John Taylor's Mango Relish is a great accompaniment. If you can't come up with ripe mangoes, mix up some yogurt with minced onion, chopped seeded cucumber, and more fresh mint. Choose any of the fruit desserts in this book.

Jeffrey Buben

Washington, D.C.

---

*Chilled Cucumber Soup
A puree of yogurt and cucumber with scallions, garlic, and mint

Grilled Salmon Steaks au Poivre
The pepper-crusted salmon is served with a mustard and Vidalia onion cream

Red Swiss Chard and Dilled New Potatoes

Field Greens Salad with Vidalia Onion Vinaigrette

*Lemon Chess Pie with Fresh Berries and Raspberry Sauce

Wine:

Carmenet Meritage White, Paragon Vineyard 1992
Pierre Ponelle, Beaune "1er Cru" Clos du Roi 1990

*I*n his professional odyssey from the Big Apple to the Big Onion, Jeffrey Buben left an awesome pile of peelings in some of America's best kitchens. After graduating from the Culinary Institute of America at Hyde Park, where he learned *la technique* and *le service,* he spent fifteen years gaining the practical experience and creative credibility necessary to open his own place in Washington—a restaurant called Vidalia.

Vidalia is a winsome restaurant with a softly southern accent reflecting both Jeffrey's mother's culinary heritage and that of his North Carolinian wife and business partner, Sallie. No surprise that the chef's favorite dish is Carolina barbecue. But the Bubens didn't open a gentrified pig stand or a monument to the sweet Georgian onion. Jeffrey's menu is a sophisticated blend of his own creative intensity and traditional training along with Sallie's down-to-earth humor and practicality. This is country comfort food with an urbane spin—dishes like fried oysters stuffed with crabmeat, fennel, and spinach or apple onion upside-down cake with caramel sauce.

Since Jeffrey's pleasure is cooking for his patron friends every night at the restaurant, he seldom cooks at home. He confesses that it's because he hates to clean up, but Sallie tells us he spends every spare moment planning his second restaurant. The Bubens live forty-five minutes away in the Virginia countryside, where their children are active in team sports, so on Sunday, chef's only night off, the whole family often goes out to eat after a game. If Jeffrey were cooking at home, though, and pressed for time as he is constantly, here's what he'd serve—a remarkably simple menu to prepare with perfectly balanced and delicious flavors.

Chilled Cucumber Soup

The soup is a sparkling light preface to the filling main course and can be prepared the night before. Yogurt soups deserve more attention—they're versatile, only seemingly rich, and uncomplicated to prepare.

4 small to medium cucumbers, peeled,
    seeded, and diced
½ cup diced sweet onion
2 garlic cloves, blanched
2 tablespoons chopped parsley
1 tablespoon chopped fresh mint
2 cups yogurt
2 tablespoons fresh lemon juice
salt, freshly ground pepper,
    Worcestershire sauce, and Tabasco
    sauce

Garnish:

1 heaped tablespoon minced fresh mint
1 ripe tomato, peeled, seeded, and finely
    chopped
¼ cup minced sweet onion

Puree all the soup ingredients in a food processor or blender. Season to taste. Make up to a day ahead. Chill for at least 1 hour before serving. Garnish each bowl with mint, tomato, and onion.

- *To blanch the garlic cloves, drop them into boiling water for 2 minutes.*
- *It's tempting to be generous with the Tabasco, but remember that the salmon is* au poivre.
- *This soup would make a lovely summer main course for a luncheon or casual supper. Change the mint to fresh dill (or half mint and half dill) and float steamed shrimp, split lengthwise, around the edge of the soup plate. Mound the garnishes in the center. Serve a simple platter of sliced farm-ripe tomatoes, both yellow and red, a chunk of Greek or Bulgarian feta cheese accented with Kalamata olives, and a handsome*

loaf of semolina or walnut bread. A bowl of fresh apricots (or plumcots) chilled in ice water would be a welcome finale.

- *Transform this soup by substituting 3 medium peeled and seeded tomatoes (red or yellow) for the cucumbers. Use either mint and/or dill to season and garnish.*
- *For a breeze of a brunch, serve this soup (with the dill variation) with black bread or bagels and plenty of smoked salmon and whipped cream cheese. Danish Marys— with aquavit—to start.*

Grilled Salmon Steaks au Poivre

*T*his recipe may seem almost too simple to be memorable, but the blending of flavors is just right, and the onion mustard cream sauce is delectable.

Sauce:

2 tablespoons unsalted butter
¼ cup minced Vidalia or other sweet
    onion
2 cups dry white wine
4 fresh thyme sprigs
1 bay leaf
2 tablespoons Dijon mustard
2 cups heavy cream at room temperature

Salmon:

6 salmon steaks, about 6 ounces each
1 spice jar of mixed or black peppercorns
pinch of salt
1 tablespoon vegetable oil

Melt the butter in a small saucepan and sauté the onion over medium heat until soft and transparent, about 2 minutes. Add the white wine, thyme, and bay leaf. Keeping the sauce at a steady simmer, reduce the volume by half. This wine reduction can be done as far ahead as you like. There is no need to refrigerate it, just keep the pan handy on the back of the stove. When you're ready to cook the salmon, discard the thyme sprigs and bay leaf and bring the reduction back to a simmer. Add the mustard and cream and reduce the sauce by one third. Remove it from the heat and pass it through a fine-mesh strainer. Taste and adjust the seasoning if necessary. Keep the sauce warm or reheat briefly on low power in the microwave.

Bring the salmon steaks to room temperature. Coarsely crack the peppercorns in a spice mill or small coffee grinder, an ounce at a time as needed. Mix the pepper and salt with the vegetable oil and press the mixture into both sides of the steaks. If you're barbecuing, burn the charcoal until covered with white ash; otherwise preheat the broiler. Cook the fish for about 3 or 4 minutes per side or until just opaque in the center. Drizzle some sauce over the salmon and pass around additional sauce at the table.

&

Red Swiss Chard and Dilled New Potatoes

Chard:
3 bunches of red Swiss chard
¼ cup olive oil
2 garlic cloves, sliced
2 or 3 drops of liquid smoke, a natural
   hickory seasoning (optional)

Potatoes:
4 tablespoons butter
2 tablespoons minced fresh dill
24 Red Bliss creamers or 12 regular
   small Red Bliss new potatoes,
   scrubbed
salt and freshly ground pepper

Remove the thickest part of the chard stems and discard. Cut out the rest of the stems about halfway up the leaf by slicing alongside them and severing them with a diagonal cut. Chop and set aside. Stack the leaves and roll them up lengthwise as tightly as you can, holding the roll in shape with your fingers as you cut them across into approximately 2-inch-wide ribbons.

Put some of the oil and garlic in a wok or large sauté pan over high heat. Mash the garlic a bit with the back of a wooden spoon and stir to release the flavor. Remove the garlic and reduce the heat to medium-high. Toss in the stem pieces and sauté, tossing to coat with the oil. Turn the heat down and cook for about 5 minutes. Transfer to a large bowl. Add more oil and garlic, repeating the seasoning process. Add a drop of liquid smoke. Heat the pan to very hot and put in half of the chard leaves, tossing them around with a pair of tongs as they sizzle. When they have collapsed, transfer them to the bowl and repeat the process for the second half. Put all the leaves and the stems back into the pan over medium heat and cook the chard for about 5 minutes more. All of this goes quickly. It's only the volume of the raw leaves that makes it necessary to work in batches. Searing the chard over high heat in this manner and adding a drop or two of liquid smoke produces an intensified earthy flavor and keeps the color bright.

Put the butter in a glass measuring cup with the dill and melt it in the microwave on high. Set aside and reheat before serving if necessary.

Put the tiny creamers in a single layer in a rectangular glass baker with water in the bottom to cover about a third of the potatoes. Cover with plastic wrap and steam in the microwave on high in brief increments until the tip of a sharp knife slides easily to the center, approximately 5 minutes in two batches. Drain. If you're using regular small new potatoes, cut them in half before steaming, again keeping the water to a minimum. Serve dipped in dill butter and sprinkled with salt and pepper, on a nest of chard.

- *Both the potatoes and the chard can be prepared ahead and reheated.*
- *The tiny creamer potatoes are sometimes hard to find, but look for them in gourmet shops and at farm stands. They're as sweet as cream, as their name implies, and look very attractive on the dinner plate.*

Field Greens Salad with Vidalia Onion Vinaigrette

Some produce markets carry mixed field greens ready to use. Otherwise, mix your own varied selection from the freshest and most tempting greens available. The dressing is an appropriately assertive one and needs a salad to match. No floppy butter lettuce allowed—try to find some dandelion leaves, baby spinach, and/or arugula and toss it in with mesclun, which already has bitter greens and radicchio included.

Vidalia Onion Vinaigrette:

6 tablespoons safflower or mild olive oil

2 tablespoons red wine vinegar

1 large garlic clove, minced

1 teaspoon Dijon mustard

1 tablespoon minced fresh chives

2 tablespoons minced Vidalia onion

1 tablespoon minced Anaheim pepper

pinch of sugar

salt and freshly ground pepper

Whisk all ingredients together and toss half of the vinaigrette with the chilled greens at a time to avoid overdressing the salad.

℃

Lemon Chess Pie with Fresh Berries and Raspberry Sauce

*W*ho doesn't love a good lemon pie? Jeffrey reports his customers often ask for a second slice of this one. A splash of raspberry puree and a topping of mixed fresh berries make it a worthy dinner party dessert.

Raspberry Sauce:

1 pint raspberries

½ cup superfine sugar

2 teaspoons fresh lemon juice

Chess Pie:

4 extra-large eggs

1½ cups sugar

2 tablespoons cornmeal

2 tablespoons cider vinegar or malt vinegar

1 teaspoon vanilla extract

3 tablespoons fresh lemon juice

6 tablespoons butter, melted and cooled

1 9-inch piecrust, prebaked

1 cup mixed fresh berries

Puree the raspberries in a food processor with the sugar and lemon juice. Strain through a fine-mesh strainer to remove the seeds. Or use frozen raspberries; if they're sweetened, omit the sugar. Raspberry sauce can be made well ahead and stored in the refrigerator.

Preheat the oven to 350°F. Combine the eggs, sugar, and cornmeal and beat vigorously with a wooden spoon. Mix together the vinegar, vanilla, and lemon juice and add to the egg mixture. Fold in the melted butter. Pour the mixture into the prebaked shell and bake for 25 minutes. Cool. Drizzle some raspberry sauce over the top and garnish with the berries. The pie shell can be baked in the morning, filled in the afternoon, and sauced after dinner.

- *If the thought of making a piecrust gives you a chill, make a crumb crust by combining 2 cups coarsely ground almond biscotti with 1 stick of melted butter, 3 tablespoons light brown sugar, and a pinch of salt. Spoon the crumbs into a buttered 9-inch pie plate and press them down evenly over the bottom and sides. Chill the crust for at least 30 minutes and then bake at 325°F for 10 minutes or until golden brown. Prepare the filling and bake as instructed.*
- *If the thought of paying for all those almond biscotti gives you an even bigger chill, use zwieback or vanilla wafers or make the pie with no crust at all. Simply bake the filling in a 9-inch glass pie plate. Chill, cut, and serve over a pool of sauce with the berries on top.*
- *You can make your own superfine sugar by whirling regular sugar in a food processor for a minute.*

Mix-and-Match Menus

A SULTRY-EVENING SUPPER

Jennifer Brennan's appetizer Ginger Shrimp Salad would be a refreshing choice for a summer main dish. Leave out the cucumbers in the salad and start off with Jeffrey Buben's Chilled Cucumber Soup. To tie the menu together, bake a quick batch of Jean-Marie Josselin's muffins, using only the curry for seasoning. Paul Bertolli's Raspberry Tart would be just right after this light and simple meal.

Bright Ideas

HORS D'OEUVRES

It's important, not to mention hospitable, to have a little something with drinks when company comes to dinner. Most of the cooks in this book favor something very simple, like a selection of special olives, seasoned nuts, or fresh vegetables—these are certainly no-fuss, but it's also fun to search out alternatives. Here are some quick fixes:

Asian Crispies: Japanese and Indian savory crackers and spicy nibbles are sold at Asian markets and often at gourmet specialty stores. These tend to be addictive, and some are really incendiary, so taste them first and warn your guests.

Rosemary Walnuts: Mix 2 cups shelled walnuts with 2 tablespoons olive oil, 2 teaspoons crumbled dried rosemary, 1 teaspoon salt, and ½ teaspoon cayenne. Toss to mix, then bake on a baking sheet at 350°F for 10 minutes (a variation on a recipe from *The Pink Adobe Cookbook* by Rosalea Murphy).

Chèvre Truffles: Make little balls of goat cheese and roll them in olivada (commercial olive paste) or minced parsley. Stick them on the ends of bread sticks to serve.

Pepper Boats: Core sweet bell peppers of different colors and slice them from stem to stern along their rib lines. Remove the inner ribs and seeds. Use the boats to scoop or carry well-seasoned crab, shrimp or chicken salad, tabbouleh, herbed fresh cheese, corn relish, hummus, or chunky salsa mixed with a little sour cream.

Belgian Endive Boats: Separate the leaves and place a dollop of either smoked trout or smoked salmon mousse on the stem end, leaving the pale green leaf end for the "handle." Decorate the mousse with a little tuft of any pretty sprout. Make the mousse in a food processor with the fish and cream cheese, loosened with a drizzle of heavy cream.

Bean Spreads: Canned cannellini, black beans, or chickpeas all make wonderfully quick and tasty spreads for pita crisps, tortilla chips, garlic toast, or packaged and flavored crostini. Rinse and drain the beans or peas. Dump them into a food processor with some chopped onion, minced garlic (or garlic paste in a tube), fresh lemon juice, thyme, salt and pepper, and enough olive oil to make the mixture creamy.

Stuffed Dried Fruit: Stuff orange-flavored prunes with cheese: poke some Bucheron or peppered chèvre into them with the tip of a knife or a demitasse spoon. Fill jumbo dates: halve them and remove the pits, stuff the halves with a little mascarpone cheese, and stick on a shard of Parmesan. For a spicy version, mix softened cream cheese with finely minced pickled or fresh (red and green) jalapeños. Be sure the mixture is quite spicy to balance the sweetness of the dates. Mound the cheese onto each date half, then put them cheese side down on a plate of chopped pistachios to coat the cheese. Apricot halves: add a dollop of Saga blue cheese or any other creamy blue.

Crayfish Tails and Popcorn Shrimp: These delicate critters need a light dipping sauce: fresh herb mayonnaise (dill, tarragon, basil, chives) with a dash of Tabasco.

Smoked Trout Sushi: Take a smoked trout to a sushi bar and ask them to make up sushi with cucumber or asparagus and the smoked trout fillet. Top each piece with a tiny squeeze of wasabi—which should be in the package when you pick it up, along with the leftover trout. A whole trout will make about 50 sushi.

Cheese Cushions: In the food processor, cream 1 cup grated sharp Cheddar with 4 tablespoons butter, a pinch of salt, and cayenne to taste. Sift in ½ cup flour and pulse on and off until blended. Refrigerate for an hour, then pinch off walnut-size balls and space them out on a cookie sheet. Brush with an egg yolk whisked with a teaspoon of milk, then sprinkle with sesame seeds. Bake at 425°F for 10 to 15 minutes, until golden. Makes 2½ dozen.

Oyster Shooters: Toss oysters in minced shallots, cracked black pepper, and a little fresh lemon juice. Serve them in shot glasses. These are perfect with Bloody Mary chasers for brunch.

Basil Leaves with Feta: New Hampshire baker Ken Haedrich's excellent idea uses big fresh basil leaves. Crumble some feta cheese and mix it with yogurt until you have a smooth paste, then form a little mound of cheese on each leaf. Press in a seedless grape and arrange the filled leaves on a serving tray.

HUGH CARPENTER

& Oakville California

Southwest Caesar Salad with Chile Croutons

Romaine lettuce hearts, white corn, minced red pepper, piquant croutons, and grated Parmesan are tossed with a creamy lemon vinaigrette

Grilled Chinois Rack of Lamb

The marinade is a Provençal-Asian blend of red wine, hoisin, rosemary, and mustard

*Thai Rice Pilaf

Jasmine rice with lime, orange, currants, and fresh herbs

*Kahlúa Chocolate Decadence

An intense chocolate truffle–like indulgence accented with raspberries

&

Wine

With the first course: Cakebread Cellars Sauvignon Blanc

With the main course: Cakebread Cellars Cabernet

*I*t's certainly no surprise that Hugh Carpenter's current books are the *Fusion Food Cookbook* and *Hot Wok*. Undoubtedly Hugh is an "old soul" whose former incarnations were spent dining his way into the next life through the Orient, the Mediterranean, the Caribbean, the American Southwest, and the Bayou. What more earthly explanation could there be for his inherently easy cross-cultural cooking style? Four inspired cookbooks and six acclaimed L.A. restaurants all about this sparkling East/West culinary synthesis say that it's not just a New Wave food fad with Hugh— it's downright transcendental. Fusion cooking didn't originate with Hugh Carpenter, of course, but what makes him unique is the fact that no matter how he startles you with his diverse ingredients, everything always tastes great.

Hugh and his wife, Teri Sandison, food photographer, live the California good life. Hugh hosts Napa Valley food and wine seminars and teaches special cooking classes at the Cakebread Cellars vineyard. He also tours extensively to appear as a teaching guest chef and lecture at food conferences.

When he does manage to make his way home to the hills above the charming town of Oakville, Hugh and Teri entertain casually, on short notice, and usually encourage their professional friends to join in the fun and help put together one more smashingly attractive tour de force of fusion cuisine. Teri, a great cook in her own right (says Hugh), steadies the cooking melee by making the dessert and salad.

Once you get a handle on the conglomerate of ingredients and loosen up to the sheer fun and visual excitement of it all, this menu will delight you and your guests. Everything can be made ahead, leaving only the meat to cook and the salad to assemble.

Southwest Caesar Salad with Chile Croutons

*T*ypically, Hugh's salads are delicious enough, and handsome enough, to be a main course. This one's no exception. Try it sometime with slivers of carry-out Peking duck on top. The tiny bit of mayonnaise in the dressing is a sly alternative to the raw egg traditionally used to emulsify a Caesar salad dressing.

In the summer, when farm-stand corn is available, the just-picked sweetness of the raw kernels is a surprisingly pleasant foil for the lemon vinaigrette. As soon as corn is picked, however, its natural sugar turns quickly to starch, so the fresher the corn, the better this salad will taste. In winter, or whenever you're limited to supermarket corn, switch to the sweet, tender white corn kernels that have been flash-frozen at their peak.

Croutons:

1 French baguette or sourdough loaf, 2
    days old

½ cup olive oil

2 garlic cloves, finely minced

1 teaspoon coarse salt

2 teaspoons Asian hot chile sauce

Dressing:

⅓ cup fresh lemon juice

1 tablespoon light brown sugar

1 tablespoon low-sodium soy sauce

1 tablespoon mayonnaise

2 tablespoons finely minced fresh chives

1 garlic clove, finely minced

½ cup extra-virgin olive oil

salt and freshly ground pepper

Salad:

2 ears of sweet white corn, or ½ cup
    thawed frozen kernels

3 romaine lettuce hearts

1 large red bell pepper, cored, seeded,
    and cut into small dice

½ cup grated Parmigiano-Reggiano

Preheat the oven to 350°F. Cut the bread into ½-inch cubes. You should have about 4 cups. Heat the olive oil and garlic in a small saucepan over medium heat until the garlic begins to sizzle. Strain the oil into a mixing bowl and add the salt, chile sauce, and bread cubes. Toss to coat. Spread the bread cubes out on a cookie sheet and bake until very golden, about 20 minutes. Remove from the oven and cool. Store the croutons in an airtight container. You will need only about 1½ cups for this recipe. Keep the rest in a screw-top jar or in the freezer and use them in other salads or to float in soups.

Place all the ingredients in a blender and blend at high speed until emulsified. Add salt and pepper to taste. Put the dressing in a screw-top jar and set it aside for later use. When you're ready to assemble the salad, shake the dressing vigorously.

Husk the fresh corn and, standing each ear on end, strip the kernels from the cob with a sharp knife without cutting into the cob. Or thaw frozen kernels.

Toss the torn romaine leaves in a large salad bowl with the dressing and croutons and half the corn. Transfer the greens to 6 chilled salad plates and garnish each serving with the rest of the corn, the minced red pepper, and the grated Parmesan.

To capture and intensify the remaining sugar in not-quite-fresh or frozen corn, toast the kernels in a skillet over medium-high heat, with or without a little oil, just until the hulls are flecked with brown. We often improve on Mother Nature by adding a pinch of sugar, which instantly caramelizes on the surface and helps to restore the lost sweetness.

- *Many supermarket produce sections now carry packages of romaine lettuce hearts. If you can't find them, buy whole heads and save the heavy outer leaves for another day.*

⌒

Grilled Chinois Rack of Lamb

*T*his grilled rack of lamb is utterly delicious, but it can just as successfully be oven-roasted; or you might choose a butterflied leg to roast indoors or out; loin chops or brochettes to grill. It's the memorable French-Asian marinade that makes this dish. There is enough marinade for a butterflied leg and more than enough for a rack. Make the whole recipe and heat up any left over to serve as a sauce—that's how good it is!

2 racks of lamb, a butterflied leg, 6 to 8 loin chops, or 2½ pounds of loin cubes

½ cup olive oil

1 tablespoon dried rosemary or 3 tablespoons minced fresh leaves

1 head of garlic, finely minced

1 8-ounce jar of hoisin sauce

¾ cup dry red wine

½ cup Dijon mustard

3 tablespoons dark soy sauce

2 teaspoons hot Asian chile sauce

Bring the meat to room temperature. Put the oil in a glass cup with the rosemary and garlic and heat on high in the microwave for 1 minute to infuse the oil with the seasonings. Cool. Whisk in all the other ingredients and marinate the lamb in a large bowl or roasting pan for an hour or two at room temperature. If you're using a rack, be sure to push the marinade down to the meat between the chops since the bones won't absorb flavor. If you're making brochettes, marinate the meat cubes before stringing them on the skewers. In any case, reserve any excess marinade as a sauce.

If you're grilling, let the coals burn down until they're covered with white ash before putting on the meat. If your grill has a lid, pull it down for a couple of minutes at a time throughout the grilling to impart a slight smoky taste to the meat. Keep brushing the meat with the marinade while grilling. Use an instant-read thermometer to tell when the meat has reached an internal temperature of 140°F.

To cook a rack of lamb indoors, preheat the oven to 475°F. Put the racks in a shallow roasting pan and bake for 10 minutes. Turn the oven down to 375°F and bake for 15 to 20 minutes more. The easiest way to test for doneness is to cut along one of the end rib bones. Meat thermometers tend to hit the bone and give an inaccurate reading.

If you're cooking a butterflied leg of lamb in the oven, Hugh suggests putting the meat on an elevated rack to prevent steaming from the marinade. Roast at 450°F for 30 to 35 minutes.

Thai Rice Pilaf

*T*his aromatic pilaf is a perfect foil for the rich hoisin lamb. It's also a joy for the cook because it can be made entirely ahead and reheated in the oven or microwave.

2½ cups chicken stock or canned broth

2 tablespoons Thai fish sauce (nam pla)

1 teaspoon Asian hot chile sauce

2 teaspoons finely grated lime zest

2 teaspoons finely grated orange zest

¼ cup peanut oil, safflower oil, or clarified
    butter

2 garlic cloves, finely minced

1½ cups jasmine or basmati rice

⅓ cup dried currants

Garnish:

2 bunches of scallions, minced

¼ cup minced fresh basil leaves

¼ cup minced fresh mint leaves

3 tablespoons sesame seeds, toasted

Combine the stock, fish sauce, chile sauce, and grated citrus. Put the oil in a 2½-quart saucepan and sauté the garlic over medium-high heat for about 15 seconds. Add the rice and currants and sauté for 5 minutes. Add the stock and seasoning mixture, bring to a low simmer, cover the pot, and cook on the lowest possible heat for 20 minutes. The rice is ready when all the liquid is gone and the rice is tender and fluffy.

If done up to 2 hours ahead, set it aside at room temperature. If done further ahead, cool, cover, and refrigerate. Reheat in a 325°F oven for 20 minutes or in the microwave. When you're ready to serve it, stir in the scallions, herbs, and sesame seeds.

- *Hugh suggests a variation on this pilaf: Fold in 3 cups of cooked wild rice 5 minutes before you remove it from the oven.*
- *Turn this into a main dish by adding ½ pound each of shrimp, crab, and sliced salmon fillet along with enough additional chicken stock to transform the pilaf into a thick soup. Serve in wide-rimmed soup bowls with garlic bread. Add minced cilantro to the garlic butter.*

- *Toast sesame seeds in a small dry skillet over medium heat until they begin to turn golden or toast on a plate in the microwave for a minute or two on high.*

Kahlúa Chocolate Decadence

8 ounces imported dark chocolate, chopped

2 tablespoons unsalted butter

½ cup heavy cream

2 extra-large egg yolks

¼ cup confectioners' sugar

¼ cup Kahlúa or other coffee liqueur

1 cup heavy cream

½ pint fresh raspberries

6 fresh mint leaves or tiny sprigs

Place the chocolate, butter, and cream in a glass measuring cup and melt the chocolate in the microwave on high for 2½ minutes. Whisk the mixture until smooth and glossy. Cool. Whisk the egg yolks briefly, then stir them into the cooled chocolate mixture. Sift in the sugar and stir, then stir in the Kahlúa. Divide the mixture among 6 small (½-cup) dessert cups, filling them only halfway, and refrigerate for at least 2 hours. Just before serving, whip the cream and top the cups with it. Decorate each cup with raspberries and a mint leaf.

- *This sublime dessert is very rich and is best served, and savored, in small portions. The ½-cup fluted white soufflé cup is a good choice, and demitasse spoons would be appropriate for letting this confection melt in your mouth between sips of espresso or dessert wine.*
- *You can whip the cream earlier in the day if you store it in the refrigerator in a strainer lined with a double thickness of cheesecloth set over a bowl to catch the liquid.*
- *The mixture keeps in the refrigerator for several days covered with plastic wrap. It also keeps indefinitely in the freezer, and because of the alcohol in the Kahlúa it never hardens. An alternative and attractive way to serve this: Freeze the mixture and scoop it out with a small oval ice cream scoop dipped in hot water. Nestle the oval in*

the middle of a mound of whipped cream and dot the cream with the fresh raspberries or sliced strawberries.

- *Leftovers are great over coffee ice cream. A brief melt in the microwave makes it easy to pour. Or spread a chilled spoonful between two crispy oatmeal cookies.*
- *Try using cognac or Grand Marnier in place of Kahlúa and stuff a room-temperature knob of it into a poached pear half, sprinkle with chopped toasted hazelnuts, and garnish with a mint leaf. Or simply roll it into large marble-size balls and then into cocoa. Serve each truffle surrounded by blood orange segments, if available. Keep them in the freezer until ready to serve.*

Mix-and-Match Menus

SIMPLY SOUTHWEST

Present a centerpiece version of Hugh Carpenter's colorful Southwest Caesar Salad ringed with skewers of alternating grilled shrimp and chicken interlaced with lime slices and squares of fresh poblano peppers. Brush the skewers with fragrant oil made by infusing olive oil with split garlic cloves, a pinch of dried sage, and poblano trimmings in the microwave. Infuse the oil at least several hours ahead and let it sit in a screw-top jar to develop full flavor. Serve with warm tortillas or garlic toast. Dessert: coffee ice cream sundaes with a drizzle of Kahlúa.

Susan Feniger and Mary Sue Milliken

Santa Monica
California

Susan's Menu

*Edamame (Boiled Soybeans)

*Red Cabbage and Sprouts with Sesame Dressing

Spaghetti with Feta, Fresh Tomato, Spinach, and
Kalamata Olives

*Steamed Artichokes with Lime and Cracked
Pepper Mayonnaise

*Date Bars or Chocolate Chip Cookies with Yogi Tea

Wine:
Robert Mondavi Cabernet or Kenwood Merlot

Mary Sue's Menu

*Lime and Chile Roasted Pepitas and Cashews

Crispy-Bottomed Basmati Rice with Lamb
and Tomato
*A golden mound of aromatic rice hiding a center layer of seasoned ground
lamb and diced tomatoes*

*Yellow Split Pea Puree with Garlic and Basil

Red and Green Romaine Salad with
Lemon Vinaigrette

*Orange Pistachio Cake

Wine:
Duckhorn Sauvignon Blanc or Kenwood Merlot

*S*usan Feniger and Mary Sue Milliken, former owners of the trendy multiethnic restaurant City in Los Angeles, are currently owners and cochefs of the hip and happy Border Grill in Santa Monica, where they practice their alchemy on the simple, sensual food of Mexico and Latin America. They are the coauthors of the cookbooks *City Cuisine* and *Mesa Mexicana*, they were participants on Julia Child's PBS series *Cooking with the Master Chefs,* and they have even set their food to music on a CD.

These two transplants from the Midwest to L.A. were destined to be partners. They met as the first two women to cook at Le Perroquet in Chicago. Susan went from there to Wolfgang Puck's Ma Maison while Mary Sue stayed in Illinois—but their paths would soon cross again. Unaware of each other's plans, they simultaneously left for working sabbaticals in France and met once more in Paris. They knew then that they would work together someday back home. Susan made it happen when she became a partner at City and called Mary Sue to L.A.

Feniger and Milliken. It has the euphonic cadence of success—like Gilbert and Sullivan—but their personalities are antithetical. Susan is intense with a guilty fondness for certain junk food, and Mary Sue is easygoing, with a zeal for healthy food. Although they both love to cook for friends at home, Susan admittedly has to struggle to make time for company in her fifty-five-hour workweek. Mary Sue, on the other hand, just lets it happen even though she has an equally busy life.

Josh Schweitzer, the architect who designed both restaurants, converted an old swim club into a home for himself, Mary Sue, and their small son. The original snack bar, where the Fudgsicles and Dixie cups were once sold, is now Mary Sue's kitchen, where she and Josh like to have their friends join them to peel and chop. They use these occasions to experiment with new recipes using less red meat and more vegetables and grains but always reaching for Mary Sue's hallmark—full tastes.

Susan relaxes best through deliberate escape from the food world and prefers a quick fix of her own favorite simple flavors when she's home—invariably to the accompaniment of classical music. Her menu is admittedly idiosyncratic. For dessert she might just pluck a Milky Way from the freezer or scoop out a dish of frozen yogurt— or just snitch some date bars or chocolate chip cookies from the restaurant on the way home. (To finish the meal, Susan likes to serve yogi tea, which is available at health food stores.) And although for this menu she suggests edamame with a welcoming glass of cabernet or merlot, she'd be equally happy with an icy beer with lime and salt, a dish of imported olives, great cheese, and pickled vegetables.

A word about edamame: boiled soybeans sound pretty unappealing, but in fact they're a great discovery—bright green, soft as butter, and better than limas. We urge you to put these delicious beans on your next Asian market shopping list. You'll find them in the freezer section.

℃

Red Cabbage and Sprouts with Sesame Dressing

*T*his salad really surprised us. It's a welcome new way to use sprouts, virtually any kind that's good and fresh at the market. Part of our delight was the way this looked— pretty and original. Next time we might serve it in front of a creamy Thai chicken coconut curry or with a big platter of Chinese barbecued ribs or as a crunchy accompaniment to braised duck. You can slice the cabbage and prepare the dressing early in the day.

Dressing:
1 tablespoon Thai fish sauce (nam pla)
1 tablespoon fresh lemon juice
1 tablespoon rice vinegar
2 tablespoons vegetable oil
1 tablespoon soy sauce
1 tablespoon Pernod or ouzo (optional)

2 tablespoons Asian sesame oil
2 teaspoons finely grated fresh ginger

Salad:
½ head of red cabbage, finely sliced
4 cups sunflower sprouts

Put all the dressing ingredients in a screw-top jar. Shake and set aside, but use the same day.

Toss the cabbage with the dressing and toss in the sprouts at the last minute.

Spaghetti with Feta, Fresh Tomato, Spinach, and Kalamata Olives

*A*lthough this pasta sounds ordinary, it tastes unusual, and it's incredibly easy. It would be a great starter for a grilled leg of lamb or roasted chicken oregano.

4 quarts water
salt
1 pound spaghetti
4 tablespoons unsalted butter
4 garlic cloves, minced
1 bunch of flat-leaf spinach, stemmed
     and coarsely chopped

3 large tomatoes, peeled, seeded, and
     diced
3 to 4 ounces feta cheese, crumbled
freshly ground black pepper
12 Kalamata olives, pitted

Bring the water to a rapid boil, add salt, and cook the pasta until al dente. Drain. Heat the butter in a large sauté pan over high heat until it's light brown. Add the garlic and toss and cook briefly without browning. Add the spinach and stir it around until it's limp. Toss in the tomatoes and cook just until they release their juice. Add the drained spaghetti and most of the crumbled feta. Add salt and pepper to taste. Serve in heated flat pasta bowls, garnished with the olives and the rest of the crumbled feta.

• *If flat-leaf spinach—sold in bundles with the roots still on—is not available, start pestering your produce manager. He can get it, and that variety makes the best salads. Cut off the stems all at once before removing the twister band.*

Steamed Artichokes with Lime and Cracked Pepper Mayonnaise

These artichokes are just as good at room temperature as hot—so they can be made in advance, sauce and all.

Mayonnaise:
2 egg yolks
1 teaspoon red wine vinegar
juice of ½ lemon
½ teaspoon salt
½ teaspoon cracked black pepper
dash each of Tabasco and
  Worcestershire sauce

1 cup olive oil or half safflower oil if you
  prefer

Artichokes:
6 medium artichokes
4 limes
salt

Whisk together all of the mayonnaise ingredients except the oil. Gradually add the oil, first by drops and, after it starts to thicken, in a steady, thin stream, whisking constantly. Taste and adjust seasonings. It will keep in the refrigerator for 3 or 4 days.

Carefully trim the artichokes and drizzle the juice of ½ lime over each to prevent discoloring. Salt them and steam on top of the stove or microwave-steam* them until

*To steam in the microwave, stand the six trimmed artichokes side by side in a covered dish in enough water to cover the bottoms. Cook on high for 15 minutes. Check doneness by pulling a leaf. If it doesn't release easily, continue cooking in 3-minute increments.

the leaves pull out easily. Let cool enough to remove the chokes with the tip of a tea-spoon and serve with a lime wedge and a dollop of pepper mayonnaise inside each.

- *If you're really rushed, squeeze ½ lemon into a cup of Hellman's mayonnaise, then whisk in an egg yolk and the pepper, Tabasco, and Worcestershire. If you're watching the fat and are nervous about raw egg yolks, use half Hellmann's Light and half well-drained yogurt. Skip the egg yolk and lemon and just stir in the seasonings.*

Lime and Chile Roasted Pepitas and Cashews

*T*his mix is a tasty palate teaser and an imaginative alternative to the uninspired bowl of mixed nuts. You can make this snack well ahead and store it in an airtight storage bag, lidded tin, or jar. You can substitute your favorite nuts and seeds or add others.

1 cup each raw cashews and pepitas (pumpkin seeds)
2½ tablespoons fresh lime juice, from 1 or 2 limes

2 teaspoons paprika
1 teaspoon cayenne pepper
salt

Preheat the oven to 350°F. Toss all the ingredients together, spread out on baking sheets, and toast for 10 to 15 minutes, until lightly browned, checking regularly to prevent burning. Let cool and add salt to taste.

- *We've made these several times and keep varying the seasonings. Try curry powder or chili powder and delete the cayenne. The paprika adds an appetizing color.*
- *If you like the sheen (and enrichment) of a little oil on this mix, toss the nuts and seeds with 2 teaspoons safflower or canola oil before toasting them. If you have pure lime oil (page 32) in your pantry, add a couple of drops to the safflower or canola oil and omit the lime juice.*

- *The next time you see those packages of Japanese roasted hot green peas in an Asian food shop, buy some. They mix in with these nibbles perfectly and add a sparkling color accent.*

⌒

Crispy-Bottomed Basmati Rice with Lamb and Tomato

*T*his is the closest thing to the bottom of the Iranian rice pot we've ever tasted, and there's a lot more of it. Be sure to serve it on a beautiful round platter—this golden, crispy mound deserves attention.

3 cups basmati rice, rinsed

2 tablespoons plus 2 teaspoons sea salt or coarse salt

¼ cup olive oil

2 medium yellow onions, finely diced

2 pounds lean ground lamb

6 garlic cloves, crushed and chopped

2 teaspoons sea salt or coarse salt

1 teaspoon freshly ground black pepper

1 tablespoon hot Hungarian paprika

3 tomatoes, juiced, seeded, and chopped,

or a 14.5-ounce can Muir Glen diced tomatoes, drained

10 cups water

1 tablespoon sea salt or coarse salt

2 tablespoons butter

Minted Yogurt:

2 cups yogurt, drained

1 bunch of fresh mint, leaves only, roughly chopped, or 1 tablespoon crumbled dried

Soak the rice with I tablespoon of the salt in plenty of lukewarm water to cover for 45 minutes or overnight in cold salted water. Drain and rinse.

Heat half of the olive oil in a large heavy skillet over medium heat and sauté the onions until they start to become transparent, about I0 minutes. Add the lamb, garlic, 2 teaspoons salt, the pepper, and the paprika and stir and cook until the meat is well browned. Drain off any excess fat. Add the tomatoes and cook for another 2 or 3 minutes. Set aside.

In a well-seasoned or nonstick 4-quart saucepan with a tight-fitting lid—8-inch diameter is just right—boil the water with the remaining tablespoon of salt and add the drained rice. Bring back to a boil and cook, uncovered, for 10 to 12 minutes, stirring occasionally. The rice is ready when there is still a small firm kernel in the center. Empty the rice into a mesh colander or a handled sieve and rinse briefly with cool water, shaking it gently to drain.

Melt the butter and remaining olive oil in the same saucepan. Add 2 tablespoons of water and sprinkle the cooked rice evenly onto the bottom of the pan, a spoonful at a time, until two thirds of the rice has been used. Spread the meat and tomato mixture over the rice. Cover the meat with the remaining rice, mounding it slightly in the center. With the handle of a wooden spoon, poke about 5 holes from the surface of the rice to the bottom of the pot. Cover the pot with a thick cotton kitchen towel or two and place the lid on tight. Cook over medium-low heat for 35 to 40 minutes, turning the pot around occasionally to encourage even browning. The rice will look dry on top, and a crust will have formed on the sides and bottom.

Partially fill the sink with enough cold water to come up to the level of the rice in the pot. Uncover the rice and have the serving platter ready. Dip the pot in the water and hold it there for 30 seconds to cool the metal. Dry the bottom of the pot, then invert the rice onto the platter. It should release in one crispy, golden-brown piece.

Mix together the yogurt and mint and serve with the rice and lamb.

• *For a creamier texture and only a slight enrichment, whisk ½ cup sour cream into the yogurt.*

Yellow Split Pea Puree with Garlic and Basil

*M*ary Sue likes to spread this unctuous puree on her breakfast toast. We like to turn the leftovers into soup and float chunks of spicy smoked chicken sausage and crispy homemade croutons on top. This dish can be prepared up to a day ahead.

1 cup yellow split peas

3 cups water

3 tablespoons olive oil

1 medium yellow onion, diced

1½ teaspoons salt

1 teaspoon freshly ground black pepper

4 large cloves garlic, slivered

1 cup slivered fresh basil leaves

Cover and simmer the peas in the water for 45 minutes to an hour or until the peas are completely soft. Heat the olive oil in a large sauté pan and add the onion, salt, and pepper. Cook over low heat for about 10 minutes, until the onion is soft but not brown. Add the garlic slivers and continue cooking for 3 to 4 minutes more. Add the peas and continue cooking, stirring and mashing the mixture until smooth and creamy. Add or drain liquid to produce a loose puree, which you want to be able to mix easily into the crispy rice. Just before serving, stir in the basil.

Orange Pistachio Cake

At last, a cake you can actually make without sifting flour all over the kitchen and filling the dishwasher with every measuring spoon, cup, and bowl you own. This one is prepared totally in the food processor—a real gift to the busy cook.

1 cup raw pistachios, toasted, or unsalted
    roasted pistachios

¼ cup flour

¾ cup sugar

1 teaspoon ground cinnamon

2 teaspoons baking powder

pinch of baking soda

½ teaspoon salt

4 extra-large eggs

1 rounded tablespoon frozen orange juice
    concentrate

6 tablespoons unsalted butter, melted
    and cooled

Preheat the oven to 325°F. Butter and flour a 9-inch round cake pan. Put all the dry ingredients into the bowl of a food processor and let it run until the mixture is powdery and the nuts are finely chopped. Dump the mixture into a medium bowl. Return the processor bowl to its base (you needn't wash it first) and add the eggs, orange juice concentrate, and cooled butter. Whip the mixture well. Fold into the dry ingredients, blending well, and pour into the prepared cake pan. The batter will be very loose. Bake for 30 minutes or until a cake tester comes out clean. The center of the cake may fall a little.

In summer, serve wedges of this cake with sliced juicy-ripe strawberries and a puff of vanilla whipped cream.

* *Look for shelled pistachios in Middle Eastern markets or health food stores. Toast them in a 350°F oven, or a lightly oiled skillet, until they start to color, about 8 minutes.*
* *This cake is wonderful for breakfast with a steamy cup of café au lait.*
* *If you don't have orange juice concentrate in your freezer but you do have a fresh orange, finely grate a teaspoon of the zest and use that to flavor the cake instead. Or, if you have a bottle of Boyajian pure orange oil (available at Williams-Sonoma) in your pantry, 2 drops will do it.*
* *For Hazelnut Cappuccino Cake, use toasted hazelnuts instead of pistachios and add ¼ cup Dutch process cocoa plus 2 tablespoons instant espresso to the dry ingredients. Increase the sugar to 1 cup and melt 4 ounces chopped semisweet chocolate with 1 stick butter. Serve with whipped cream sweetened with confectioners' sugar and flavored with powdered instant espresso to taste.*
* *For Pecan Bourbon Cake, use toasted pecans, substitute 1 cup light brown sugar, loosely packed, for the white, and add 2 tablespoons bourbon to the egg mixture.*

Carol Field

San Francisco
California

Antipasto

Broiled eggplant with balsamic vinegar, roasted onions, olives scented with orange and lemon zest, cherry tomatoes, asparagus spears with extra-virgin olive oil, country bread

Penne with Bitter Greens, Mozzarella, and Toasted Walnuts

Salad of Mixed Lettuces

*Vanilla Ice Cream with Crumbled Panforte

Wine:

Rosso di Corinaldo, Le Marche
Taurasi Mastroberardino
Brentino, Maculan

*C*arol Field discovered Italy almost by accident, when she and her husband, John, went there to work on his PBS film *Cities for People*. She gained so many pounds eating the amazing food that most of her wardrobe no longer fit when she left. It was a fateful trip, the beginning of a passionate association with Italian food that has given her lucky readers several extraordinary cookbooks. She had fallen in love with Italy and has returned more times than she can count to learn as much about it as she can. She's still dazzled that the food varies from village to village, even when a dish has exactly the same name, and she's determined to taste all the variations, looking for the secrets of the many natural cooks who seem to have food wisdom in their DNA.

Perhaps best of all has been her work on Italian baking—her glorious breads and her wonderful cookies, from biscotti to ricciarelli. Carol has made so much bread in the big open kitchen of her San Francisco town house that now she can just mix flour, water, and salt and there's enough wild yeast in the air to make bread.

This dinner begins with a welcoming array of antipasto dishes—slices of broiled eggplant drizzled with balsamic vinegar, roasted onions, scented olives, tiny red or yellow cherry tomatoes, steamed asparagus spears served with extra-virgin olive oil, and, says Carol, "good country bread, of course." Though they're most easily served at the table or on a buffet, these dishes could also be served on a large coffee table, with little plates for guests to help themselves. One of the joys of antipasto is that everything can be served at room temperature, and some elements can be prepared well ahead. And of course some things can simply be acquired from a carryout store and just served along-side a couple of homemade dishes. You can expand the cornucopia almost infinitely—you might consider a good dry salami here or some interesting Italian cheeses. There are recipes for the onions and the olives, and you can just add whatever other elements you like. When Carol's in a great rush, sometimes it's just a little something to go with good Italian wine—two colors of cherry tomatoes, for instance, with a block of fine aged Parmigiano-Reggiano to nibble.

Roasted Onions

6 small yellow onions
3 tablespoons olive oil

salt and freshly ground pepper
balsamic vinegar

Preheat the oven to 400°F. Cut the onions in half crosswise and trim away any onion roots, but don't peel them. Rub the onion skins well with olive oil. Place the onions in an oiled baking dish, sprinkle them with salt and pepper to taste, and bake for I to I¼ hours, until soft enough for a knife to pierce them easily. Drizzle balsamic vinegar to taste over the tops and with the tip of a knife encourage it to penetrate the roasted onion a bit. Serve hot or at room temperature.

Olives Scented with Orange and Lemon Zest

zest of ½ orange, cut into julienne strips
zest of ½ lemon, cut into julienne strips

½ tablespoon fennel seeds
2 cups plump oil-cured olives

At least several hours before you plan to serve them, mix the orange and lemon zests and fennel seeds with the olives. Leave at room temperature for several hours. You may also cover the olives with plastic wrap and store in the refrigerator for up to 2 weeks. Serve at room temperature.

⁓

Penne with Bitter Greens, Mozzarella, and Toasted Walnuts

This is an intriguing pasta with the slightly bitter greens and walnuts—a favorite Italian taste—playing against the mild mozzarella and the unexpected anchovies and hot pepper. It's important to use good mozzarella from an Italian market or a gourmet store. And don't be tempted to stint on the anchovies; they're the secret indiscernible ingredient that pulls it all together.

1 large bunch of broccoli rabe, chicory, dandelion leaves, or other bitter greens
1 pound spaghetti, fusilli, or penne
3 anchovy fillets in oil, drained and mashed
3 to 4 tablespoons extra-virgin olive oil
¾ pound mozzarella, cut into small dice
1 cup walnuts, toasted (see page 126)
⅛ teaspoon hot red pepper flakes
salt and freshly ground pepper
½ cup freshly grated Parmigiano-Reggiano cheese plus more for serving

Wash the greens. If you're using the broccoli rabe, remove the tough leaves and large stems and separate into florets. Wash the greens well in several changes of cold water. Bring a large pot of salted water to a boil and cook the greens until they are barely tender, just a few minutes. Remove them from the pot with a strainer—don't dump out the water—and set aside to keep warm. Cook the pasta in the same water until it is al dente.

Meanwhile, warm the platter on which you will serve the completed dish. Combine the mashed anchovies and olive oil. Drain the pasta, reserving 3 or 4 tablespoons of the cooking water. Mix everything together on the platter except the Parmigiano. Add the reserved pasta water, season with salt and pepper, and toss well again. Sprinkle the Parmigiano over the top, toss again, and serve immediately. Pass more Parmigiano at the table.

- *If you don't have any anchovies, squeeze out an inch or so of anchovy paste from a tube.*
- *You can speed things up a little by buying your mozzarella in the form of bocconcini, little mozzarella balls that have been seasoned with olive oil, red pepper flakes, parsley, and garlic. In that case, leave out the red pepper (unless you want more) and a spoonful of the olive oil.*
- *If you're not fond of bitter greens, try this recipe with flat-leaf spinach or chard sautéed with garlic in olive oil.*

Vanilla Ice Cream with Crumbled Panforte

*T*his ice cream, with its simple but sensational spice mix, is incredibly good. Panforte is a dessert from medieval Siena that falls somewhere between candy and fruitcake, flavored with cinnamon, cloves, coriander, and nutmeg. It's crammed with nuts and candied fruit, sweetened with honey, and sparked with white pepper. Grab panforte when you see it, which is usually around Christmas—but it keeps for a very long time. Otherwise just substitute a good brand of biscotti, about one per serving. Or plan ahead and order the excellent panforte made by Margaret Fox at Cafe Beaujolais in Mendocino, California (800-332-3446), or the chocolate-glazed version in 2-ounce bars or 8-ounce cakes from Coffaro's Bakery in Seattle, which can also be mail-ordered (206-869-1936).

1 quart vanilla ice cream
½ pound panforte or chocolate-covered
    biscotti, cubed

¼ to ⅜ teaspoon ground cinnamon to
    taste
⅛ teaspoon ground cloves

Soften the ice cream in the microwave for 30 seconds on high or put it in the refrigerator for 15 minutes. Put the cubed panforte in a food processor fitted with the steel blade and pulse for about 1 minute. Add the softened ice cream and spices, then process until the pieces of panforte are well distributed through the ice cream. You may need to pulse frequently at first. Transfer the mixture to a freezerproof container and return to the freezer for at least ½ hour before serving.

- *Coffee, chocolate, or honey vanilla ice cream or frozen yogurt would also be delicious this way—or try a mix of coffee and chocolate.*

Mix-and-Match Menus

A KITCHEN PICNIC

Fill a handsome kettle or stockpot with a soup version of Mary Sue Milliken's Yellow Split Pea Puree with Garlic and Basil, thinning it to the right consistency with chicken broth. Hang a generous ladle right on the edge of the pot and stack the soup bowls next to it. Fill a basket with chunks of olive, walnut, and sourdough farm breads from the bakery and arrange a tempting platter of country cheese, prosciutto, and cervelat around a bouquet of crispy vegetables. For dessert, a bowl of clementines accompanied by Jo Bettoja's Dark Chocolate Brownies.

EDMOND FOLTZENLOGEL

Washington, D.C.

*Cervelat and Provençal Olives

Herbed Fresh Cheese with Radishes

Romaine Lettuce with Sherry Vinaigrette, Mint, and
Garlic Croustades

Couscous Chez Edmond
*Parisian-style couscous with grilled lamb and seafood brochettes, served with
onion confit*

*Strawberries and Oranges with Red Wine Sauce

Wine:
Pinot Blanc d'Alsace, Domaine Lucien Albrecht
Vin Gris, Domaine de Triennes

*O*nce upon a time, in the tiny Alsatian village of Lembach, Henri Foltzenlogel lowered his evening paper and listened with dismay while his only son told him he wanted to quit his job and move to America. *Mon Dieu!* What about the tenure he'd earned teaching at the Paris and Strasbourg hotel schools? What about all those years he'd spent peeling, chopping, and sautéing his way from young apprentice to master chef in the near-great and great restaurants of Paris and the Rhine country—the Contrexéville spa, the Alpine ski resorts, and the summer playpens of Deauville? How could he abandon such a solid career?

But, Edmond explained, he'd fallen in love with an American. What's love got to do with it? Quite a lot as it turns out. So, leaving all paternal words of caution in Lembach and able to speak only three words of English, Edmond left for America in 1984 to become executive chef at the French Embassy in Washington. Six months later he and his lady love, Leslie Blakey, opened their restaurant, Le Caprice, another impulsive act of love, which she manages and where he does what he loves most—cooks divinely—which we all know is done best with a loving heart.

This menu is a good example of how well these two treat their friends—either inside their gracious turn-of-the-century town house in the Adams Morgan section of Washington or outside on their patio. Couscous is the perfect year-round casual meal—easily prepared ahead, effortlessly presented, and a lot of fun to eat. Their lucky guests enjoyed these feasts so much that Edmond decided to feature couscous at Le Caprice one night a week. Now a veritable army of couscous aficionados lines up at the restaurant door.

With the guests' choice of liquor or wine, and in keeping with the provincial menu, Edmond assembles a couple of casual, help-yourself hors d'oeuvre trays—one of thin slices of cervelat or dry salami and a mix of French and Moroccan olives and the other with chunks of crusty French bread to slather with a soft herbed cheese. For contrast, he tucks in plenty of crispy radishes with some of the stems or leaves still on, in neat little green ponytails.

The cheese could be any one of the following: fromage blanc, chèvre, cottage cheese or ricotta whipped up with sour cream or yogurt, or chèvre mixed with natural cream cheese. The flavor enhancers should start with either finely minced garlic or roasted garlic puree, a touch of salt and pepper, and then minced fresh herbs such as parsley, chives, mint, and/or basil.

Romaine Lettuce with Sherry Vinaigrette, Mint, and Garlic Croustades

*E*dmond likes to serve this lively salad as a first course. The refreshing aroma of the chopped mint seems to stimulate the appetite, and it's the perfect preface to the spicy meal to follow. We find romaine lettuce a forgiving choice for company salads if it has to stand at room temperature for a while before it's served.

Croustades:
2 garlic cloves, minced
¼ cup olive oil
12 ¼-inch slices of a French baguette

Dressing and Salad:
1 tablespoon Dijon mustard
3 tablespoons sherry vinegar

½ cup plus 1 tablespoon extra-virgin olive oil
salt and freshly ground pepper
2 medium heads of romaine, well trimmed
3 tablespoons chopped fresh mint leaves

Preheat the oven to 250°F. Add the minced garlic to the olive oil and let sit while the oven preheats. Brush the bread slices lightly on both sides with the garlic oil. Put the bread on a baking sheet and slowly bake the croustades until they're dry and crisp throughout. Break one in half to test in about 20 minutes. You can make the croustades ahead and store them in an airtight container.

Whisk the mustard and vinegar in the bottom of the salad bowl. Add the olive oil and whisk again. Add salt and pepper to taste. Gently tear the romaine leaves and drop into the bowl. Add the chopped mint. Toss the greens with the vinaigrette and arrange on serving plates, placing 1 or 2 croutons alongside the salad.

- *If you trim, wash, and spin-dry salad greens the day you buy them and store loosely packed in a resealable perforated plastic bag, salad making can always be spontaneous.*
- *Look for the ready-to-serve romaine lettuce hearts now available in some supermarkets.*
- *For the best control over the amount of dressing to use, measure all ingredients into a screw-top jar and shake well before pouring over the greens. Make this the last thing you do before your guests arrive.*

℃

Couscous Chez Edmond

*T*his Parisian-style couscous should be presented with the grain separate from the meat and the vegetables. You'll need a tureen or a deep bowl and ladle for the vegetables in broth, a platter to mound up the couscous and garnish, and another for the brochettes. Each guest piles up a portion of couscous, makes a little well in the center, spoons in a few vegetables, moistens the grain with a ladle of broth, and tops it all with the meat and/or seafood. Serving brochettes, let alone combining seafood and meat, is not the traditional couscous presentation, but it gives the dish a contemporary lift. Harissa is the volatile Moroccan condiment each guest mixes in according to incendiary preference, and the sweet onion raisin confit is a French touch that makes a perfect counterpoint alongside.

The Vegetables in Broth:

3 tablespoons olive oil

1 medium onion, chopped

2 teaspoons épices de couscous (a
  specialty spice mixture) or 1
  teaspoon chile powder blended with
  1 teaspoon Chinese five spice
  powder

1 cup canned crushed tomatoes

bouquet garni: 3 parsley sprigs, 2 thyme
  sprigs, and 1 bay leaf tied together
  with a long string

2 14½-ounce cans chicken broth and 1
  14½-ounce can beef broth
  combined or 1 quart homemade
  chicken stock plus 2 cups
  homemade beef stock

2 small turnips, peeled and diced

3 medium carrots, cut into rounds

2 celery ribs, chopped

1 cup finely sliced savoy cabbage

1 large red bell pepper, cored, seeded,
  and diced

3 small zucchini, halved lengthwise and
  sliced crosswise

1 16-ounce can chickpeas, drained and
  rinsed

The Couscous:

3 cups water

2 cups quick-cooking couscous

1 tablespoon vegetable oil

1 tablespoon butter

1 teaspoon salt

The Brochettes:

12 bamboo or wooden skewers, soaked
  in water for an hour to prevent
  scorching

18 1-inch chunks boneless lamb loin,
  about 1½ pounds

12 ½-inch slices merguez (spicy North
  African/French sausage), about 1
  pound (optional)

12 large shrimp, about ½ pound

12 sea scallops, about ½ pound

olive oil for brushing the meat and
  seafood

The Garnish and Condiments:

¼ cup sliced or slivered almonds, toasted
  (see footnote, page 217)

½ cup harissa, thinned out with a little of
  the vegetable broth

Onion Raisin Confit (recipe follows)

First make the vegetables in broth. This is essentially vegetable soup and can be prepared a day or two ahead and reheated.

Pour the olive oil into a large soup pot and sauté the onion over medium heat until wilted and golden. Add the couscous spice and stir to release the scent and flavor. Add the tomatoes and simmer to soften them. Tie the bouquet garni to the pot handle and toss it into the pot. Pour in the combined broth and bring it to a simmer. Add the turnips, carrots, and celery and simmer for 10 minutes. Add the cabbage, red pepper, zucchini, and chickpeas and simmer for 10 minutes. Test for doneness—all vegetables should be well cooked, not crisp. You can cook the vegetables ahead, too.

Start the grill or preheat the broiler.

Now make the couscous. Each brand seems to bear a different set of instructions, but we recommend 1½ cups water to 1 cup couscous. Bring the water to a boil in a 2-quart saucepan. Add the couscous, stirring slowly with a fork. Add the oil, butter, and salt, remove the pan from the heat, cover tightly, and let it sit for 5 or 10 minutes. When all the liquid is absorbed, fluff the grains with a fork and keep warm in a 250°F oven for up to 30 minutes. To serve, mound the couscous on a platter and sprinkle the toasted almonds on top.

For the brochettes, thread 6 skewers with 3 lamb chunks and 2 sausage slices and thread the other 6 skewers with 2 shrimp and 2 scallops. Brush the brochettes with olive oil. Put the meat on first—it should take 2 to 3 minutes on each side, while the seafood should be done after only 1 minute on each side.

- *If you double the quantity of vegetables and broth, you'll have a delicious soup to serve the next day with cooked barley or pasta. You could also freeze it for future couscous dinners.*
- *Harissa is available in cans or tubes at specialty stoes and some supermarkets. If you can't find it, make your own with a thick Asian chili sauce (not paste or liquid) and add a little ground cumin and a touch of crushed caraway and anise seeds for a fair pass at authenticity.*
- *If you're not fond of lamb, use steak—and you may certainly use all scallops if you don't fancy shrimp.*
- *There is also nothing sacred about the selection of vegetables in the broth. If there's no savoy cabbage in the market and the flat-leaf spinach looks beautiful, go ahead and switch. If you hate turnips, use parsnips. Just don't use a vegetable that tastes better crisp.*

Onion Raisin Confit

1½ cups diced onion

3 tablespoons olive oil

½ cup golden raisins

3 tablespoons water

salt

In a small saucepan over medium heat, cook the onion in the olive oil until lightly browned, about 10 minutes. Add the raisins and water, cover, reduce the heat to low, and simmer until the raisins are plumped, about 5 minutes. Add a pinch of salt. Set aside for serving with the couscous.

• *Try doubling this recipe so you can keep the condiment for other uses. We added a drop of mesquite smoke essence and a dash of chile sauce to the leftovers and served it warm as a topping for dishes as various as lamb burgers, roast chicken, and apple/chicken sausage—all with great success. The confit keeps well in the refrigerator for a couple of weeks and reheats quickly in the microwave.*

Strawberries and Oranges with Red Wine Sauce

*T*his fruit salad dessert requires a little time to assemble attractively and is easier to compose on one large serving plate, preferably glass.

2 cups dry red wine

1 cup sugar

1 small vanilla bean, split

3 oranges

1 cup water

vegetable oil for frying

2 pints strawberries, sliced lengthwise

fresh mint sprigs

In a small saucepan, boil the wine, ½ cup sugar, and vanilla bean together until the sauce is reduced by half and is slightly syrupy. Set aside to cool.

Peel the zest from the fruit in wide ribbons with a sharp vegetable peeler. Trim away the uneven edges with the tip of a sharp paring knife and cut the neat rectangles into very thin strips. Store the fruit in the refrigerator until the day you're serving it. Bring the water and remaining sugar to a simmer in a small saucepan and simmer until the sugar melts. Put half of the strips into the simple syrup and boil for 5 minutes. Allow them to cool in the syrup and then spread them out on a piece of wax paper to dry off.

Make crispy peels with the remaining zests by quickly shallow-frying them in ½ inch of vegetable oil in a small skillet.

Arrange the sliced strawberries in overlapping concentric circles in the center of the platter. Drizzle with the wine reduction and place one gorgeous stem-on berry in the bull's-eye position. Trim the reserved oranges of all white pith and cut into sections. Place the orange sections around the outside of the berry circle and decorate the edge of the platter with the mint sprigs. Sprinkle the candied and crispy orange peels all over the fruit.

- *Both candied and crispy orange peels can be made well ahead and stored in screw-top jars. Try not to eat them all before your dinner party.*
- *This is a good opportunity to remind you to keep your kitchen knives sharpened. Spiral-cutting the pith from an orange is quick and easy with a keen-edged paring knife. Otherwise you'll end up with a juicy bowl of debris.*
- *You can slice the well-peeled oranges instead of sectioning them. Be sure to remove the little central white core.*

Bright Ideas

STARTERS

Of course you don't have to serve a first course, and a lot of famous cooks we know don't—Diana Kennedy usually doesn't, for instance. But having a starter makes dinner seem like a special occasion, and if that's what you're after, here are some simple ideas.

Mixed Green Salad with Smoked Salmon: You can use baby salad greens (mesclun) for this or almost any mixed greens with a simple vinaigrette dressing. On top of the tossed salad on each plate, seductively drape a couple of slices of smoked salmon. Add some rings of red onion and a few olives.

Scallop Seviche: In wine goblets, make parfait layers of tiny Cape scallops, hot red and green pepper, fresh lime juice against diced avocado, papaya, and jícama.

Prosciutto with Dried Fruit and Chèvre: Soak chopped dried apricots in white wine with a dash of cassis for 20 minutes. Stuff prunes with chèvre. Ruffle up a couple of slices of prosciutto on each plate; garnish with a tiny pyramid of the drained apricots and a couple of stuffed prune halves. Place a garlic croustade on each serving.

Mushrooms Stuffed with Clams: Mix canned minced clams, a little garlic, parsley, some grated Parmesan, canned roasted red peppers, bread crumbs, and a little crumbled crisp bacon. Stuff mushroom caps with the mixture. You can make these well ahead and bake them at 350°F for 10 minutes just before serving.

Sweet Red Pepper Soup: This delectable soup comes from Chef Jimmy Sneed of Virginia's The Frog and the Redneck restaurant (Jean-Louis Palladin is the frog; Jimmy's the redneck). In its entirety, here is the recipe: "Remove seeds from peppers. Cover with heavy cream. Simmer until soft. Puree. Season. (Secret: use sea salt.)" This is very appealing—start with 1 pepper and about ⅓ cup of cream per person. Especially wonderful served with a few lumps of fresh crab floating on top.

Grilled Asparagus with Toasted Sesame Seeds and Pear Tomatoes: Paint medium asparagus spears with olive oil and put them in the toaster oven for 2 minutes or until they are tender. Lightly salt them and roll the butt ends in toasted sesame seeds (you can buy these or toast your own in a dry skillet, watching carefully to be sure they don't burn). Garnish with tiny pear tomatoes.

Melon with Black Olives: California cook Susan Costner taught us this unusual light sweet-and-salty Provençal dish: Mix cantaloupe balls with some Niçoise olives, toss, and marinate in the refrigerator for at least half an hour. Grind a little pepper over just before serving in small glass bowls. Add a garlic croustade spread with tapenade or olive paste.

Smoked Trout: Peel off the skin and pull apart the fillets. Cut the fillets in half along the backbone groove. Pull the fillets apart into natural chevrons and serve a few pieces over individual watercress salads. Make a creamy mustard vinaigrette by adding a dash of heavy cream to the oil, lemon juice and/or vinegar, Dijon mustard, salt, and pepper. Shake it up in a screw-top jar and drizzle over the salad.

Stuffed Avocado: Shred or finely julienne a daikon (white radish). Toss it with a dressing of soy sauce, rice vinegar, and grated fresh ginger. Fill the cavity of a ripe Haas avocado half with the daikon salad and garnish the top with one butterflied cooked shrimp with its tail intact. Serve one stuffed avocado half per person.

Vodka Shrimp: Sliver a few sun-dried tomatoes and use some of the packing oil to sauté medium peeled shrimp with their tails still on. When the shrimp are pink and springy to the touch, splash them with Absolut Peppar Vodka, and when the vodka is warm, tip the sauté pan into the gas flame to ignite the shrimp—or light them with a match. Serve over a small nest of angel hair pasta or simply on top of a garlic croustade.

Green Chile Crab on Corn Buckwheat Waffles: Make the waffles ahead—from Aunt Jemima's buckwheat pancake and waffle mix, adding drained cooked corn kernels (frozen are fine) and snipped chives or scallion tops for color. Reheat the waffles in the oven and serve one warm crisp waffle section per person with a mound of fresh crab (or shrimp or scallops) sautéed in garlic butter. Park a spoonful of green chile to one side.

Iced Yellow Tomato Soup: Peel and seed ripe yellow tomatoes and puree them in the food processor with enough plain yogurt (half sour cream is good, too) to thin the mixture out. Salt and pepper the soup and mix in a lot of snipped fresh dill. Refrigerate for at least 2 hours before serving.

Suzanne Hamlin

Brooklyn
New York

---

*Cold Sesame Noodles
Thin egg noodles are tossed with a peanut dressing, cilantro, scallions, and crispy vegetables

Baked Chicken in a Salt Crust with Soy-Ginger Dipping Sauce

Perfect Chinese Rice

Stir-Fried Broccoli

*The Frozen Mango and Fortune Cookies

Green Tea

Wine:
Gruet Sparkling Wine from New Mexico

As the ex–food reporter of the New York *Daily News* in its heyday and current food writer for *The New York Times*, native Kentuckian Suzanne Hamlin has been on the cutting edge of the evolving American food scene for a couple of decades. Above all she's curious, pursuing stories to their ultimate sources and in the process finding out crucial information that the general food press misses entirely. Thanks to Suzanne we know how to enjoy wine with our artichokes: short-circuit the chemical reaction that usually ruins the taste of wine by cooking the artichokes with orange juice. Suzanne's also the expert on baking with olive oil, a subject of great interest as we move further toward the Mediterranean diet—but with our sweet tooth still demanding satisfaction. Her deep interest in healthy good eating has led to her forthcoming book, on the world's most nutrient-rich foods and how to incorporate them into your everyday cooking.

You might expect a healthy menu from Suzanne, and you'd be right: this one is brimming with antioxidants and very low in fat. But that's more or less beside the point. The chicken is a fascinating recipe, a technique that appears in several cuisines but has nearly disappeared from the canon. Somehow the salt crust produces a chicken that's the essence of itself, a taste so succulent and pure you may think you've never before known what chicken really tastes like. This ancient Chinese recipe was once done in a wok over an open fire, but Suzanne has updated it to use a foil-lined roasting pan, which provides the same result with no cleanup and no pot watching. We know you think the chicken will be unbearably salty, but that's not the case at all—it's just moist, exceptionally tender, and unbelievably flavorful. And best of all it's dramatic, unlike most simple dishes: for the full impact, take the chicken to the table and crack the crust in front of your guests.

The rest of this menu is simplicity itself, so easy that you can walk into the kitchen with the ingredients and serve dinner an hour and a half later. At the Hamlin house in Brooklyn Heights, Suzanne's two grown children still turn up unexpectedly with friends—and even these committed vegetarians are happy with this multichoice meal.

A game plan: Freeze the mangoes first, then prepare the chicken and start cooking it. Make the noodles and the dipping sauce, then wash and cut the broccoli. When the chicken is done, take it out to rest and start the rice. Serve the noodles. When the rice is ready, serve the main course and cook the broccoli while the dishes are being passed around the table. And use chopsticks; everything will taste even better.

℘

Cold Sesame Noodles

½ pound Chinese egg noodles,
    Japanese udon, vermicelli, or
    angel hair pasta

Dressing:

2 scallions, white part only, chopped

⅓ cup vegetable or chicken stock or
    canned broth

¼ cup tahini or smooth peanut butter

¼ cup cider vinegar or rice wine
    vinegar

½ cup low-sodium soy sauce or tamari

2 teaspoons Asian sesame oil

Any or All
of the Following Additions:

1 cucumber, peeled, seeded, and cut into
    small pieces

1 cup sliced red radishes

1 bunch of scallions, including most of
    the green, trimmed and cut into thin
    rounds

1 cup bean sprouts

1 carrot, shredded

1 cup slivered snow peas

½ cup roughly chopped cilantro

¼ cup toasted sesame seeds

Incredibly thin Chinese egg noodles are usually packed in coiled rings, like nests. These will come apart when boiled. Cook them in a large pot of boiling salted water, stirring occasionally, for 3 or 4 minutes or until tender. Pour them into a colander and run cold water over them until cool. Pick them up by the handful, shake them dry, and transfer to a large shallow bowl.

Blend all the dressing ingredients in a blender or food processor and pour over the noodles, turning them over and over with your hands until they have absorbed most of the dressing. Add the additions now or cover and chill. When ready to serve, mix in the additions and toss together well.

- *Whatever else you leave out, we urge you not to drop the cilantro and the scallions.*
- *If you have any high-quality peanut oil around (Loriva makes a good one), add a spoonful to the dressing.*

Baked Chicken in a Salt Crust

*B*earing in mind that you're going to taste just the essence of chicken, with a little lemon to freshen it, it's worth tracking down a very good chicken for this dish. Free-range, organic, whatever's best in your local markets is what you should buy.

3½-pound chicken	6 cups kosher salt
1 lemon	1 cup tepid water

Preheat the oven to 450°F. Remove the giblets from the chicken and save for another use. Rinse the chicken under tepid running water, shake, and pat dry with paper towels.

Cut a thin slice off both ends of the lemon and use the knife to make 5 or 6 deep incisions around the lemon. Put the lemon in the cavity of the chicken. Truss the cavity with a trussing needle and soft twine or tie the legs together with twine. Use kitchen scissors to cut off the wing tips.

Line a large shallow roasting pan with a sheet of heavy-duty aluminum foil. Using rubber gloves (salt can be abrasive), pour a cup of the salt into the center and spread it out in a thin layer slightly larger than the chicken. Put the chicken breast side down in the center of the salt. Pour the rest of the salt into a mixing bowl and stir in the cup of water. Start packing it all over the chicken, just like making an igloo or a snowman with wet snow. Pack it evenly so that the chicken is totally encased in salt and somewhat resembles a football.

Put the pan on the middle oven rack and roast for I hour. Remove from the oven and let rest for at least 10 minutes or up to 30 minutes.

When ready to serve, bang the top of the rock-hard crust with the handle of a heavy knife. The crust should fall off in 3 or 4 pieces. Discard them and pat the chicken with a paper towel to get rid of any lingering salt. Cut the trussing string and remove and discard the lemon.

If you're adept with a Chinese cleaver, whack the chicken into bite-sized pieces with the bones still in. If you're not, cut the chicken in the kitchen once you've cracked through the crust at the table. With heavy kitchen scissors or poultry shears, cut the chicken into halves, then quarters. Then, using a chef's knife or scissors, cut the chicken across the grain into 1½- to 2-inch pieces. Some of the skin will fall off, which is fine—you can discard all of it if you want. Serve the chicken on a platter and put out the bowls of dipping sauce.

- *Suzanne warns not to skip trussing the chicken—otherwise salt might get into the cavity, and the delicious juices may escape altogether.*
- *For maximum drama, remove the chicken still in the foil and place it on a serving platter, tucking the foil under the chicken. Surround it with watercress sprigs and proceed with the whacking.*
- *The chicken doesn't have to be Chinese. Try adding a head of garlic cloves, separated and with the outer skin peeled off, over the bed of salt on the foil. Tuck a sprig or two of thyme inside the cavity. You may end up cooking chicken this way often, it's so delicious and clean—just pick up the foil and toss it out.*
- *Chicken roasted this way isn't at its best cold, so plan to serve it hot.*

Soy-Ginger Dipping Sauce

½ cup low-sodium soy sauce

2 tablespoons plus 2 teaspoons rice wine
  vinegar

2 tablespoons freshly grated ginger

1 tablespoon plus 1 teaspoon Asian
  sesame oil

4 garlic cloves, minced

Mix all the ingredients and divide among 6 little bowls, one for each guest.

Perfect Chinese Rice

*T*his recipe contains no salt, because the Chinese feel that rice should be neutral, a complement to other foods.

2 cups long-grain converted white rice

6 cups water

Put the rice in a bowl and cover it with tepid water. Drain off the water in a sieve. Do this 2 or 3 times until the water is clear.

Drain and put the rice in a deep heavy pot with the 6 cups water. Bring to a boil, reduce the heat, cover, and simmer for 18 to 20 minutes, until the rice is cooked.

Stir-Fried Broccoli

2 bunches of broccoli, about 2 pounds

2 tablespoons olive oil

2 garlic cloves, slivered

½ cup vegetable or chicken stock or
  canned broth

¼ teaspoon fine sea salt or to taste

pinch of hot red pepper flakes

1½ tablespoons fresh lemon juice

Wash the broccoli and cut it into small florets. Peel the stalks and cut them on the diagonal into 1½-inch pieces.

Heat the olive oil and garlic briefly in a large skillet or wok. Add the broccoli pieces and stir them constantly over high heat for a minute with a spatula or spoon. Add the stock, salt, and red pepper. Cover the pan and steam over medium heat for about 2 minutes. The broccoli will be crisp-tender and bright green. Sprinkle with lemon juice and serve immediately.

⁓

The Frozen Mango

A magic trick: this recipe turns a simple mango into a velvety, creamy dessert. To make it into ice cream, use the evaporated milk. Of course you can keep mangoes in the freezer, ready to make this dessert at a moment's notice. The recipe is per person, so plan accordingly.

1 ripe mango
1 tablespoon fresh lemon juice

1 to 2 tablespoons canned evaporated skim milk or low-fat milk (optional)

Peel the mango. Working over an open plastic food storage bag, cut the flesh away from the pit in chunks, dropping the pieces into the bag. Sprinkle with lemon juice, seal tightly, and freeze—90 minutes or more. Put the frozen mango pieces in a food processor and blend until smooth and thick. To heighten the mango flavor, add a bit more lemon juice when blending. To make it even richer, add the milk.

Serve immediately, with fortune cookies.

- *Obviously you can make this richer with a little cream if you'd rather—but Suzanne says the more cream or milk, the more distant the intense taste of mango becomes, so be sparing.*
- *We're crazy about lime with mango, which is another option instead of the lemon.*

REED HEARON

San Francisco
California

Mixtec Guacamole with Tortilla Chips

Spicy Grilled Yucatán Chicken with Caramelized
Onions

Grilled Corn with Lime and Chiles

Mexican Sundaes with Cajeta or Tropical Fruit
Salsa

Beverage:
Negro Modelo Beer

*R*eed Hearon cooks lusty country food from Italy and France over a giant open wood fire at his restaurant Lulu—and something completely different across town at Cafe Marimba, where the specialty is Mexican food with an emphasis on Oaxaca and the Yucatán. (There's another Cafe Marimba in Burlingame.) Marimba is wildly colorful, with Mexican folk art lining the walls and intense hues everywhere. There are lots of surprises, like fresh strawberry juice and intriguing dishes you haven't seen on other Mexican menus.

Hearon grew up in Texas—he's the son of novelist Shelby Hearon—and he's always had a passion for Mexican food. Hearon's way with Mexican cuisine does stir up soul-food feelings; these are dishes you'll make often if you can find (or mail-order) a couple of key ingredients: achiote paste and cajeta. Both are available at Mexican groceries or can be mail-ordered from Marimba Products (415-776-1506). Achiote paste is a blend of spices with a bright orange color that comes from annatto seed—it has an indefinable taste that's instantly recognizable as authentic. And it keeps for a very long time in the refrigerator, so it's worth ordering.

You probably won't have cajeta around long enough to worry about how to store it. This caramelized goat's milk sauce is addictive and makes ordinary caramel sauce seem completely inadequate. The brand Reed Hearon likes is Coronado, with a little goat's face on the label.

You'll notice right away that this isn't your ordinary guacamole—roasting the tomato makes a big difference to the flavor, but probably the biggest surprise here is using the jalapeño seeds. For salad, Reed likes to use cactus paddles (nopales), but we'll settle for a simple green salad or a side dish of Drew Allen's sliced tomatoes with nothing but lime juice and salt.

⌒

Mixtec Guacamole with Tortilla Chips

2 ripe medium Haas avocados, halved
    and pitted

1 small ripe tomato, roasted under the
    broiler until blistered, black, and soft

1 jalapeño chile, diced, with the seeds

1 tablespoon minced white onion

2 teaspoons minced cilantro

¼ teaspoon salt

Scoop out the avocado flesh into a molcajete (a Mexican basalt mortar) or a bowl. Mash together the avocado, tomato, and chile with a pestle or the back of a fork until chunky-smooth. Stir in the remaining ingredients. Serve immediately with crisp tortilla chips.

- *If you don't like too much heat, minimize or cut out the chile seeds, which are the hottest part of the pepper, along with the ribs (aka veins).*

⌒

Spicy Grilled Yucatán Chicken with Caramelized Onions

*R*emember to start this recipe the night before you plan to serve it so the chicken can marinate. You might as well cook the onions while you're in the kitchen. Reed Hearon likes fiery Roasted Habañero Salsa (page 237) alongside the chicken.

Achiote Marinade:

1 cup achiote paste

2 cups fresh orange juice, from about 5
  oranges

1 cup water

2 tablespoons ground New Mexico chile,
  such as Chimayo

1 tablespoon salt

Chicken:

6 whole chicken legs

3 chicken breasts, split

salt and freshly ground pepper

Caramelized Onions:

1/4 cup vegetable oil

4 medium white onions, sliced into thin
  rings

salt and freshly ground pepper

Combine all the marinade ingredients in a blender and process until smooth. Keep refrigerated until ready to use.

Rinse and wipe the chicken dry, then cover it with the marinade and keep it refrigerated in a covered bowl overnight. Bring to room temperature before grilling. When the barbecue is ready—the ash should be white-hot—brush the grill with oil. Season the chicken with salt and pepper and grill it skin side down first. Start with the legs, which take longer to cook. After about 10 minutes on one side, turn the legs over and add the breasts, skin side down, and cook for another 20 minutes, turning the breasts once. Test with a skewer to be sure the juices are running clear.

Meanwhile, cook the onions if you didn't get around to them the night before. Heat a large nonstick skillet until very hot. Add the oil, then the onions, salt and pepper to taste, and cook them over medium heat, stirring from time to time, until they turn soft, tender, and golden brown, about 20 minutes.

Serve the chicken with the onions spilling over it.

- *If you cook the onions the night before, your house won't smell like cooking onions during the party.*
- *There are simply never enough onions, and leftovers are wonderful on burgers, baked potatoes, pork . . . so think about doubling the recipe.*

Grilled Corn with Lime and Chiles

6 ears of corn   New Mexico chile powder
vegetable oil   1 lime, cut into small wedges

Remove the husks from the corn and brush the ears with oil. Cook on the grill, rotating the corn until all sides are lightly charred and the corn is tender. Remove from the grill and sprinkle chile powder all over the corn. Serve with the lime wedges.

Mexican Cajeta Sundaes

*R*eed uses Häagen-Dazs vanilla ice cream—because it's less sweet than other brands, it's a good foil for the cajeta.

2 cups cajeta (Mexican caramel sauce)   1 quart vanilla ice cream

Heat the cajeta until it's smooth and creamy—the microwave can do this. Pour it over scoops of ice cream in sundae dishes.

• *You can also use half chocolate sauce and half cajeta.*

Tropical Fruit Salsa Sundaes

*I*f cajeta is out of the question, here's another exhilarating sundae based on tropical fruit. Passion fruit is a delectable element here, but if it's unavailable, just skip it—the salsa will still be terrific.

½ cup chopped ripe mango

½ cup chopped ripe papaya

¼ cup chopped ripe pineapple

½ cup chopped ripe banana

2 passion fruits, pulp and seeds

2 tablespoons fresh lime juice, from 1 or 2 limes

2 fresh mint leaves, minced

1 quart vanilla ice cream

Mix everything but the ice cream together in a bowl. Spoon the salsa over scoops of the ice cream and serve immediately.

✆

Mix-and-Match Menus

UPSCALE STEAK AND POTATOES

Tenderloin with Rosemary, Garlic Chips, and Beet and Potato Puree: Cut thick fillet steaks into ¾- by 3-inch strips. Finely mince some parsley for garnish and set aside. In a large sauté pan, shallow-fry thinly sliced garlic, at least one or two cloves per person, in ¼ inch of olive oil. Set aside on paper towels to drain. Pour off all but a couple of tablespoons of oil, saving the flavored oil for other uses. Add some chopped fresh rosemary to the remaining oil and quickly sauté the fillet strips over high heat, tossing and browning on all sides. Arrange the steak strips on a platter or dinner plates, salt and pepper them, and dust with the minced parsley. Top with the crispy garlic chips. Serve with beet and potato puree: 4 large baked beets and 2 baked potatoes pureed and combined with butter, warm half-and-half, salt and pepper, and a little freshly grated nutmeg. Toss up a mixed green salad and pick up a fancy bakery dessert.

Jean-Marie Josselin

Kapaa
Hawaii

Sesame Soba Noodles with Tempura Vegetables

Buckwheat noodles with ginger and roasted sesame seeds with crisp mixed vegetables

*Seared Swordfish with a Tomato and Kalamata Vinaigrette

Strips of swordfish fillet on a mesclun salad topped with a fresh tomato, basil, and Greek olive vinaigrette

*Ginger Curried Muffins

*Sliced Peaches with Fruited Red Wine

A red wine reduction flavored with citrus, honey, and vanilla over peach slices garnished with fresh mint

Wine:

1992 Vouvray Sec Domaine Bourillon
1990 Savennières Domaine des Baumaro

*J*ean-Marie Josselin, French born and trained, has adopted the Hawaiian Islands—and Kauai has adopted him. His emigration from his native Provence, via the U.S. mainland, to this unique multiethnic society in the middle of the Pacific Ocean was an easy assimilation. Jean-Marie married a Hawaiian, is raising his family there, and owns and operates his own acclaimed restaurants, A Pacific Cafe, in Kapaa and Kihei, Maui. The native Hawaiians' deep spiritual connection to nature and their contagious joy in its beauty is a very nourishing environment for a creative young chef—we've noticed Jean-Marie is constantly beaming.

In fact Hawaii is a paradise for fine-food aficionados—if they know how to get past the stereotypical. Not only do the islands abound with glorious fruit and vegetables and the waters around them teem with the world's most delectable fish, but a spectrum of culinary repertoires from Portuguese to Japanese flourishes there. So it's amazing to realize that for decades the talented European chefs who headed up tourist hotel kitchens virtually ignored the generous local bounty. But Jean-Marie couldn't resist exploring the free-form cooking of the real Hawaii. Soon he started breaking away from his classical restraints and began experimenting—embracing lower-fat cooking styles and moving in step with contemporary American trends—with a definite island beat.

Jean-Marie is particularly fond of fish—especially tropical fish, which we're just beginning to appreciate—and has won accolades for his innovative ways of preparing it. His cookbook, *A Taste of Hawaii*, brilliantly showcases that talent. The glorious photography also proves his dedication to fanciful presentations with natural ingredients.

This simple summery at-home menu is a good example of the multiethnic Hawaiian style. The Japanese noodle (pasta) and tempura (fritto misto) first course echoes the Italian vinaigrette for the swordfish. Jean-Marie's recipe calls for onaga, a long-tailed red snapper, but a swordfish is also superb here. Best of all, this entire menu can be served at room temperature and can be made ahead, except for the tempura—the only element you'll have to cook after your guests arrive. See page 219 for tips on how to make deep-frying simple.

Sesame Soba Noodles with Tempura Vegetables

The intriguing contrast of slithery noodles and crispy vegetables is perfectly complemented by the ginger vinaigrette. Almost any vegetables will do for this tempura, but select at least one colorful one for visual appeal.

Noodles:

½ pound Japanese soba (buckwheat) noodles

2 tablespoons sesame seeds, toasted

2 tablespoons olive oil

1 teaspoon Asian sesame oil

1 tablespoon fresh lemon juice

1 tablespoon rice vinegar

4 slices of pickled ginger, cut into julienne strips

1 teaspoon minced fresh ginger

2 scallions, green parts only, cut into julienne strips

1 tablespoon chopped cilantro

Tempura Vegetables:

1 quart vegetable oil

1 egg

½ cup plus 1 tablespoon water

½ cup flour

¼ cup cornstarch

1 red bell pepper, cored, seeded, and cut into 6 lengthwise strips

1 yellow squash, cut into ½-inch rounds, or 6 broccoli florets with 1 inch of stem

1 Japanese eggplant, cut into thick sticks (optional)

Garnish:

fresh chives or mint or basil sprigs

Drop the noodles into a large pot of rapidly boiling water and cook until al dente, 2 to 3 minutes. Rinse in a colander or sieve under cold water to stop the cooking. Drain well. Toast the sesame seeds in a dry skillet over medium-high heat until they start to color and pop. In a large bowl, toss the noodles with the remaining noodle ingredients until the seasonings are distributed and the noodles are coated. Set aside until ready to serve.

Heat the oil to 375°F in a wok or a deep-fryer. Mix the egg and water with a fork. Add the egg mixture to the combined dry ingredients and mix lightly. Ignore lumps, which will drop off in the hot fat. Dip the vegetables into the tempura batter, coating them well, and fry in small batches until pale gold and crisp. Turn them out onto paper towels or a rack over a shallow pan and keep warm in a low oven until all vegetables are cooked.

Put a serving of noodles in the center of each plate and arrange a few vegetables on either side. Garnish with 3-inch-long chives or a sprig of mint or basil.

- *Look for Hime tempura batter mix (dry) in Asian markets or specialty stores. It's excellent.*

Seared Swordfish with a Tomato and Kalamata Vinaigrette

This main course hits every target—it's delicious, unusual, visually enticing, simple to prepare, and can be made well ahead. Snapper, swordfish, tuna, salmon, and mako are all good choices because they all have enough character to hold up to the assertive vinaigrette.

2½ pounds swordfish or onaga, cut into 6
    servings
olive oil
salt and freshly ground pepper
1 pound mesclun

Vinaigrette:
6 medium tomatoes, peeled, seeded, and
    diced
5 shallots, minced
¾ cup Kalamata olives, pitted and chopped

6 large fresh basil leaves, slivered

¾ cup extra-virgin olive oil

2½ tablespoons red wine vinegar

1½ tablespoons balsamic vinegar

¼ cup chopped flat-leaf parsley

salt and freshly ground pepper to taste

Rub the fish with a little olive oil, salt, and pepper. Either grill or sauté it until just cooked through and set aside—not more than an hour before serving. The fish should be either warm or just at room temperature when you serve it.

Combine the vinaigrette ingredients and set aside.

To serve, cover the plate with a generous nest of mesclun, place the fish on it, and spoon the vinaigrette over the fish.

• *If you plan to light an outdoor grill to cook the fish, you might consider cutting it into chunks and skewering it.*

Ginger Curried Muffins

These wonderful muffins appear regularly in the baskets of assorted bread at A Pacific Cafe. They are so popular that the restaurant sells them by the dozen for clients to take home.

MAKES 12 MUFFINS

1 tablespoon minced red ginger
   (available in jars at Asian markets)
   or fresh ginger

6 slices of pickled or fresh ginger, minced

1 tablespoon Thai red curry paste
   (available at Asian markets and
   some supermarkets)

¼ cup minced cilantro

½ cup (1 stick) butter

2 tablespoons sugar

3 eggs

1 cup milk

about ¼ cup flour

pinch of baking soda

pinch of salt

2 rounded teaspoons baking powder

Preheat the oven to 350°F. Have ready a greased 12-cup muffin pan. Puree the gingers, curry paste, and cilantro in a food processor. Cream the butter and sugar in a bowl with an electric hand mixer. Add the eggs one at a time and beat in. Mix in the milk and pureed ginger mixture. Add the remaining ingredients and mix until blended; do not overmix. Pour into the prepared pan and bake for 30 minutes. Let the muffins cool in the pan before removing.

- *You can change the flavor of these muffins in many ways—simply substitute different seasonings for the ginger mixture. Try mint and/or basil instead of cilantro or use only fresh ginger and add a tablespoon of curry powder to the butter as you cream it. Try roasted garlic and sun-dried tomatoes or use unsweetened coconut milk instead of regular milk and use 2 teaspoons of grated lime zest instead of the seasoning paste.*
- *If you double this recipe, use only 5 eggs and 1 heaped tablespoon of baking powder. You can buy the pickled ginger at a sushi bar.*

Sliced Peaches with Fruited Red Wine

This dessert is a nostalgic throwback to Jean-Marie's childhood summers in the south of France, where everyone lingered over the table and dinner went on into the night. More peaches, more wine, more good conversation.

1 orange, unpeeled, sliced
1 lemon, unpeeled, sliced
¼ cup honey
seeds scraped from 1 vanilla bean

1 quart dry red wine
6 ripe peaches, peeled and sliced
6 fresh mint sprigs

Combine all ingredients except the peaches and mint in a 2-quart nonreactive saucepan. Bring to a boil and let the alcohol burn off for 2 or 3 minutes over medium-high heat. Remove from the heat and let cool completely. Divide the sliced peaches among 6 large wineglasses. Strain the red wine syrup over the peaches and garnish with a mint sprig.

Mix-and-Match Menus

DIM SUM

Pick up fresh or frozen uncooked shrimp or pork dumplings from the Chinese restaurant or Asian market—about 8 to 10 per person. Start off with Jimmy Sneed's Sweet Red Pepper Soup (page 78) and then serve the steamed dumplings (you can do this in the microwave with a little chicken broth) on a bed of Diana Kennedy's Sautéed Spinach with Chiles. For a dumpling dipping sauce, mix a little rice vinegar and a few drops of Chinese sesame oil into a small bowl of soy sauce, adding plenty of minced fresh ginger and garlic. Don't forget the chopsticks. Patrick O'Connell's Ginger Ice Cream is a good dessert even without the rhubarb sauce—add a plate of toasted-nut cookies.

DIANA KENNEDY

Zitacuaro, Michoacán

Mexico

Fish Shehadi with Tahini and Pecans
Baked red snapper with a tahini, garlic, and lime sauce topped with fried onions and pecans

*Brown and Wild Rice Pilaf

Sautéed Spinach with Chiles

Asian Watercress Salad

*Sliced Oranges with Almond Brittle

Wine:
1993 Gewürztraminer Trembach

If you come to dinner at Diana Kennedy's ecological ranch in the foothills of the Mexican Sierra, you might plan to come early enough to be in time for tea. Sometimes it's hard to remember that this ultimate authority on Mexican cooking, the author of the legendary *Cuisines of Mexico* and five other classic cookbooks, is actually British. But every afternoon without fail there's tea at Diana's, proper tea with tea-cloths and scones, homemade jam, and cup after cup of perfectly brewed tea—half Assam, half Darjeeling. This will brace you for the tour of the ranch—rough-hewn acres of extraordinary growing things, from asparagus to rare chiles to hoja santa leaves the size of elephant ears to giant trees. If it's Christmas, the lanes that lead to the house will be jammed with Ozlike poinsettias the size of dinner plates; if it's the rainy season, the hedgerows will be bursting with wildflowers.

Here you'll eat as you would nowhere else—not only because Diana is one of the world's great cooks but also because so much of what turns up on her table has spent its life growing on her property. To begin, there might be some smoky Oaxacan guava-flavored mescal, distilled in a small village famous for its product—which of course never gets exported to the United States. There might be tacos made with blue corn tortillas and local wild blue mushrooms, served with a brilliant salad that's a tangle of young greens from the garden, with strips of jícama and homemade sun-dried tomato dressed with a little oil and Diana's own mild pineapple vinegar. Intense tropical fruits, either fresh or in sorbet, might finish the meal—possibly passion fruit plucked from the vines that meander along her fences. And there are always goodies tucked away to be had with the fruit. Coffee is her own homegrown, and later she might bring out a plate of succulent guava paste—homemade, of course. In fact, Diana's kitchen is a little treasure trove of things put up and things put away for company, so much so that a good friend, asked what he'd like to be left in her will, stipulated "the contents of your refrigerator."

So a typical dinner is completely irreproducible here. And it must seem as though Diana would be the last person in the world to consult about no-fuss cooking. But in fact the only way she can do so much is to use her time efficiently and to get her priorities completely in order. She doesn't cut corners, but when a simple recipe is entirely delicious, she adopts it. Here, for instance, is a favorite dish that can be made when she's away from her extraordinary resources. The fish is Middle Eastern, a recipe from her Lebanese friend Norma Shehadi. It's very rich, and you may want to have just plain white rice with it. Otherwise, just mix wild rice with brown rice and cook them together. The chiles have snuck into this mostly Middle Eastern menu, but we think you'll agree with Diana that the spinach is much livelier with them; they also balance out the richness of the fish dish. Just to completely mix cuisines, Diana's given us an Asian watercress salad, another lively note. And for dessert, the astringent oranges are perfect—and back to the Middle East.

This meal is served with warm tortillas or pita bread, of course.

Fish Shehadi with Tahini and Pecans

This dish looks spectacular made with a whole red snapper—with its head on, naturally. The squeamish, or hosts expecting the squeamish for dinner, can opt for very large fillets instead.

1 large onion, roughly chopped
4 garlic cloves, roughly chopped
1 teaspoon sea salt or to taste
1 whole red snapper, about 4½ pounds,
    cleaned but head and tail left on, or
    2½ pounds fish fillets

3 tablespoons fresh lime juice, from 2 or
    3 limes
2 tablespoons olive oil

Topping:
6 tablespoons unsalted butter
10 ounces onions, about 2 medium,
    thinly sliced
¾ cup roughly chopped pecans

Tahini Sauce:
rounded ½ cup tahini
2 garlic cloves, mashed
½ cup fresh lime juice, from 6 to 8 limes
sea salt to taste

Put the onion, garlic, and salt in the food processor and process for 30 seconds. Spread this mixture on the inside and outside of the fish. Set the fish in an ovenproof dish into which it will just fit; if there's a lot of space around it, the juices will tend to dry up. Cover and set aside in a cool place to season.

Preheat the oven to 350°F. Sprinkle the lime juice and olive oil over the fish. Cover loosely with foil and bake for 20 minutes. Turn the fish over and bake for 20 to 25 minutes longer, depending on the thickness. The fish will be cooked when it just comes away from the bone—if it flakes easily, it is overcooked.

While the fish is baking, prepare the topping. Melt the butter in a frying pan, add the onions, and cook gently until softened and then browned, about 20 minutes. Push the onions to one side of the pan and tilt so that the butter drains out. Fry the pecans in this butter; they will be browned in about 5 minutes.

Beat the ingredients for the tahini sauce together with the juices from the fish. Cover the fish with the sauce and warm through for 15 minutes.

When the fish is ready to serve, strew the top liberally with the fried onions and pecans.

૮ᴏ

Sautéed Spinach with Chiles

*D*iana sometimes makes this spinach with a little grated fresh ginger instead of the chiles—either way, it's a great fresh take on spinach.

1½ pounds flat-leaf spinach
1½ tablespoons oil

3 tablespoons unsalted butter
½ cup finely chopped onion

4 garlic cloves, chopped

3 serrano chiles or any fresh hot green
chile, finely chopped

2 tablespoons chicken stock or canned
broth

finely ground sea salt to taste

Pick over the spinach and remove any tough stalks. After washing, spin for a few seconds in a salad spinner to remove excess water. Chop roughly. Heat the oil and butter together in a heavy pan or large wok. Add the onion, garlic, and chiles and cook over high heat until the onion is translucent, about 3 minutes. Add the chopped spinach and stir briefly. Add the broth and cook over high heat, turning the spinach over until wilted, about 3 minutes. Adjust the seasoning. Cover the pan and let it sit off the heat for 5 minutes before serving.

℃

Asian Watercress Salad

3 cups firmly packed watercress, thick
stems removed

3 tablespoons roughly chopped cilantro

3/4 teaspoon finely chopped fresh ginger

5 small scallions, both white and green
parts, finely chopped

2 tablespoons Asian sesame oil

4½ tablespoons rice vinegar, preferably
Japanese

1½ tablespoons soy sauce

2½ tablespoons sesame seeds, lightly
toasted in a skillet

Wash the watercress well and spin dry. Put it in a bowl with the cilantro and set aside. Beat together the ginger, scallions, oil, vinegar, and soy sauce until well amalgamated. Toss the salad with this dressing and the toasted sesame seeds.

Sliced Oranges with Almond Brittle

*T*his refreshing orange dessert has a couple of unusual elements—the almond brittle and the orange zest, which give it crunch and punch. This is an interpretation of a dessert Diana had at the home of Gerald Asher, the wine connoisseur. She particularly likes it with mixed tangerines and oranges—fruit, juice, and peel.

Diana doesn't bother sectioning the oranges—she says she hasn't the patience—but just thinly slices them and enjoys their chewy texture. Fussers may want to section them anyway, of course.

6 large oranges
1 cup fresh orange juice
scant ½ cup sugar
butter for the baking sheet
3 heaped tablespoons blanched and
   slivered almonds

6 fresh mint sprigs
3 tablespoons Cointreau or Triple Sec
   (optional)

Peel the oranges over a bowl, removing all the white pith. Cut into very thin rounds. Arrange the orange slices, no more than 3 deep, in a shallow dish. Pour the orange juice over them and set aside to macerate. Cut the orange zest into julienne strips. Put in a small saucepan with cold water to cover and bring to a boil. Drain and add the strips to the oranges.

Put the sugar in a frying pan and dissolve over low heat.

Lightly grease a baking sheet and set aside.

When the sugar has melted, raise the heat and cook, stirring, until the sugar turns a dark caramel color. Stir in the almonds. Pour onto the greased sheet and allow to cool. As soon as it is cool and brittle, cover with an old cloth and crush roughly with a hammer—do not process or blend. Reserve until ready to serve the oranges. Then sprinkle the almond brittle over the oranges and decorate with the mint sprigs. Add Cointreau or Triple Sec to taste if you wish.

- *Instead of using the almond brittle and mint, just before serving stir in 3 tablespoons sliced preserved or crystallized ginger and 3 tablespoons slivered and roasted almonds.*

- *Making the caramel for the almond brittle couldn't be simpler, but if you're nervous about caramelizing, you can do the same thing in the microwave. It will take about 4 minutes, but do it in spurts the way you melt chocolate so you can control how quickly it goes.*

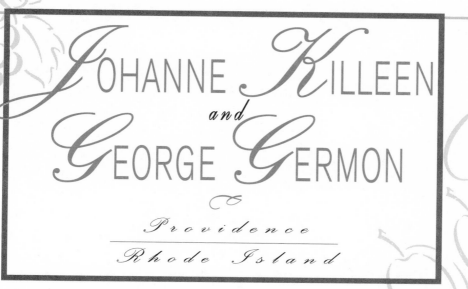

JOHANNE KILLEEN
and
GEORGE GERMON

Providence

Rhode Island

*White Peaches in White Wine

*Red Creamer Potatoes with Anchovies

Spaghettini with Littleneck Clams *Macchiato*

Spicy Braised Lobster

Corn on the Cob

*Soused Peaches with Mascarpone Amaretti

Wine:

For the peaches: Tocai, Eno Fivlia, or Pinot Bianco, Tiefenbrunner

For the pasta course: Verdicchio di Matelica, La Monacesca

For the main course: Greco di Tufo, Mastroberardino

*P*oor little Rhode Island—snipped off the coastline by pinking shears run amok and hiding in the fold of every map from New York to the Cape. In truth it's a gem, little known and unsullied.

The Rhode Island School of Design in Providence is partly responsible for the large cadre of artists and designers who live there—some of whom stay on after graduation, like Johanne Killeen and George Germon. The Johnson & Wales College of Culinary Arts also contributes to the good-life atmosphere of Providence. Then there are the naturalists, the sport boat enthusiasts, the fishermen, the history buffs, the craftsmen, the vintners and farmers who find the temperate weather on the coast as ideal for crops and grapes as it is for people. The proof is in Little Compton, the picture-perfect coastal village where Johanne and George live in bucolic bliss and the Sakonnet Vineyards press delicious wine from contented grapes.

For Al Forno, the restaurant conceived and designed by Johanne and George at the start of 1980, this gentle fertile land and its abundant waterways are always inspirational. They use their kitchen like an artisan's studio, where they skillfully craft that sensory loop of nature from the earth to the table. For them, cooking is all about basic instinct—offered up by two very generous spirits. No wonder they run off to Italy, the land of *abbondanza,* whenever they can. They've even outdone the Italians with their incomparable grilled pizza—its sheer beauty and perfection would make Neapolitans weep.

Here's their jeans and T-shirt al fresco New England dinner. It's messy, finger-lickin' summer fun—as George says, "Sometimes we all need to be reminded that lobsters have shells."

We appreciate the value of that reminder, but don't forget to have on hand lobster shears and picks or lobster crackers or at least a communal hammer or two. You'll need lots of large and sturdy paper napkins, a big bowl for tossing in the shells and the corn cobs, and naturally no fine linens for this feast.

If you plan to have this party on your patio or in the yard and have a large grill, there's no reason not to cook the lobsters outdoors as well. In fact, George would probably say that squealing while you watch the pot lid jiggle is all part of the fun. One of those huge enamel canning pots would be just the thing to fit on the grill.

White Peaches in White Wine

*T*he peaches in the aperitif for this menu turn magically into dessert, so put them where no wandering guests will snitch them.

1 bottle Italian dry white wine　　　　*1 10-ounce bottle tonic water (optional)*
8 white peaches, unpeeled and quartered

Half-fill a large pitcher with the wine and add the peaches. Allow the fruit to perfume the wine for at least 30 minutes. Add ice cubes to fill the pitcher. Put a little ice into the wineglasses. Pour and top with a splash of tonic if desired. Reserve the soused peaches for dessert.

Red Creamer Potatoes with Anchovies

12 Red Bliss creamer potatoes (the tiny ones), unpeeled
freshly ground black pepper

½ cup extra-virgin olive oil
6 whole anchovies preserved in salt
6 lemon wedges

Cook the potatoes in a steamer or in the microwave: put them in a single layer in a microwave-safe dish, add water to come a third of the way up the potatoes, cover the dish tightly with plastic wrap, and cook on high power for 5 to 8 minutes, until the tip of a sharp knife pierces them easily. Turn and shake the dish halfway through the cooking. Use the potatoes still warm or at room temperature.

To serve, place 2 quartered potatoes on each plate, grind a little pepper over them, drizzle with olive oil, and drape an anchovy fillet over each potato. Garnish with a lemon wedge.

- *Johanne and George specified salted anchovies for this recipe because they feel they are superior in both flavor and texture. If you agree, and don't mind cleaning them, by all means use them. See our rap on anchovies on page 178.*
- *If you think someone has an aversion to anchovies, fix an emergency plate or two of potatoes with tissue-thin slices of prosciutto. To assure totally free choice for all, arrange the well-drained anchovies, prosciutto, and a chunk of Parmigiano-Reggiano or ricotta salata on a separate platter. Dust the potatoes with finely minced Italian parsley and offer them in a shallow bowl next to a small carafe or pitcher of extra-virgin olive oil, coarse salt, and a pepper grinder.*

Spaghettini with Littleneck Clams
Macchiato

*T*his white clam sauce is stained (*macchiato*) with tomato. The lightly dressed pasta needs to be served piping hot. The informality of this gathering allows you to serve this dish yourself—*trattoria* style—right from the sauté pan. Now's the time to polish that copper. Have a stack of heated wide-rimmed pasta bowls next to you and use tongs or salad scissors to quickly portion out the pasta, placing the clams on top.

salt

6 quarts water

¼ cup virgin olive oil

1 large garlic clove or more to taste, sliced

¼ cup finely minced onion

1½ cups dry white wine

1 cup peeled, seeded, and chopped ripe plum tomatoes or well-drained Italian canned

24 to 36 littleneck clams, scrubbed clean

1 pound imported spaghettini (DeCecco or Del Verde)

In a large pot over high heat, bring the well-salted water to a rolling boil.

Heat the olive oil in a large sauté pan with a tight lid. Add the garlic and onion and sauté over medium heat until golden. Add the wine, increase the heat, and bring to a boil. Adjust the heat to medium-high and reduce the liquid until only 2 or 3 tablespoons remain. Add the tomatoes and bring back to a boil.

Add the clams, cover, adjust the heat to medium-high, and cook until the clams open. They won't open all at once. Check in 5 minutes and then at 2-minute intervals and keep removing the open ones to a heated stainless-steel bowl (heat by filling it with very hot water before you start). Fashion a loose foil lid to keep the clams warm and place the bowl close to your sauté pan, which will help keep it warm and make it easy to toss in the clams.

As the clams begin to open, drop the pasta into the boiling water and cook at a rapid boil for 5 minutes. Meanwhile, continue to cook and remove the clams, keeping the remaining broth at a simmer. Drain the pasta. It will be very firm. Turn it into the broth and toss gently to coat the strands. Reduce the heat to medium, cover, and cook for 1 minute. Remove the cover, toss again, and continue cooking, uncovered, for 1 or 2 minutes or until the pasta is al dente. Garnish the top of the pasta with a few clams and bring the rest to the table in the heated bowl along with the skillet of pasta.

∽

Spicy Braised Lobster

A lobster dinner is a wonderful gift to your friends—it's just that it comes in such a wacky wrapper. The main obstacle is getting it cooked without fuss. This recipe is an interesting alternative to the traditional boiled or steamed lobster, and it precludes having to ingest all that melted butter.

6 1¼-pound lobsters

1 cup loosely packed flat-leaf parsley
    leaves

1 tablespoon finely minced garlic

¼ cup virgin olive oil

½ teaspoon hot red pepper flakes

You'll need 2 large covered sauté pans or 1 large pot that will cover 2 burners to fit 6 lobsters in without layering the bodies.

Coarsely chop the parsley. If you prefer to use a food processor, pulse the motor on and off to keep from mincing it and releasing moisture, which will cause the parsley to steam when cooked instead of char. Blot it lightly with a paper towel to be certain.

Heat the olive oil in the pan(s) until very hot. Add the red pepper, garlic, and parsley. Stir quickly until the garlic is golden and the parsley darkens. Add the lobster, cover, and cook over medium-high heat for about 10 minutes or just until the lobster is cooked. Serve immediately with the pan juices on the side for dipping. Add a little more olive oil to each serving if desired.

- *Don't forget to remove the rubber bands from the claws before cooking!*
  This is a perfect recipe for using culls, which are usually cheaper. Ask if your lobster

purveyor has them or can order them. These lobsters have only one claw, sometimes none at all—alas, lobsters are cannibals, but that little fact always eases our angst over cooking them live.

- *A reminder: Chicken lobsters weigh between ¾ and 1 pound; quarter lobsters weigh between 1 and 1¼ pounds; selects weigh between 1½ and 2 pounds, and jumbos are anything over that. Ask your purveyor which size is the current best price. Lobster is available all year, but it does get scarce, therefore more costly, in the dead of winter.*

- *If you want to grill your lobsters, bring the fire down to medium heat (white ashes over the coals) and split the lobsters in half, starting at the tip of the spine where the tail meets the body and bringing the cleaver sharply forward to the head. Then turn the critter around and split the tail. Or ask the market to do it if you're coming straight home to cook. Remove the head sac and intestinal tract. If it's a female and there's roe, remove it and set aside. Heat the oil-garlic-parsley sauce in a small pan on the grill. Cook the roe in it if you like. Cook the lobsters shell side down, brushing the sauce over the meat and saving some for dipping. If you bring the lid down on the grill for about 5 minutes, the lobsters will have a slightly smoky (and totally delicious) flavor. If you have no lid, lay a piece of heavy-duty foil over the lobsters for this final cooking. They are done as soon as the flesh turns white and firm.*

Soused Peaches with Mascarpone Amaretti

peaches reserved from the aperitif
6 to 8 amaretti cookies, crumbled

1 cup mascarpone cheese, sweetened
with superfine sugar to taste

Divide the peaches among 6 dessert dishes. Sprinkle the crumbled amaretti on top and top with the sweetened mascarpone.

DEBORAH MADISON

Santa Fe

New Mexico

Baked Ricotta and Goat Cheese with Thyme

*Olives with Roasted Cumin and Paprika

*Fennel Crudités with Sea Salt

Saffron Noodle Cake

Herb Salad with Roasted Walnuts

*Caramelized Pineapple with Vanilla Ice Cream

Wine:
1992 Long Sauvignon Blanc, Sonoma

*D*eborah Madison is largely responsible for the twinkle of anticipation we now feel when we hear the word *vegetarian*. As the founding chef of the legendary Greens restaurant in San Francisco, she transformed vegetarian food into a full-fledged cuisine with its own exciting tastes and textures. The depth of her understanding of kitchen garden plants probably owes a great deal to her childhood in the fertile farmland of northern California, where her father was a botanist. Her training at Chez Panisse refined her palate, and the organic bounty of the Zen Center's Green Gulch Farm, which supplies the raw materials for Greens, inspired it.

One of the most remarkable aspects of Deborah's cooking is her ability to see things in a new way; slicing into a Belgian endive, she'll cut the leaves lengthwise instead of horizontally, creating a different edge to the taste—a little sweeter—and a fresher shape. Possibly it's her Zen background that has strengthened her ability to focus on the essential nature of a given vegetable or fruit, to capture and enhance it. She also has a well-developed sense of finesse, the quality of perfect balance and subtle seasoning that takes a dish to another level. Her cookbooks—*The Greens Cookbook* and *The Savory Way*—have become bibles for hundreds of thousands of cooks, vegetarian and not.

But Deborah also likes to have fun in the kitchen, and she particularly loves impromptu meals that are improvisations. At home in Santa Fe she's likely to begin with a trip to the farmer's market, where the produce itself inspires her. It might be heirloom beans in a rainbow of colors, spanking-fresh herbs, or local specialties like dozens of kinds of chile peppers, dried squash blossoms, or Indian red peaches. But this menu doesn't depend on such rare bounty—everything you need can be found at virtually any supermarket. And it's a meal that spans several seasons, from early spring to fall.

This light menu is filled with fresh herbs and exhilarating tastes, perfect for brunch or late supper. To make it even easier, skip preparing the olives and just toss some olives with good olive oil and a pinch of crushed fennel seeds. Best of all, you can prepare everything ahead.

࿄

Baked Ricotta and Goat Cheese with Thyme

*T*his terrific baked cheese goes together in about 3 minutes and comes out of the oven with a delectable golden top sprinkled with herbs. Serve it warm on crackers or just stick the cheese diamonds with toothpicks and serve along with the olives and fennel. You probably won't have leftovers, but if you do, crumble them and add to pasta or soups, where they turn into tender cheese dumplings.

extra-virgin olive oil
½ pound ricotta cheese
½ pound fresh goat cheese
8 fresh thyme sprigs

freshly cracked pepper
1 to 2 teaspoons chopped fresh thyme
leaves to taste

Preheat the oven to 375°F. Lightly oil a 2-cup baking or soufflé dish—large enough to hold the cheese in a layer about an inch thick. Mix the cheeses well and spread them evenly in the dish. Brush a little more olive oil over the cheeses and scatter the thyme sprigs on top. Season with pepper, then bake uncovered until the top is golden and the cheese is starting to pull away from the dish, about an hour. Brush with oil again and add the thyme leaves. Let the dish cool for 10 minutes, then cut into squares or diamonds and serve on a plate. If there's any milky liquid around the cheese, just pour it off.

- *It's worth searching out a high-quality ricotta for this dish, but low-fat ricotta will also work. If the ricotta is very moist, drain it before baking. Line a sieve or colander with cheesecloth or a kitchen towel and set it in a bowl or in the sink. Add the ricotta, stir it with a wooden spoon, and turn a plate over on top of it. Weight the cheese by setting a heavy can or skillet on top. Let it drain for at least an hour.*
- *Crack peppercorns in a spice or coffee grinder or roll them in a kitchen towel and give them a few smacks with a hammer or a meat mallet.*

Olives with Roasted Cumin and Paprika

*T*hese zesty olives can be made several days ahead or at the last minute, but they need at least an hour to develop their flavors. The paprika turns the oil a lovely red.

1 pound Kalamata, oil-cured, or cracked green olives	several pinches of hot red pepper flakes
1 teaspoon cumin seeds	4 ½-inch-wide strips of lemon zest
2 teaspoons paprika	1 tablespoon extra-virgin olive oil
2 garlic cloves, thinly sliced	juice of 1 lemon
	1 tablespoon chopped parsley

Taste the olives; if they're very salty, rinse them. Toast the cumin seeds in a dry pan until fragrant, then bruise them with a pestle or a large kitchen spoon. Add them to the olives with the remaining ingredients except the parsley and toss. Let stand for an hour or more before serving, then toss with the parsley and transfer to a serving bowl.

Fennel Crudités with Sea Salt

Slice a small head of fennel into quarters, then slice each piece lengthwise into long batons. Set them in a bowl and serve with a little dish of sea salt.

Saffron Noodle Cake

This crispy little cake has a golden crust, a moist interior, and a beautiful saffron color flecked with green. The recipe is for a single cake, which will serve four; make two cakes for six people. Don't worry about flipping the cake; it's easy once you've done it—try it once before you make it for guests.

salt and freshly ground pepper
2 pinches of saffron threads
½ pound very fine egg noodles
1 or 2 eggs, beaten
½ cup grated dry Jack, Parmesan, or smoked provolone cheese
1 garlic clove, minced or pressed
2 shallots or white parts of 4 scallions, finely diced

¼ cup finely chopped fresh basil
¼ cup finely chopped parsley
1 tablespoon each olive oil and butter for frying

Garnish:
1 red bell pepper, roasted and diced
½ cup mayonnaise with 1 minced garlic clove mixed in

Bring a large pot of salted water to a boil. Put the saffron threads in the bottom of a large bowl with a few spoonfuls of the boiling water to soak. Boil the noodles until al dente, then drain and rinse in cold water and shake dry. Add them to the saffron with the remaining ingredients, except the oil, butter, and garnish, stir well, and season with salt and plenty of pepper.

Heat the oil and butter in a 10-inch cast-iron or nonstick skillet. Add the noodles, pat them down, and cook over medium-high heat without disturbing them until golden on the bottom, about 5 minutes. Turn the cake out onto a plate, slide it back into the pan, and cook on the second side until crisp and golden, about 5 minutes longer. Serve it cut into wedges with a little mound of diced peppers and a spoonful of garlic mayonnaise.

• *You can use canned roasted peppers for the garnish.*

Herb Salad with Roasted Walnuts

*T*his unusual potpourri of greens and herbs is delightful in the amazing range of its elements. It's worth tracking them down, but if time is short you can just use the gourmet mixed salad greens (mesclun) that are ready to serve. The dressing is made by tasting as you go along.

5 cups flat-leaf spinach leaves

2 cups arugula or frisée leaves

3 scallions, thinly sliced

1/3 cup each roughly chopped flat-leaf
   parsley leaves, cilantro leaves, and
   dill

3 tablespoons chopped fresh mint

15 pale celery leaves

3/4 cup chopped toasted walnuts (see
   directions, page 126)

salt

2½ tablespoons walnut oil or extra-virgin
   olive oil

sherry vinegar or fresh lemon juice to
   taste

Tear or cut the spinach and arugula into bite-size pieces. Toss the scallions, all the herbs, and the walnuts together with a few pinches of salt. Add the oil, then toss again with a little vinegar——start with a scant tablespoon.

• *Prepare the salad greens ahead and keep them in a plastic bag in the refrigerator. Roast the walnuts earlier in the day and set aside. Toss everything together at the last minute.*

Caramelized Pineapple with Vanilla Ice Cream

*T*his is a lovely dessert that somehow seems to be more than the sum of its parts. Be sure your pineapple is ripe and sweet—even this technique won't rescue a tasteless, woody pineapple.

1 tablespoon butter

5 tablespoons sugar

12 ½-inch-thick fresh pineapple slices,
    from 2 peeled and cored pineapples

1 quart vanilla ice cream

You'll need to cook the pineapple in batches. Melt the butter in a heavy (not nonstick) skillet over medium heat, sprinkle about half of the sugar evenly over the bottom in a thin layer, and add the pineapple. Cook over medium-high heat until the sugar has caramelized and the bottom side is richly glazed—just a few minutes. Sprinkle the top surface of the pineapple with sugar, turn the slices over, and cook until the second side is also caramelized. Serve warm with a small scoop of vanilla ice cream

* *Nonstick skillets aren't good for caramelizing because the sugar beads up on the surface of the pan.*
* *You can caramelize the slices on a broiler rack lined with foil. Keep the oven door ajar to avoid smoking and watch the fruit closely.*
* *You can make the pineapple slices ahead and place them on a baking sheet. When you're ready to serve dessert, run the sheet under the broiler until the pineapple slices are heated through, just a few minutes.*

CARLO MIDDIONE

San Francisco
California

Veal Carpaccio on Crostini with Lemon Mascarpone

Salmon with Red Cabbage Sautéed with Orange
and Capers

*Poached Pears Filled with Apricots and Hazelnuts
on Raspberry Sauce

Wine:
Lacryma Christi del Vesuvio Bianco, Mastroberardino
or
Rosato, Regaleali

With dessert: Malvasia delle Lipari, Hauner

*C*arlo's sheer joy in the magnificent but simple Italian food he cooks at his San Francisco restaurant/take-out store, Vivande Porta Via, and at Vivande Ristorante is contagious. When you learn that he's the youngest of thirteen children born to Sicilian immigrant parents—both accomplished restaurant and pastry cooks—you begin to get the picture. Both Carlo's ebullience and his well-trained palate come straight from that Italian heritage. It's his instinctive passion for culinary purity, and his drive to share it, that makes him not only a great chef but a great teacher as well. The popularity of his weekly PBS television cooking show, *Cooking with Carlo*, attests to that.

It even feels like Italy in Carlo's huge home kitchen in the hills near Twin Peaks, with windows looking out across the city on one side and to the ocean on the other. Of course the kitchen is the heart of the Middione home—all parties begin there, with Carlo and his wife, Lisa, who's a partner at Vivande, making sure the wine flows as fast as the conversation. A parade of little hors d'oeuvres comes out of the oven, all completely irresistible, and then it's time to repair to the baronial dining table. All this expansiveness barely keeps pace with the southern Italian hospitality.

Pure, honest, simple—Carlo's style seems perfect for the no-fuss approach, but oddly enough he does like to fuss a bit for his friends. So this menu is not quite typical of Carlo in the kitchen, though it's certainly typical of his sensational palate. As with everything simple, the quality of ingredients is crucial—this menu requires the whitest veal, the freshest salmon, great bread, and imported mascarpone. And be sure there's plenty of wine, as there always is at Carlo and Lisa's bountiful table.

Veal Carpaccio on Crostini with Lemon Mascarpone

*T*his delicate veal sandwich with lemon zest and lemon-spiked mascarpone is entirely different from the classic raw beef carpaccio invented at Harry's Bar in Venice, with its mayonnaise-Worcestershire-lemon sauce. And it's versatile: suitable for a sit-down dinner, it can also be passed with cocktails. You need a premium-quality veal here (look for Provimi), or beef tenderloin can be substituted.

12 veal scallops, about 9 ounces

12 thin slices of Italian-style bread, about
    2 by 3 inches

¼ pound mascarpone cheese

1 tablespoon fresh lemon juice

zest of 1 lemon

plenty of freshly ground white pepper

sea salt to taste

2 large garlic cloves, peeled

shaved Parmigiano-Reggiano cheese
    (optional)

Have the butcher (if you have one) pound the scallops thin or do it yourself with a mallet, the flat side of a cleaver, or a rolling pin—they should be about ⅛ inch thick. Set aside. Cut the bread no more than ⅜ inch thick. Set aside. Mix the remaining ingredients together, reserving half the lemon zest, the garlic, and the Parmigiano.

    Toast the bread until it's lightly golden—on a stovetop grill, in the broiler, or in a toaster. While the slices are hot, rub them briskly and quickly on one side with the whole garlic cloves. Immediately spread the mascarpone mixture over the garlic-scented side of the toast, ruffle a piece of veal over each toast, then scatter on the remaining lemon zest. Serve immediately, with or without the shaved Parmigiano on top.

- *You can make the mascarpone mixture a day ahead and store it in the refrigerator, well covered with plastic wrap.*
- *To shave Parmigiano curls, use a vegetable peeler on the flat side of a block of cheese.*
- *For a sit-down dinner, a little salad of baby arugula or frisée dressed with extra-vir-*

gin olive oil, a few drops of balsamic vinegar, salt, and freshly ground pepper makes
a pretty accompaniment. In that case you might put the Parmigiano on the salad in-
stead.

- *Make veal tartare: cut the veal into small pieces and process in the food processor*
  until you have little bits—don't let it go so far that it turns into paste. Fold in the
  mascarpone mixture and pile it onto the crostini. Garnish with Parmigiano curls.

∽

Salmon with Red Cabbage Sautéed with Orange and Capers

This dish has the typical sweet-sour-salty aspect of Sicilian cuisine, provided here by orange, vinegar (itself both sweet and sour), and capers. This dish is almost instant, and you'll find yourself making the cabbage frequently, it's so easy and delicious.

Other firm fish will work here, but salmon is especially gorgeous against the intense purple of the cabbage, and the flavors are perfect together too. Of course Alaskan salmon will be even more wonderful than farm-raised, a pleasure for which you'll pay dearly. You can sauté the salmon if your pans are big enough or broil it or grill it.

6 pieces of salmon fillet or steaks, each about 6 ounces and 1 inch thick, skinned

¼ cup extra-virgin olive oil

sea salt to taste

plenty of freshly ground black pepper

1 red cabbage, cored and sliced ¼ inch thick

zest of 2 oranges

juice of 1 orange

1½ tablespoons small capers

2 tablespoons balsamic vinegar

Dry the salmon well. Lightly rub it with about half of the olive oil. Sprinkle on some salt and plenty of pepper. Set aside for about 5 minutes.

Put the remaining oil into a medium-hot large nonreactive sauté pan and add the sliced cabbage. Toss well. Cook the cabbage over medium heat, stirring gently now and then until it is tender and slightly collapsed, just a few minutes. Add half the orange zest and the remaining ingredients and stir well. Cook until the orange juice reduces to just coat the cabbage. Keep the cabbage hot or make ahead and reheat.

Meanwhile, cook the salmon. Either preheat the broiler or heat a large sauté pan until medium-hot and add the pieces of fish. Let them cook on one side for about 3 minutes, then turn them over carefully and let cook another 3 or 4 minutes or until they are just opaque at the center. (Broiling time is roughly the same.) A 1-inch-thick salmon steak shouldn't cook longer than 10 minutes.

Divide the cabbage among 6 hot dinner plates, spreading it out well. Place the cooked salmon on top and garnish the cabbage and salmon with the remaining orange zest.

- *The technique of seasoning the salmon with an extra-virgin olive oil rub and salt and pepper, then letting it sit for a few minutes, is an excellent flavor-enhancing one for almost any fish—a good thing to keep in mind.*
- *If Alaskan salmon isn't in the budget, look for Icelandic salmon, which is sweet and mild.*

Poached Pears Filled with Apricots and Hazelnuts on Raspberry Sauce

Even though plain fresh fruit is served for dessert after a typical Italian meal, sometimes it's cooked and made fancy. Carlo feels that European fruit is best enjoyed raw, whereas American fruit tends to be too acidic and picked too immature to be savored in its natural state. This dessert takes the fancy approach to American pears, which tend to arrive in the market as hard as rocks. The apricot-hazelnut filling atop each pear half is intensely delicious, and the pears look fetching sitting in their pool of raspberry essence.

All the elements of this dish can be made a day ahead. Cover the pears, the apricots, and the raspberry sauce separately with plastic wrap and refrigerate them; leave the nuts at room temperature. Bring everything to room temperature before you're ready to serve, then just assemble the dish.

6 ripe but firm medium pears such as
    Bosc, Bartlett, or Comice
1 cup dry white wine
½ cup dry Marsala wine
2 cups water

up to ½ cup sugar, to taste
6 large dried apricots or more to taste
½ cup hazelnuts
2 pints raspberries
fresh mint sprigs for garnish

Peel the pears, cut them in half lengthwise, and core them. Set aside. Mix the white wine, Marsala, water, and sugar in a saucepan. Bring to a simmer and add the pears. Poach the pears until they are just tender, about 10 to 12 minutes. Test by stabbing them with the tip of a sharp knife or a skewer. Remove them from the liquid with a slotted spoon and leave them to drain on a rack or a plate.

Put the apricots into the hot liquid until they are soft, about 10 minutes. Remove the apricots with a slotted spoon and drain them on the rack. You can discard the poaching liquid or save it to drizzle over cake or fruit—in which case reduce it by about two thirds or until syrupy and store it covered in the refrigerator.

To toast the nuts: Preheat the oven, or toaster oven, to 350°F. Put the hazelnuts in a pie pan and toast them for 15 to 20 minutes, shaking the pan often. Or micro-wave them on high power on a plate for 2 or 3 minutes. When they start to smell good and look toasty, remove them and let them cool. Rub off as much of the skin as you can with a clean towel and chop them medium-coarse. Chop the apricots medium-coarse and mix with the hazelnuts. Taste: if the mixture needs some sugar, add as much as you like—but remember, this isn't an American dessert, and it shouldn't taste really sweet.

Puree the berries in a food processor and push them through a sieve with the back of a wooden spoon. Sweeten the berries if you need to. Fill the pear hollows with equal portions of the apricot/nut mixture. To serve, coat 6 dessert plates with some of the berry puree and set 2 pear halves on each plate. Garnish with a sprig of mint on each plate and pass plain cookies at the table.

- *You can chop the nuts and apricots in the food processor, but pulse in short bursts to preserve the coarse texture—don't turn it into mush.*
- *If fresh raspberries aren't available, use frozen raspberries.*

- *The apricot-hazelnut mixture is so delicious we started thinking of other ways to use it: in little puff pastry turnovers (use frozen puff pastry, fold squares in half into triangles over a spoonful of the mixture, and bake at 375°F for 10 minutes); or tuck it into little chocolate dessert cups; or spread a thin layer over cheesecake.*

Bright Ideas
PICK UP A CHICKEN

When you're seriously rushed, count on a good rotisserie chicken. With clever costuming you can transform this staple into a star. Plan a half chicken for each guest. Slit the skin down both sides of the backbone with a sharp paring knife and remove the backbone and center breastbone with poultry shears or a knife, making an easy-to-eat portion with a neatly carved appearance. Reheat the birds in a 350°F oven under a loose tent of foil.

• Platter the chicken on a bed of soft polenta made with half chicken broth and half light cream (leave out the butter). Smother the chicken with mixed wild mushrooms quickly sautéed in butter or light olive oil with fresh rosemary, thyme, and chives. Tuck in a little bouquet of stemmed flat-leaf parsley for each guest.

• Serve the chicken with Faith Willinger's White Beans with Garlic, Oregano, and Tomato along with a spinach salad with Eileen Weinberg's Creamy Lemon Vinaigrette sprinkled with finely diced pancetta, fried crisp.

• Cut the chicken into leg, thigh, and breast portions, rub very lightly with walnut oil mixed with grated lemon zest and coarse salt, and serve at room temperature with Susan Feniger's Steamed Artichokes with Lime and Cracked Pepper Mayonnaise and big alternating slices of farmstand red, yellow, and pink (if you're lucky) tomatoes garnished with slivered scallions and whole chives. For the best show, nest it all together on one large tray thinly lined with mesclun. Serve a separate bowl of peppered mayonnaise and chunks of sourdough bread.

• Make a quick coconut curry sauce using Michael Min Khin's recipe as your guide and drizzle it over the hot chicken halves or parts. Accompany it with rice stick noodles (follow the package instructions) strewn with crisp sautéed sweet red peppers.

• Make this delicious Spanish sauce for chicken hot off the grill: In the blender or food processor, puree peeled and seeded tomatoes with a little olive oil, garlic, sherry vinegar, and salt and pepper. Skin the chicken and marinate it in this sauce for several hours. Serve at room temperature with a hot casserole of John Taylor's Black Beans and Rice, garlic bread, and a green salad.

Michael Min Khin

Key West
Florida

**Spicy Fish Steamed in Lettuce Parcels*
Leafy packages of minced white fish seasoned with garlic, lemongrass,
cilantro, and chiles

**Burmese Chicken Curry with Noodles*
A mild coconut chicken curry over soft egg noodles with toppings of fried onions
and garlic, crispy noodles, herbs, and hot pepper sauce

**Tropical Fruit and Ginger Crisps*

Beverage:
Pinot Gris, King Estate
Fumé Blanc, Hogue Cellars
Icy Cold Thai Beer

*M*ichael Min Khin is an anomaly, and so is his restaurant, but we decided not to try filling in the blanks—it would only spoil the fun. He grew up in Rangoon of Burmese and French-American heritage and went to college at American University in Washington, D.C.—where he somehow became a cop in the inner-city Third Precinct. At some point he lived in Hawaii and eventually resurfaced in Washington on the Georgetown restaurant scene. In the seventies Georgetown's chic restaurants were overstaffed with talented, entrepreneurial postgraduates awaiting their destinies.

Fourteen years ago three of the more adventurous types, Michael among them, followed the conch shell trail to Key West and opened their own places. Instead of depending on the traditional cuisine of the Keys for his success, Michael built Dim Sum, an Asian-style teahouse with typical seamless wood joinery, sliding bamboo screens and windows, a thatched roof, and the seductive purr of overhead fans. The restaurant's bar is handmade of local almond tree wood, and the Pan-Asian menu is the perfect match for Michael's background and improvisational style of cooking.

When the restaurant is closed for the summer, Michael and Christine (his wife and the restaurant's hostess) either travel to the Far East for inspiration or stay home and succumb to the pleasures of Key West. Staying home on vacation provides the only chance they get to invite friends in for dinner, which follows a toast to that famous sunset. This is the kind of casual and convivial menu Michael usually chooses. It's a simple and easy-to-prepare menu that deserves some pizzazz in the presentation. Consider

130

getting into the spirit a little with a batik cloth, tropical flowers, and votive candles. All the little *tolee molee* (Burmese for bits and pieces or condiments) do look more appetizing in shallow Asian bowls.

⁊

Spicy Fish Steamed in Lettuce Parcels

1 stalk of lemongrass, trimmed
2 medium onions, chopped
2 garlic cloves, crushed
½ teaspoon Thai fish sauce (nam pla)
2 fresh hot chiles, minced
1½ pounds white fish fillets, minced

¾ cup unsweetened coconut milk as
  needed
romaine lettuce leaves
1 small bunch of cilantro
hot dipping sauce: soy sauce and chile
  sauce mixed to taste

Trim the lemongrass about 4 to 5 inches from the white bulb base. Peel off the toughest outer shell and finely mince a teaspoonful from the white end. Reserve the rest for another use.

Put the lemongrass, onions, garlic, fish sauce, and chiles in a food processor or blender and process to a fine mince. Add the minced fish, pour in a small amount of coconut milk, and pulse once or twice. Keep adding coconut milk and pulsing on and off until you have a thick mixture.

Spread a tablespoon of the mixture in the center of a lettuce leaf and place a sprig of cilantro on top. Make a flat, square package, folding in the sides to keep the filling in while steaming. Secure with a toothpick if necessary. Don't fret if the packages aren't perfect or look ruffly. Steaming will flatten the lettuce. You'll have to fold a couple of these to get the hang of it—just make as tight a little package as you can. A lot depends on the characteristics of the leaf—older leaves have heavy spines that break before they bend, and tender leaves are easier to fold but harder to fasten.

Steam the packets over simmering water in a steamer insert for 15 minutes or steam in a tiny amount of water in the microwave for 3 minutes.

Serve 3 or 4 per person along with the hot dipping sauce.

- *The bright green parcels look most attractive with a stripe of Sriracha Thai chile sauce from the nozzle-tip plastic bottle. We drizzled a little soy sauce over the packages first to save the guests from having to dip.*
- *If you don't want to fuss with a first course at all, just zap some frozen shrimp shao mai in the microwave, decorate the plate with a sprig or two of cilantro, and give each guest a small dish of soy/chile dip.*

☙

Burmese Chicken Curry with Noodles

*B*urmese curries are soupy and best served in flat-rimmed soup or pasta bowls. Guests are supposed to serve themselves to a small amount of noodles and chicken on the first helping and then test their own ability to mix in the *tolee molee* for a great taste. It's considered perfectly polite for novices to ask to taste another guest's creation so you can build an even better dish the second time around! You can see now why the size and shape of the bowl is important. Resist cutting back on the number of condiments—they really give this dish its character.

3 medium onions, finely chopped

4 garlic cloves, smashed

4 quarter-size slices of fresh ginger, peeled and finely chopped

1 teaspoon ground turmeric

2 teaspoons paprika

1 tablespoon Asian sesame oil

2 tablespoons vegetable oil

2½ pounds skinless, boneless chicken breasts, cut into ½-inch cubes

3 tablespoons Thai fish sauce (nam pla)

1 quart unsweetened Thai coconut milk

2 cups chicken stock or canned broth

1½ pounds fresh Chinese egg noodles or vermicelli, cooked and drained

Puree the onions, garlic, and ginger in a food processor. Mix in the turmeric and paprika. Heat the oils in a large sauté pan over high heat until very hot. Averting your face, add the seasoning paste. Reduce the heat to low and simmer, covered, scraping the pan frequently with a wooden spoon to prevent sticking. Add splashes of water if needed. The paste will be ready when the onions are transparent, the paste is richly colored, and the oil is visible again, 15 minutes or more.

If you're preparing this curry to serve immediately, add the chicken cubes and fish sauce to the pan and stir-fry until the meat turns white. Add the coconut milk and chicken broth. Bring it quickly to a simmer, lower the heat, cover the pan, and cook for 15 to 20 minutes, stirring occasionally. Serve the curry and the noodles in separate bowls.

If you're making the curry sauce ahead, add the coconut milk, the chicken broth, and the fish sauce to the cooked seasoning paste. Simmer for 5 minutes, cool, and store as long as 4 days. When you're ready to serve, stir-fry the chicken in a little oil, then add the curry sauce, simmer, and serve with the noodles and the following accompaniments:

> chopped scallions—all the white and half the green
> chopped cilantro
> thin slices of lime
> crushed dried red chiles or minced fresh
> fried onion slices
> fried garlic chips
> crispy noodles
> hard-cooked egg slices
> Thai fish sauce (nam pla)

- *Fried onions can be thinly sliced or finely chopped. Press or twist the onions in paper towels to blot out as much moisture as possible—they'll cook faster and crispier. You can fry them in a skillet in enough hot oil to cover, regulating the heat so that they don't burn but just slowly dry-fry.*
- *To fry garlic, slice the garlic thinly, rinse it in cold water, and then dry the slices between paper towels, pressing out any moisture. Fry the slices as you did the onions, in the same pan, until they're golden. Let them cool in the oil—strain, reserving the oil for other uses. Drain the slices on paper towels. The Italian garlic slicer gadget makes this garnish a snap.*
- *You can buy fried onions and garlic in Asian or Indian markets in cellophane packages, although they're never as good as fresh—particularly the garlic.*

- *For the crispy noodles, Michael says you can also use ordinary chow mein noodles.*
- *If you like, you can make a thin crepelike flat omelet out of fork-beaten fresh eggs, using a tad of Asian sesame oil to cook it in. Slide it from the pan and sliver into fine strips. Replace the hard-cooked eggs with these omelet ribbons.*
- *For a vegetarian alternative, replace the chicken with tofu. You can also use any seafood or firm-fleshed fish.*

Tropical Fruit and Ginger Crisps

Burmese dinners do not normally end with a sweet, since sweets are reserved for between-meal snacks. Fresh fruit or digestives such as candied ginger are more traditional. We suggest a tropical fruit or sorbet, such as mango or coconut, garnished with a sprig of fresh mint and served with crispy Swedish ginger cookies.

Michael's restaurant serves a steamed banana and coconut "custard" that is totally addictive and a simple little miracle. It's on page 228 because this menu uses so much coconut. However, if you love coconut as much as we do, by all means serve it after this meal, particularly if your guests enjoy their curry with lots of chiles. The cool banana-coconut custard is a great palliative after a spicy meal.

Nancy Oakes and Bruce Aidells

Berkeley
California

*Southwest Turkey and Sausage Pie
An updated tamale pie with a chile-and-cheese corn bread crust

*Jícama, Red Onion, and Orange Salad

*Nancy's Coconut Pudding with Lime

Beverage:
1992 Ravenswood Zinfandel, Sonoma
Icy Cold Mexican Beer

*B*ruce Aidells, whose first career was as an endo-crinologist, is the jolly bearded man on the label of his Aidells Sausage Company, which produces a breathtaking array of interest-ing sausages, from andouille to chicken-and-apple to Burmese curry. Most of his sausages are also very low in fat, amazingly. Of course his home freezer is always filled with his sausages, and he can't seem to stop coming up with terrific recipes that use them in new ways. The New Mexico sausage is the secret ingredient in this delicious new version of tamale pie.

Bruce's wife, Nancy Oakes, is the chef-proprietor of Boulevard, her restaurant in San Francisco, where she's famous for her simple, soul-warming food. When they en-tertain at home, they usually prepare easygoing one-pot dishes that can be made ahead of time and reheated. In this household, food is king—but not less important than the guests; Bruce and Nancy would much rather spend their time talking with friends than chained to the stove trying to produce an extravaganza.

There's only one rule: since they're both accustomed to being the boss, they can't work on the same recipe, so this main-dish recipe is perfect for them. Because Nancy's the family baker, she makes the corn bread crust while Bruce makes the sausage filling.

The salad is simply crisp cubes of jícama with slices of sweet red onion, oranges, and a little minced cilantro in a vinaigrette.

One of the joys of this menu is that the pie can be done a day ahead, or just the sausage filling can be prepared ahead. The coconut pudding can be made a day ahead too, so that all you have to do on the day itself is put together the salad, which will take about 5 minutes, reheat the pie (half hour at 350°F), and set the table.

Southwest Turkey and Sausage Pie

*L*eftover turkey is the no-fuss ingredient here. If you're fresh out, you can splurge and buy cooked turkey and/or chicken at the deli or spend a few extra minutes cooking fresh turkey or chicken thighs (see the note at the end of the recipe). Poach them for 45 to 55 minutes in lightly salted water or stock. Let them cool in the pan, then pull off the skin and pull away the bones. Chop the meat coarsely and save the broth for the filling.

This may seem like a very rich dish, and in fact the crust *is* rich, but the Aidells poultry sausages are very lean, as is the turkey, and there's only a tablespoon of additional oil here.

This pie looks particularly wonderful baked in a Mexican earthenware cazuela if you have one.

½ cup blanched almonds

5 garlic cloves, peeled

1 pound Aidells chicken New Mexico
    sausage, Mexican-style chorizo, or
    hot Italian sausage, removed from
    casing and coarsely chopped

1 tablespoon olive oil

1 large onion, finely chopped

1 cup canned crushed tomatoes in puree

1 cup turkey or chicken stock or canned
    broth

2 teaspoons ground coriander

pinch of ground cinnamon

½ cup chopped Mexican canned green
    chiles

2 tablespoons chile powder

½ teaspoon salt

¼ cup bread crumbs as needed

3 to 4 cups diced cooked turkey or
    chicken

freshly ground pepper to taste

1 recipe Chile Corn Bread (recipe
    follows)

¾ cup grated sharp Cheddar cheese

In a small heavy frying pan over medium-high heat, toast the almonds and garlic cloves (without oil), shaking the pan continuously until the nuts are lightly browned and the garlic is beginning to color—they'll start to smell good when they're ready. Transfer to the bowl of a food processor and process until finely chopped but not pureed. Set aside.

In a large heavy skillet or Dutch oven, fry the sausage in olive oil over medium-high heat for about 5 minutes. Add the onion and cook 5 minutes more, stirring frequently. Add the tomatoes, stock, coriander, cinnamon, chiles, chile powder, and salt. Bring everything to a boil and then reduce the heat to a simmer. Cook for 10 minutes. Add the garlic/nut mixture and just enough bread crumbs to thicken the sauce. Stir in the diced poultry. Taste for salt and pepper. Set aside to cool or refrigerate overnight.

When you're ready to bake the pie, put the filling into a 3- to 4-quart casserole and cover with the corn bread batter. Sprinkle with the reserved cheese. Bake at 400°F for 45 minutes to an hour, or until the crust is golden. This dish reheats well and is excellent as leftovers.

• *Leftover roast pork will also work in this recipe.*

Chile Corn Bread

3 tablespoons melted butter

1 cup yellow cornmeal

1 tablespoon baking powder

1¼ cups grated sharp Cheddar cheese

2 eggs, lightly beaten

1 cup sour cream or yogurt

1 8-ounce can creamed corn

1 cup chopped Mexican canned green
  chiles, drained

1 fresh jalapeño chile, seeded and finely
  chopped

½ teaspoon salt

Put the melted butter in a large bowl and stir in the remaining ingredients. Mix all the ingredients thoroughly. Use this batter to finish the pie as directed or for corn bread or muffins:

To make corn bread, pour the batter into a hot buttered 10-inch cast-iron skillet and bake for 20 minutes at 400°F or until the sides of the corn bread start to come away from the pan and the top is a lovely golden brown.

To make muffins, fill 12 muffin cups three-quarters full and bake at 400°F for 15 minutes. Reduce the heat to 375°F and bake for another 5 to 10 minutes, until the muffin tops feel springy. Cool on a rack for 5 minutes before serving.

Nancy's Coconut Pudding with Lime

To get a real head start on this recipe, you can make the coconut mixture up to a week ahead of time and refrigerate it until you're ready to proceed with the rest. You can serve the pudding warm or cold—we liked it best cold.

2 cups unsweetened grated coconut

6 cups half-and-half

12 egg yolks

1½ cups sugar

¼ cup flour

2 tablespoons cornstarch

½ teaspoon salt

6 tablespoons fresh lime juice, from about 4 to 6 limes

2 teaspoons vanilla extract

slices of mango, banana, or strawberry for garnish (optional)

Combine the coconut with the half-and-half in a large heavy saucepan. Bring just to a boil, then turn down to a simmer and cook for 20 minutes. Strain the liquid into a bowl, pressing the coconut with a wooden spoon to extract all the flavor. (Toss out the coconut.)

In a medium heavy saucepan, combine the egg yolks, coconut mixture, sugar, flour, cornstarch, salt, and lime juice. Whisk together until very smooth. Over medium heat, cook until a thick custard forms, stirring constantly—about 5 to 8 minutes. Be careful not to let it boil. Add the vanilla and strain into a bowl—be sure to scrape off the custard on the underside of the strainer. Divide the custard into individual cups, wineglasses, or a serving dish.

• *Unsweetened coconut can be hard to find—try a natural foods store.*

Mix-and-Match Menus

A TEX-MEX DO-IT-YOURSELF BUFFET

Early in the day, crisp-fry flour tortillas, two per guest, in an inch of oil, drain on paper towels, and store in an airtight container. Set a colorful table with baskets of the crisp tortillas and the following toppings. Let guests build their own tostadas: hot refried beans (you can use canned refried beans or pintos, but mash the whole beans and slowly refry either of them—use a little lard for best taste; warm crumbled sautéed chorizo; a choice of warm shredded pork (salted roasted country ribs work well), cooked chicken, and/or minced beef moistened and heated with a little prepared red or green chile sauce; room-temperature garlicky sautéed shrimp cut in half lengthwise; very thin romaine lettuce ribbons (stack the leaves, roll them up lengthwise, and cut into ⅛-inch strips); a hand-mashed, chunky guacamole; a good spicy salsa fresca; grated *Manchego* or grated moist or dry Monterey Jack cheese. Set out the bowls in that order so that the tostadas build up from the hot beans to the cold toppings. Pitchers of iced margaritas or sangria and a platter of Drew Allen's Sliced Tomatoes with Lime are natural companions. Dessert: Put out a bowl of scooped vanilla and chocolate ice cream with more do-it-yourself toppings, like cajeta or a drizzle of deKuypers *Hot Damn* cinnamon liqueur.

Patrick O'Connell

Washington Virginia

Soft-Shell Crabs with Toasted Hazelnuts
Sautéed crabs topped with toasted hazelnuts, tomato, and cilantro

*Garden Tomato Salad
Watercress, sliced tomatoes, grilled red onions, ribbons of Asiago cheese, and fresh basil

Grilled Cornish Hens with Blueberries and Wild Mushrooms
Boned Cornish hens marinated in an herbed blueberry vinaigrette and served with sautéed mushrooms and blueberries over a crispy potato galette

*Ginger Ice Cream with Rhubarb Sauce

Wine:
With the first course: 1992 Morgan Sauvignon Blanc, Sonoma County

With the main course: 1991 Bethel Heights, "Southeast Block Reserve," Oregon

*T*he spate of accolades from critics and patrons for The Inn at Little Washington and the heavy-medal culinary awards for Chef Patrick O'Connell are all deserved. But what's really interesting about Patrick and his partner, Reinhardt Lynch, is not that they are good at what they do—it's that they *are* what they do. They live and work on the same stage—like the elegant hosts of Fantasy Island awaiting "the car . . . the car. . . ." They're the witty masters of sleight of hand who completely reinvented their world. With the talent of world-class set designers, they transformed a rural American general store into a restaurant and inn of uncommon European charm and sophistication.

If you don't look sharp, you could cruise right past Washington, Virginia (pop. 250)—a sleepy Shenandoah Valley community only an hour or so's drive from the maelstrom of Washington, D.C. From the moment you step into Patrick and Reinhardt's alluring oasis and bask in their welcome, all of your senses are pleasured in a way that says surely you deserve to be there.

But the dinners Patrick puts before his guests reveal the flip side—the real side. There's nothing "faux" about this food. His playful drizzles, squirts, and crunches never obscure quality or flavor, and however artful they are, they never pull him far from the familiar and seductive. In spite of his lofty reputation, Patrick is incapable of pretension—because just beneath that decorous smile lurks a magnetic sense of the absurd.

Like most summer menus, the success of this very elegant one lies in the quality of the ingredients. It's easy for Patrick, out there in the countryside, to have his blueberries plucked right from the bush, his tomatoes sunning on the vine awaiting his knife, and his shiitake mushrooms personally delivered by the local cultivator. No doubt his watercress grows along the banks of a meandering stream. We city folk just have to do the best we can.

This isn't a difficult menu to produce. It involves no unfamiliar ingredients or techniques—it just has many parts. Read through the recipes and you'll see that most of the components can be made ahead—the marinades, sauces, garnishes, nuts—all but the last-minute sautéing of crabs and grilling of hens.

Mix-and-Match Menus

A CRAB FEAST

Turn Patrick O'Connell's first course, Soft-Shell Crabs with Toasted Hazelnuts, into a meal. Balance it with Diana Kennedy's Brown and Wild Rice Pilaf or, if you're feeling guiltless, fill a basket with crisply fried shoestring potatoes sprinkled with a little chili powder. Make Eileen Weinberg's Raspberry Shortcake for dessert.

Soft-Shell Crabs with Toasted Hazelnuts

Soft-shell crabs are a generous treat for guests—yes, they're expensive, and most of us shy away from preparing them, even for ourselves. We're still unaccustomed to cooking food that can stare us down or, in this case, sidle away. A few of the squeamish may not realize that the fish market will cheerfully dress the crabs—you need only pop these delectable critters into a pan. The summer shedding season is all too short.

Sauce:

6 tablespoons mayonnaise

juice of 1 lemon

5 teaspoons Dijon mustard

2 teaspoons dry mustard

salt and freshly ground pepper

Crabs:

flour seasoned with salt and pepper for
    dredging crabs

6 soft-shell crabs, dressed

4 tablespoons butter

2 small tomatoes, peeled, seeded, and
    diced

½ cup toasted, skinned, and slivered or
    sliced hazelnuts (page 126)

2 tablespoons chopped cilantro leaves

½ cup (1 stick) butter, melted

¼ cup vegetable oil

Garnish:

leaf lettuce or any soft deep green leaf

1 lime, cut into 6 wedges

cilantro sprigs

1 to 2 tablespoons snipped fresh chives

Mix all of the sauce ingredients and pour into a plastic squirt bottle or just set aside.

Preheat the oven to 400°F. Cover a plate with seasoned flour. Dredge the crabs in the flour, shaking off the excess.

Brown the 4 tablespoons butter in a 10- to 12-inch sauté pan over medium-high heat, pour out into a small container, and set aside with the tomatoes, nuts, and cilantro. Wipe out the residue in the pan with a paper towel. Divide the melted butter and oil between two 10- to 12-inch sauté pans with ovenproof handles. Heat the butter and oil mixture to sizzling over medium-high heat and place the crabs on their backs in the pan. Maintaining medium-high heat, sauté the crabs until lightly browned, then drain off any liquid in the pan. Turn the crabs over and add the brown butter, tomatoes, hazelnuts, and cilantro.

Place the pans in the preheated oven and bake for 2 minutes. Meanwhile, tightly roll up a stack of lettuce leaves and cut across the roll every ¹⁄₁₆ inch until you have enough chiffonade (ribbons) to make 6 small nests for the crabs.

Remove the crabs from the oven, place one on each nest, and distribute the cooked "salsa" evenly over the top. Garnish each plate with a lime wedge and cilantro sprigs.

Squirt the mustard-mayonnaise over the whole dish attractively or simply place a small dollop to one side. Sprinkle the snipped chives over all.

- *You can make the mayonnaise sauce, chiffonade of lettuce, toasted nuts, diced tomatoes, cut lime wedges, and chopped and snipped herbs ahead.*
- *If you don't have 2 sauté pans large enough to do the job, sauté 3 crabs at a time in one pan, placing them on a baking sheet as they finish cooking. Remove them all at once to the hot oven.*
- *If soft-shell crabs aren't available, this first course could be adapted as a simple jumbo lump crab salad by tossing the picked crabmeat with the mayonnaise sauce and the chopped cilantro and mounding the salad over mixed baby lettuce or watercress. Garnish with the diced raw tomato, toasted hazelnuts, cilantro, and, in this case, a scattering of whole chives. Don't serve the Garden Tomato Salad.*
- *These crabs are so delicious you might want to serve 2 apiece for a main course. If so, Patrick suggests providing a vegetable accompaniment by serving them on top of a seaweedlike tangle of French-cut green beans—cooked, cooled to room temperature, and dressed with a lime vinaigrette. Frozen French-cut green beans are fine. Be sure to keep their bright color by plunging them immediately into ice water after cooking. Dry on paper towels before dressing with the vinaigrette. Pass a basket of crispy shoestring potatoes and hot miniature corn muffins. Patrick's Garden Tomato Salad would make an excellent first course.*

Garden Tomato Salad

This is an ideal palate cleanser between the sautéed crabs and the hens. If you prefer to skip the crab first course, however, this assertive salad would make an excellent starter.

2 red onions, sliced ¼ inch thick and tossed in olive oil, salt, and pepper	2 tablespoons red wine vinegar ½ cup Italian extra-virgin olive oil salt and freshly ground black pepper

a ¼-pound wedge of Asiago, Parmigiano-
  Reggiano, or Romano cheese
2 bunches of watercress, tough lower
  stems removed
6 ripe medium tomatoes, sliced ¼ inch
  thick

salt, pepper, sugar, extra-virgin olive oil,
  and vinegar
6 fresh basil sprigs

Grill or broil the seasoned onion rings until they are just tender but not limp. Set aside. Measure the vinegar and olive oil into a screw-top jar. Add a pinch of salt and 2 or 3 turns of the pepper grinder. Shake to blend and set aside. Cut 2 or 3 ribbons of Asiago cheese per serving with a sharp vegetable peeler or a cheese plane and set aside. Everything to this point can be done ahead.

Lightly dress the watercress with a little vinaigrette and place it on the plates with the stems toward the center. Overlap the tomatoes over the stems in a triangular formation and add the grilled onion rings on top. Add salt, pepper, and a few granules of sugar over the tomatoes and onions. Arrange the ribbons of cheese on each salad and drizzle a little extra-virgin olive oil and a few more drops of vinegar over all. Garnish each plate with a sprig of basil.

☞

Grilled Cornish Hens with Blueberries and Wild Mushrooms

This is definitely a dish you eat first with your eyes. The plain little farm hen looks ravishing in her bright blue dress. Since the blueberry is the only blue food we can think of that keeps its color, we guarantee this main course will get the conversation flowing. The mushrooms and berries have a surprising affinity for each other.

Marinade:
⅔ cup red wine vinegar
1 bay leaf

2 fresh thyme sprigs or ½ teaspoon dried
2 pints blueberries, rinsed
¼ cup extra-virgin olive oil

Hens:

3 1½-pound Rock Cornish game hens,
    rinsed and patted dry
¼ cup olive oil
3 cups small shiitake or cremini
    mushrooms, stems removed
salt and freshly ground pepper

4 garlic cloves, minced
4 tablespoons butter
3 tablespoons snipped fresh chives
6 heaped tablespoons crème fraîche or
    sour cream
6 fresh mint sprigs

Put the vinegar, bay leaf, thyme, and I cup of the blueberries into a saucepan and bring to a boil. Turn off the heat and allow the berries to steep for 20 minutes or more. Strain the mixture through a sieve, pushing the pulp through with the back of a wooden spoon. Discard the skins. Whisk in the olive oil. You should have about I½ cups thin puree. If you want to buy a half pint of blueberries as much as a week ahead, you can make and store this marinade in the refrigerator.

Cutting around bones is a nuisance at the dinner table, not to mention a potential hazard with blueberry sauce to stain your linen, so we recommend partially deboning these little birds. Not to worry, the bones are very soft, the process quite easy, and it can be done the day before.

Place the hens, breast side down, on a clean cutting board. Cut off the wing tips. Cut along each side of the backbone with a sharp boning knife or kitchen scissors and discard the backbone. Open up and flatten out the bird and cut it in half down the middle of the breastplate. Now you can easily remove the tiny rib cage on each half. Leaving the leg and larger wing bones intact, turn and fold the leg and wing over the breast meat into a plump little package with the leg on top. Use the skin as a wrapper to protect the breast meat from direct heat. Marinate the hens for at least 2 hours or as long as overnight.

Grill or broil the hens until the juices from the meatiest part of the thigh run clear, about I0 minutes on each side. Keep them warm in a low oven while you prepare the sauce.

Heat the olive oil in a skillet over medium-high heat and sauté the mushrooms, shaking and tossing them in the pan until they are slightly golden. Season them with salt and pepper and toss in the minced garlic. Drain off any excess oil and turn the

PATRICK O'CONNELL

mushrooms out into a bowl. Set aside. Put the butter into the skillet and heat until it foams and starts to brown lightly. Add the remaining blueberries and the chives and just warm them through. Add back the mushrooms and garlic.

Put a hot half bird on a crispy potato galette (recipe follows), smother it with the mushroom and berry sauté, and top with a dollop of crème fraîche or sour cream. Decorate the plate with a sprig of mint.

- *An alternative to grilling or broiling the hens is to bake them in a 450°F oven for 25 minutes, basting 2 or 3 times with the marinade.*
- *To organize this dinner ahead of time even further, precook 3 marinated and split birds at a time in a covered glass baking dish in the microwave on high for 8 minutes. Either store them in the refrigerator for a day or two or leave them at room temperature for a couple of hours. Then finish them under the broiler or on the grill for only 5 minutes or so on each side. Don't forget to bring them back to room temperature before cooking,*

Crispy Potato Galette

*T*he crispiness of these French potato cakes lends such important contrast to the dish we think it's worth the last-minute fuss. If you don't have a French or Japanese mandoline, a julienne disk for your food processor, or one of those inexpensive plastic vegetable slicers, you'll need more patience to julienne these potatoes than we'd have with company coming—fry up some frozen shoestring potatoes instead.

5 white potatoes, peeled and thinly cut   *salt and freshly ground pepper*
    into matchsticks   *fresh vegetable oil for frying*

Preheat the oven to 250°F. Have ready a baking sheet covered with paper towels.

Blot the cut potatoes dry and toss them in a bowl with a little salt and pepper. Heat $1/2$ inch of oil in a medium skillet until one stick tossed in sizzles. Divide the potatoes into 6 piles. Fry one portion at a time in a thin circle in the hot oil, keeping the galette covered with sizzling oil. Hold it down with a spatula if need be. The potatoes will be crisp and golden in 3 or 4 minutes. Remove each finished galette to the baking sheet, and when they're all finished, slide them off the towels and hold them in a 250°F oven until you're ready to serve the main course.

- *These galettes can be prepared ahead and quickly warmed in a hot oven just before serving. They hold their crispiness quite well.*
- *Another worthy alternative: grate the potatoes on the largest holes of a hand grater or the food processor disk. Blot the moisture from the potatoes with paper towels (to assure crispness) and fry thin plate-size cakes in a little butter in a nonstick pan, flipping them over when the underside is golden and crisp. These will also hold in a warm oven but will lose some of their crunch as they wait.*

Ginger Ice Cream with Rhubarb Sauce

*T*his is a flavor twin of a more sophisticated dessert served at The Inn at Little Washington. Chef O'Connell spreads a light layer of cooked rhubarb over a tissue-thin pizza crust and serves each wedge with an oval of homemade ginger ice cream.

Ice Cream:

6 knobs of preserved ginger in syrup plus
   3 tablespoons syrup

1 quart honey vanilla or plain vanilla ice
   cream, softened
grated fresh ginger to taste

Finely mince the preserved ginger and work it into the softened ice cream along with the syrup. Taste. Add a little grated fresh ginger if you like it zippier. Pile the ice cream back into the container and return it to the freezer for about an hour or until it refreezes.

Sauce:

1¼ pounds rhubarb
¾ cup sugar

Chop the rhubarb and put it in a covered dish with the sugar. Microwave on high until it softens and releases its juice. Taste for sweetness and adjust. Return the rhubarb to the microwave, uncovered, and reduce it to a thick sauce, about 10 minutes on high. Spoon it into a jar and store in the refrigerator.

- *This sauce freezes beautifully, so buy rhubarb whenever it comes into the market and keep it on hand.*
- *You can make an equally delicious sauce by adding a pint of strawberries to the rhubarb. Increase the sugar to 1 cup.*
- *Reduce any leftover sauce to a jamlike consistency and use it on your breakfast toast or muffins.*
- *The dark red field-grown rhubarb makes a more vibrantly beautiful sauce, but the paler hothouse stalks available in late fall and winter taste as good. Adding frozen strawberries will brighten their pallor.*
- *For a totally no-fuss shortcut, the Trappist label has a strawberry-rhubarb preserve that can be thinned out with a little water or kirsch and melted down in the microwave for a dandy sundae sauce for the ginger ice cream.*

Michael Roberts

Los Angeles
California

*Provençal Roasted Eggplant Vinaigrette

Bow Tie Pasta with Scallops, Bacon, and Peas
A light toss of pasta with smoky bacon, tiny peas, sherry, savory, and a touch of sour cream

Mixed Green Salad

*Blueberries with Cajeta

Wine:
Schramsberg Blanc de Blanc

*T*rained as a classical musician and composer, Michael Roberts also had a rigorous classical French chef's training—everything from learning to dice carrots perfectly to making the most elaborate dishes in the cuisine. All this discipline under his belt means that now he's free to indulge his creativity and playfulness in the kitchen. This he's done brilliantly at both his first Los Angeles restaurant, Trumps, and his current Pasadena restaurant, Twin Palms. Who would have thought you could entice cool Angelenos into a restaurant for afternoon tea? But Michael made it such an event, with such sensational little treats to go with the tea, that at 4:30 in the afternoon Trumps was the place to be. At Twin Palms, where Kevin Costner is his partner, the menu is casual Provençal and the mega-restaurant seats 350 people—but people come as much to have fun as to have dinner; there's live music, and the crowd stays late.

Michael's always been an avant-garde, somewhat intellectual cook. In his first book, *Secret Ingredients,* he broke new ground exploring the components of flavor, explaining how the various elements work together and play off each other—territory no other chefs have ventured into so far. Sometimes his combinations are startling—Vanilla Saffron Lobster Soup, or his signature fried plantain slices with caviar, sour cream, and black bean puree—but they're always on target, excitingly delicious.

There aren't a lot of chefs who actually cook at home all the time, and Michael is one of them. Open his refrigerator and you'll find curious things like lamb jerky and homemade prosciutto hanging off the racks; his freezer is jammed with bases for chile and gumbo—in fact, he has a whole cookbook on the subject of cooking for the freezer. But prepared as he is for almost any eventuality, he also likes to improvise with whatever's available, as in this impromptu meal. It begins with a Provençal appetizer that's both light and deeply flavorful. As with everything Michael cooks, this dish has a little twist—briefly cooking the vinaigrette is a brilliant touch that gives it depth and sweetens the garlic. The whimsical bow tie pasta dish has a rich, faintly smoky sweetness. And dessert is simplicity itself.

Provençal Roasted Eggplant Vinaigrette

You can make this appetizer up to three hours ahead of serving.

3 medium eggplants, about 3 pounds	1½ teaspoons herbes de Provence
6 tablespoons olive oil	1½ teaspoons salt
3 garlic cloves, minced	freshly ground black pepper
3 tablespoons fresh lemon juice	6 radicchio leaves, to make serving cups
1 teaspoon red or white wine vinegar	chopped parsley for garnish

Preheat the oven to 450°F. Cut the eggplants in half and score on the cut side with a sharp knife, down to the skin but not through it. Place the eggplants cut side down on an oiled baking sheet and bake for 20 to 30 minutes, until charred and shriveled. Remove from the heat and allow to cool.

Remove the eggplant flesh from the skins and set aside in a bowl.

Combine the oil and garlic in a small saucepan and cook over medium heat until the garlic stops sizzling, about 3 minutes. Add the lemon juice, vinegar, herbs, salt, and pepper to taste. Simmer for a minute and remove from the heat.

Mix the warm vinaigrette into the eggplant. When the mixture cools, mound equal portions in the radicchio cups, sprinkle with the parsley, and serve at room temperature with garlic toasts or green and black Italian olives.

- *If you don't have herbes de Provence sitting around, make your own using dried herbs: mix 2 parts thyme and oregano to 1 part summer savory and marjoram.*
- *To dress this up a little, crisscross roasted red pepper strips (the canned ones are fine) over the eggplant or serve the puree over a fan of roasted red pepper slices.*
- *Use this puree to stuff cherry tomatoes or fill red bell pepper boats for hors d'oeuvres.*

⌒

Bow Tie Pasta with Scallops, Bacon, and Peas

*B*e sure to have everything ready to make this dish—it goes very fast.

6 quarts water

salt

1 pound bow tie pasta

6 strips of lightly smoked bacon

2 tablespoons light olive oil

1 pound bay scallops, patted dry with
    paper towels

3 tablespoons sherry or Madeira

1 cup frozen baby peas, defrosted

½ teaspoon dried savory or a mixture of
    thyme and rosemary

3 tablespoons sour cream

salt and freshly ground white pepper to
    taste

Boil the water, add salt, and cook the pasta until it is al dente.

Meanwhile, cook the bacon in a 10- or 12-inch skillet until crisp. Remove and drain on paper towels. Pour off all but a tablespoon of the bacon fat. Add the olive oil to the pan and raise the heat to high. Sauté the scallops in the oil mixture, tossing and shaking the pan for just 30 seconds, until the scallops take on a little golden color. Deglaze the pan with the sherry, lower the heat to medium, and add the peas and savory. Crumble the bacon and return it to the skillet. Cook for another 30 seconds. Take the skillet off the heat and whisk in the sour cream, salt, and pepper.

Drain the pasta and add to the skillet. Toss everything together and turn out into a warm serving dish or onto warm plates.

⌀

Blueberries with Cajeta

*I*f you're not familiar with cajeta, it's the delectable Mexican caramel made from boiling down milk—cow or goat—until the milk sugars caramelize. In America this tends to be done by boiling whole cans of condensed milk for hours in a large pot of water—but don't try that method; it's unsafe, as every can of condensed milk warns on the label. Instead, look for commercial cajeta (page 88), which is sensational with blueberries or just about anything else.

3 pints blueberries, rinsed
1 cup cajeta, warmed briefly in the
     microwave

Pick over the blueberries, discarding the stems and any mushy or little green ones. Put the blueberries in a bowl and pass the cajeta separately. (Warm it further in the microwave if it's too solid—you should be able to spoon it easily.)

• *If there's no cajeta to be had, mix the blueberries with a little lime juice and a diced banana. Add a spoonful or two of brown sugar and a pinch of cinnamon. Mix well and let sit for about 20 minutes to develop flavor. Pass a plate of cookies.*

HUBERT SANDOT

New Orleans
Louisiana

Sautéed Oysters with Cumin and Mushrooms

Beef Tenderloin Aiguillette
Sautéed fillet, sliced and sauced with burgundy- and honey-glazed shallots

Grilled Potatoes with Thyme

Soft Lettuce Salad with Balsamic Vinaigrette

*Chocolate Hazelnut Mousse

Wine:
Sancerre or Pinot Blanc

1987 Rodney Strong Cabernet Sauvignon or
Vintage Merlot

*B*orn off the coast of Mozambique on the steamy island of Madagascar . . . it sounds more like the lead-in for a Humphrey Bogart/Sydney Greenstreet movie than the cradle setting for a hot New Orleans chef.

Hubert Sandot spent most of his adult life, however, in Paris and environs, where he, like so many talented and accomplished French chefs, learned to cook in his mother's kitchen. We know this isn't just promotional palaver because when we asked him for recipes the measurements were written on the back of his restaurant's menu in soupspoons, coffee spoons, and dessertspoons, the French equivalent of "a pinch of this and a pinch of that." This charmingly casual culinary style prevails at Hubert's two New Orleans restaurants—L'Economie, a modest French bistro, and Martinique, a French Caribbean restaurant.

In real life, however, Hubert is much more of a traditionalist. He and his wife and two daughters live in a classic home with a very large formal garden. His greatest joy in cooking comes on his day off, when he either prepares dinner for his own small family or entertains guests at a proper planned sit-down dinner. The Sandots' friends "share many different horizons," and he clearly takes his mother's admirable view that the regular gathering of friends and loved ones at your table generates renewal of the spirit and brings continuity to your life.

This menu is typical of what might be served at the Sandots'. Although it wasn't conceived as such, it has all the right elements for a holiday dinner. Oysters and filet mignon are both luxe and festive, and, best of all, the menu is quite simple to prepare.

Oysters and steak are a classic combination, but this is far from a classic rendition. Hubert couples the oysters with buttery sautéed mushrooms and seasons the dish lavishly with cumin and garlic. Just before serving, he enhances the pan juices with a splash of dry white wine.

℃

Sautéed Oysters with Cumin and Mushrooms

6 tablespoons butter

1 pound medium mushrooms, about 18, sliced

2 pints select oysters, about 36, well drained

6 small garlic cloves, minced

1½ teaspoons ground cumin

⅔ cup dry white wine

Use 2 large skillets for this quick sauté. Divide the butter between the pans and lightly brown it over medium-high heat, then toss the mushrooms in the browned butter, cooking them until they develop a golden tinge. Meanwhile, drain the oysters thoroughly in a sieve, put them in a bowl, and coat them well with the garlic and cumin. Add the oysters to the hot pans and shake and toss for 3 or 4 minutes or until the edges of the oysters curl.

When the oysters are cooked, moisten the contents of each pan with the wine and let the juices bubble up and burn off the wine's alcohol for a minute. Serve immediately.

• *This dish is best served in a shallow, flat-rimmed soup bowl to accommodate the juices.*
• *Have some good French bread on the table for sopping up the sauce.*

Beef Tenderloin Aiguillette

*S*hallots, burgundy, butter, steak . . . and *honey*? It sounds bizarre but provides an intriguing dimension to the dish by adding sweetness to the shallots and tempering the acidity of the wine.

The Sauce:

6 tablespoons butter

18 to 24 whole shallots, peeled

salt and freshly ground pepper

6 tablespoons wildflower honey

2 cups dry red burgundy

The Steaks:

4 tablespoons butter or more if needed

6 beef tenderloin fillets, 6 to 8 ounces
  each

Melt the 6 tablespoons butter in a large heavy skillet and sauté the shallots over medium-high heat, tossing them often, until they are lightly browned, about 3 minutes. Salt and pepper them to taste. Reduce the heat and cook the shallots until tender, about 5 minutes. Stir in the honey and shake and toss the shallots around to glaze them. Remove the shallots from the pan and add the wine. Reduce it by half, about 10 minutes. Return the glazed shallots to the wine reduction and simmer for a couple of minutes. Set the sauce aside in a bowl or cover and hold for a day without refrigeration if you like. If you make the sauce just before sautéing the beef, simply wipe out the pan and use it for the steaks.

Melt the 4 tablespoons butter over medium heat in 2 heavy skillets or prepare a grill. Sauté the steaks for 8 to 10 minutes, turning them repeatedly and adding more butter if necessary. Transfer the steaks to a low oven (250°F) to keep warm. Deglaze each of the hot pans with some of the wine sauce—pour it all into one pan and reduce the heat to low to keep the sauce hot. When you're ready to serve, slice the steaks with the grain, into strips, and fan them out slightly on each hot dinner plate, preserving a deep overlap so they don't cool off. Spoon a couple of tablespoons of the hot sauce over each serving, letting it trickle down between the slices. Top each serving with 3 or 4 glazed shallots. Serve immediately.

- *The shallots can be peeled a day or two ahead and stored in a resealable plastic bag in the refrigerator.*
- *Glazed shallots are equally delicious with grilled lamb or veal chops and make an appealing surrounding garnish for a whole roast chicken or duck. Use a flavorful wild honey and sprinkle the shallots lightly with cayenne.*
- *If you're cooking for a larger group, consider grilling or oven-roasting a whole tenderloin. Cut off the tail and keep it in the freezer for stir-fries.*

Grilled Potatoes with Thyme

*T*hese "grilled" potatoes are actually baked, or you can put them on your charcoal grill if you decide to fire it up for the steaks. Either way, and in any culinary language, no two foods are a better match than steak and potatoes.

6 small or 4 large Idaho potatoes, peeled
olive oil to coat

salt and freshly ground pepper
fresh or dried thyme to taste

Preheat the oven to 400°F. Cut the potatoes as you like—either into lengthwise fingers like fat french fries or into crosswise chunks or simply into thick slices. Precook them until just tender either by simmering in enough water to cover on top of the stove or with minimal water in your microwave. Drain and spread out to cool. Blot the potatoes dry. Coat them well with the olive oil, salt, and pepper and dust them with thyme. Make a single layer on a rimmed baking sheet or in a shallow roasting pan and bake until crispy and golden, turning them over once or twice, about 20 minutes altogether.

- *You can cut the potatoes in the morning and keep them in a bowl well covered with cold water to prevent discoloring.*
- *You can also cut and precook them ahead of time and keep them in a covered bowl.*

Soft Lettuce Salad with Balsamic Vinaigrette

2 teaspoons Dijon mustard
2 tablespoons balsamic vinegar
½ cup extra-virgin olive oil

salt and freshly ground pepper
mixed baby lettuces or red leaf lettuce

Put all the dressing ingredients in a small screw-top jar and shake well or whisk them together in a small bowl. Taste for seasoning. Drizzle just enough dressing over the chilled greens to coat them lightly. If possible, serve this delicate salad on chilled plates.

Chocolate Hazelnut Mousse

*D*on't let the fact that this is a mousse deter you from trying it. It's very simple and well worth the bother of beating egg whites. It's also just the right ending for this dinner and can be made the night before.

1 cup hazelnuts
1 tablespoon plus 2 teaspoons unsalted
   butter
8 ounces imported semisweet or
   bittersweet chocolate, cut into small
   pieces
6 tablespoons very strong brewed coffee,
   espresso preferred

1 tablespoon sour cream
5 eggs, separated
pinch of salt
2 tablespoons confectioners' sugar
chocolate curls, confectioners' sugar, or
   whipped cream and a sprig of mint
   for garnish

Toast and skin the hazelnuts (page 126) and grind them into powder in the food processor.

Preheat a small heavy skillet, add 2 teaspoons butter, and right away toss in ½ cup of the powdered nuts, reserving any leftover for another use. Toast and stir constantly over medium-high heat for 20 seconds. Remove from the heat and turn out on a plate to cool.

In a double boiler, or on medium-low power in the microwave, melt the chocolate pieces with the coffee. Set aside to cool slightly. Add the remaining butter and the sour cream and stir well to make a smooth and glossy mixture. Cool completely. Whisk in the egg yolks one at a time, keeping the mixture smooth. Stir in the toasted hazelnut powder.

Beat the egg whites until very stiff, adding the salt and sugar halfway through the beating. Incorporate the egg whites into the chocolate mixture a little at a time with a wooden spoon. Refrigerate in a deep covered bowl or individual ramekins for several hours or overnight.

Garnish with chocolate curls and a dusting of confectioners' sugar or top with a small puff of whipped cream and tuck in a jaunty sprig of mint.

Norma Shirley

Jamaica, B.W.I.

*Red Pea Bisque Flambé

Kidney bean soup with fresh thyme, a touch of sherry, and a dark rum flambé

*Johnnycakes

Shrimp Jamaica

Fluffy Mashed Sweet Potatoes

Sugar Snap Peas and Green Beans

Green Salad with Cucumber Ribbons

*Piña Colada Mousse

Jamaican Blue Mountain Coffee

Wine:
White Côtes-du-Rhône

*N*orma Shirley has been called the Julia Child of Jamaica by *Vogue,* and indeed she has something of Julia's extraordinary presence and warmth as well as her command of French cuisine. She grew up in Jamaica, but she's also lived in France, New York, Scotland, and India, all of which have contributed to her innovative style in the kitchen. She's been an air ambulance nurse, a midwife, a food stylist, and a film caterer. Now she owns two restaurants in Jamaica—Norma and Norma at the Wharfhouse, and Norma's on the Beach in South Beach, Miami, managed by her son Delius.

Norma has devoted herself to elevating her island's culinary image above Jamaica jerk everything. When she returned to her island in the sun, she was well prepared to transform the superb local ingredients into lighter, more sophisticated fare, and her restaurant kitchen became her laboratory. The ultimate aim is to make sure her native Caribbean food doesn't become just another food fad.

Not a chance; this food is just wonderful. Norma's cuisine is elegant and homey all at the same time, the ultimate comfort food. Her menu here is for an informal dinner for six at home—different from what you'd get at her restaurants. Once you taste Norma's food, you'll be tempted as we often are to hop on a plane and go straight to the Wharfhouse, a picturesque spot on the water that used to be the center of Jamaica's famous sugar trade. If you got completely carried away, you might stay and go to Nouvelle Jamaica, Norma's culinary school in Kingston. But step one is to make this wonderful meal.

Make the mashed sweet potatoes just as you would regular mashed potatoes. Cook the peas and beans separately before mixing them together with a little butter. And use a vegetable peeler to make the long cucumber ribbons—pat them dry with kitchen towels before adding to the salad.

℘

Red Pea Bisque Flambé

In Jamaica *red peas* means kidney beans, and we've hastened Norma's recipe along by using canned kidney beans here. This soup is a winner, and it's almost instant. The flambé part is of course optional, but a flaming bowl of soup will delight your guests, and it's very easy to do.

½ cup (1 stick) butter
1 large onion, sliced
2 parsley sprigs
1 generous fresh thyme sprig
4 to 6 cups chicken stock or canned
    broth

3 15½-ounce cans red kidney beans,
    drained
2 to 3 tablespoons dry sherry
salt and freshly ground pepper to taste
minced scallions for garnish
½ cup Jamaican rum for the flambé

Heat the butter in a 1½-quart saucepan. Add the onion and sauté with the herbs over medium heat until the onion is transparent, about 10 minutes. Put the mixture in a blender or food processor and add 2 cups of stock and half the beans. Blend until smooth. Pour the mixture back in the pan and repeat the process with 2 more cups of stock and the remaining beans. Stir in the sherry. Add more stock if the soup is too thick. Taste for salt and pepper.

Bring the soup to a simmer over moderate heat. Stir and simmer for about 20 minutes. Let the soup cool and then strain it through a fine-mesh sieve, coaxing it through with the back of a wooden spoon. This can be done ahead. Just before serving, bring the bisque back up to a simmer, pour into heated bowls, and garnish with the scallions.

To flame the soup, heat the rum in a small saucepan—or in a glass measuring cup in the microwave—until it's bubbly. Rush to the table, pour a little of the hot rum into each bowl, then ignite them one by one.

Johnnycakes

These are not like Rhode Island johnnycakes (pancakes) but rather little fried biscuits or hush puppies. It may seem like frying bread is anything but no-fuss, but in fact it will take only about 10 minutes, and the crunchy results are so good and so unusual it's well worth the minimal effort.

MAKES 24 SMALL JOHNNYCAKES

2 cups flour
2 teaspoons baking powder
pinch of salt

2 tablespoons softened butter
½ to ⅔ cup milk, whole, low-fat, or skim
vegetable oil for frying

Sift together the flour, baking powder, and salt. Stir in the butter and enough milk to make a soft, loosely formed ball of dough. Turn out onto a floured board and knead the dough a few times by turning it with your left hand, folding it to the center, and pressing down lightly with the heel of your right hand. In 4 or 5 turns the ball will be solid enough to pinch off small pieces. Roll them quickly between your palms and then press them down slightly on the board to make little cakes about 1½ inches in diameter—you should have 24 of them.

Let the cakes rest for 10 or 15 minutes. Meanwhile, heat ½ inch oil in a 10-inch skillet until it's sizzling hot but not smoking. Place half the cakes in the oil so they're not touching. When the bottoms are golden brown, in about 2 minutes, turn them over with tongs. Lower the heat a little so that they don't brown before they cook through to the center. When they're puffed and golden, remove them to a double thickness of paper towel to blot off any excess oil. Fry the remaining cakes the same way.

Serve immediately or keep warm in a slow oven (250°F) for up to half hour.

- *You can reheat these in the oven at 325°F for about 5 minutes, so you can make them just before you start the rest of the dinner and reheat them.*
- *If you cut the recipe in half, you can serve a restrained foursome. These are very appealing, however, and you may be sorry you made so few.*
- *Don't be tempted, as we were, to add cornmeal to the johnnycakes (we were thinking of hush puppies). Even adding more baking powder won't make them puff well; they soak up too much oil, and they have the pitiful look of a bad idea.*
- *Of course these are just as wonderful for breakfast as for dinner. Drizzle a little maple syrup on top—they don't need butter. And they'd make great emergency canapés. Just add some minced fresh herbs and a fresh grating of Parmesan to the dry ingredients and roasted or pressed garlic to the softened butter. Pinch off little balls of dough and roll them, but don't bother flattening them—they'll cook through quickly. Use a good virgin olive oil for frying and shake a little salt over them right after they're fried.*

Shrimp Jamaica

This buttery-herby fresh-tasting shrimp is rich and delicate and peppery (if you make it that way) at the same time. Three pounds makes a lot of shrimp, but your guests are guaranteed to eat every last morsel.

4 tablespoons butter

2 tablespoons chopped scallions

1 tablespoon pressed garlic

¼ teaspoon minced scotch bonnet
    pepper or 1 jalapeño chile, minced,
    or to taste

1 tablespoon fresh thyme leaves

½ cup chicken stock or canned broth

3 pounds jumbo shrimps, peeled and
    deveined, with tails

2 tablespoons chopped parsley for
    garnish

Melt the butter in a 12-inch skillet over medium heat. Add the scallions, garlic, chile, and thyme and sauté for 2 minutes. Add the chicken stock, bring to a boil, and simmer briefly. Cool slightly, puree in a blender, and return to the skillet. Taste and adjust the seasoning.

Add the shrimp to the skillet and simmer for 5 minutes, turning once. Transfer the shrimp to a heated platter. Reduce the sauce if it hasn't already thickened. Pour the sauce over the shrimp and garnish with parsley.

- *The really jumbo shrimp, 10 to a pound, will be spectacular here. But check with the fishmonger to make sure they're tender. You'll be serving 5 of these whoppers to 6 people. You can also restrain the largesse and serve just 3, which is plenty for most sane guests. Or buy 2 pounds of large shrimp (18 to a pound), 6 apiece.*
- *Try hard to find fresh thyme leaves for this dish; it really does make a difference.*
- *You can of course tone down the heat considerably by skipping the scotch bonnet and substituting a mild green chile instead—sometimes jalapeños are amazingly mild. An innocent-looking Anaheim pepper can also bite your head off. Always slice off a piece of chile pepper and touch a moist edge to the tip of your tongue before deciding how much to use. But even without the heat, this dish is wonderful.*

Piña Colada Mousse

*T*his smooth, creamy glide of a mousse is a soothing and refreshing finish to almost any meal. You need to make it a day ahead, fortunately, and you can make it right in the serving bowl. Norma Shirley suggests a glass bowl, which is perfect.

1 coconut

1 cup water

¼ cup condensed milk

½ cup heavy cream

½ cup milk

½ cup crushed pineapple, fresh or
    canned

2 tablespoons rum or to taste

2¼-ounce envelopes of gelatin dissolved
    in ¼ cup hot water

freshly grated nutmeg

fresh pineapple slices for serving

Preheat the oven to 375°F. Pierce 2 of the coconut eyes and drain out the water. Put the coconut on the top shelf of the oven for about 15 minutes, until the shell splits. When it's cool enough to handle, hit it with a hammer and pull the meat away from the shell. Pare away the brown skin and grate the white meat—the grating attachment for the food processor works well. Dice the coconut and place it in a blender or the food processor fitted with the metal blade. Add the water and blend to make coconut milk. You should have 2 cups or more.

Place 2 cups coconut milk back in the blender and add the condensed milk, cream, milk, pineapple, and rum. It will be very full, so be careful as you blend the mixture on low speed, then slowly add the dissolved gelatin. Strain into the serving bowl. Grate fresh nutmeg to cover the top of the mousse. Cover with plastic wrap and refrigerate to set overnight. Serve with fresh pineapple slices.

- *You can minimize your efforts here by using canned coconut milk—the unsweetened kind—but you'll also be minimizing the taste of the mousse. Although it tastes a little thin by comparison, the canned coconut milk version is in fact a bit smoother.*
- *Don't skimp on the rum. If you have nontipplers coming, just heat the rum to burn off the alcohol first. We like the dark Jamaican rum for this dessert, but white will work too.*
- *If you don't have a nutmeg grater, run out and get one. Or use the finest holes on a box grater. Grating fresh nutmeg makes a world of difference.*

Martha Rose Shulman

Berkeley
California

*Olives, Tapenade on Red Pepper Squares,
Radishes, and Parmesan Curls

Fusilli with Red and Yellow Tomato Vinaigrette

*The fresh tomatoes are seasoned with a basil and balsamic vinaigrette, then
tossed with hot corkscrew pasta*

*Arugula and Mushroom Salad with Parmesan

Sourdough Baguettes

*Baked Pears with Ginger Preserves and Biscotti

Wine:
Domaine Tempier Rosé

*M*artha Rose Shulman (author of *Mediterranean Light, Entertaining Light, Provençal Light,* and *The Vegetarian Feast*) first started cooking seriously in Texas, then moved to Paris for twelve years—with many long excursions to her beloved Provence—and now lives in the Bay Area of California. Her frequent company dinners are usually inspired by one or another of these places (or Mexico, her current passion), but they're always light, usually vegetarian, and often insouciant, like this one. This menu is just right for late summer, when the tomatoes are at their best and the pears are just coming into the market.

Martha loves to entertain so much that in Paris (and earlier in Texas) she had a supper club in her rambling Left Bank apartment. She still believes strongly in sharing meals with her friends, sometimes several times a week. So she's learned how to put appealing healthy meals together without angst. This is about as close as you can get to an instant dinner; the most difficult thing about producing this meal is tracking down the ginger preserves.

In the French style, Martha usually doesn't offer too much food before the meal—just a taste or two: good Provençal olives, whole radishes with their pretty tops still on, maybe some shaved curls of Parmesan, and tapenade, the garlicky olive spread with anchovies (easy to make but also available at many gourmet supermarkets), on little squares of red pepper. To drink there's lots and lots of wine, also in the French style.

Trenchermen may find this menu a bit skimpy—and they won't be surprised to learn that Martha developed the original recipes for Dr. Dean Ornish's landmark heart study. Martha has since become one of the leading authorities on low-fat gourmet cooking, and her lusty food is always satisfying on all counts. If you're expecting trenchermen for dinner, however, you can certainly add a roast chicken perfumed with lemon, preferably also at room temperature, and/or a cheese course along with the salad and bread.

Martha loves salads made of all fresh herbs—parsley, mint, whatever's available.

℧

Fusilli with Red and Yellow Tomato Vinaigrette

This dish is beautiful, with its bright red and yellow sauce flecked with green. Marinating the vegetables in the sauce gives it a piquant depth of flavor. If you're serving the pasta at room temperature—our preference, of course, since it can all be done ahead—you might consider skipping the Parmesan and throwing it onto the salad instead.

1¼ pounds ripe red tomatoes, about 5 medium, peeled, seeded, and finely chopped

1¼ pounds ripe yellow tomatoes, about 5 medium, peeled, seeded, and finely chopped

3 large garlic cloves, minced or pressed

1 or 2 tablespoons balsamic vinegar to taste

½ teaspoon coarse sea salt or more to taste

freshly ground pepper to taste

2 tablespoons olive oil

2 to 4 tablespoons chopped or slivered fresh basil to taste

1 tablespoon salt for the pasta

1 pound fusilli

⅓ cup freshly grated Parmesan cheese

In the bowl in which you plan to serve the pasta, toss together the tomatoes, garlic, vinegar, sea salt, pepper, and olive oil. Add the basil and let sit for 15 to 30 minutes. Taste and adjust the seasonings.

Meanwhile, bring a large pot of water to a boil; add the tablespoon of salt and the pasta. Cook al dente, 8 to 10 minutes, according to the package directions. Drain, toss with the tomato sauce, and serve, passing the Parmesan at the table. Or cool and serve at room temperature.

- *Remember that it takes at least 20 minutes to boil a big pot of water for the pasta and time things accordingly if you're serving the pasta hot.*
- *Drain any juice off the tomatoes—you don't want to water down the sauce.*

Baked Pears with Ginger Preserves and Biscotti

*B*aked pears on their own are a treat, says Martha, and with ginger preserves they're really special. And they couldn't be easier to make. You can serve them hot or at room temperature—as we do, of course. But in winter a hot gingered pear might be just the thing. Martha serves the pears with biscotti.

6 firm medium Bosc pears
6 heaped teaspoons ginger preserves
2 tablespoons raw brown (turbinado)
    sugar

¾ cup apple juice

Preheat the oven to 400°F. Lightly butter a baking dish large enough to accommodate all the pears. Cut a cone out of the top of each pear and stand it in the baking dish—if the pear has a bumpy bottom, you may need to cut a little slice off so it will stand. Place a heaped teaspoon of preserves in each cavity. Sprinkle a teaspoon of sugar over each pear. Pour the apple juice into the baking dish.

Bake the pears for 10 minutes, then turn the heat down to 350°F and bake for 40 minutes, basting every 10 minutes with apple juice, or until the pears are thoroughly tender but still intact.

Transfer the pears to serving plates. Pour any apple juice remaining in the pan over the pears. Serve hot or at room temperature.

- *If the pears fall over while they're cooking, just set them upright again and spoon the preserves back on top.*
- *Ginger preserves can be hard to find, and not all gourmet stores carry them. Try a supermarket with British affiliations, A & P, for instance. If you have no luck, mince candied or preserved ginger and mix it into plain honey, omitting the sugar. Or use the ginger lemon honey that's sometimes on the supermarket shelf and skip the sugar.*

ᢒ

Mix-and-Match Menus

AN ANTIPASTO COCKTAIL BUFFET

Plan a grazing table of interesting and varied small dishes: Deborah Madison's Baked Ricotta and Goat Cheese with Thyme and Fennel Crudités with Sea Salt, Killeen and Germon's Red Creamer Potatoes with Anchovies, Olive Oil, Parsley, and Lemon, Michael Roberts's Provençal Roasted Eggplant Vinaigrette, Martha Rose Shulman's Tapenade on Red Pepper Squares, any or all of Carol Field's menu starters, and David Tanis's array of tapas. For a large crowd or a dinner buffet, fill out the spread with Faith Willinger's Tonno di Pollo and Patricia Wells's Provençal Couscous Salad.

*Tapas
Radishes, roasted almonds, green and black olives, anchovy sandwiches, steamed clams with chorizo, Spanish cheese, Serrano ham, caper berries, rustic bread

Vegetable Paella
Summer and winter versions

*Assorted Sweets
Fresh fruit, cookies, and chocolate

Wine:
Spanish Jug Wine or Chilean Cabernet Sauvignon
1985 Cousino Macul Antiguas Riserva

$\mathcal{D}$avid Tanis has been the chef of Cafe Escalera since he and Deborah Madison developed the basic Mediterranean concept there in 1991. By now the restaurant has picked up a Santa Fe imprint as David is subtly influenced by the southwestern style. He's even written a cookbook about corn. Before moving to Santa Fe, David was chef at the café at Chez Panisse in Berkeley. His personal attraction to Spain and its earthy, robust food seems a perfect match for his bearded and swarthy merry *bandido* face. The wide grin seems to say "Here's your glass—there's the bar," and at David's it's stocked with J&B scotch, chilled *fino* sherry, inexpensive red and white Spanish or Italian jug wines, a searing macho brandy for now or later. Tapas will all be set out in a utilitarian profusion of crockery—fingers are fine.

Everyone sips, snacks, and salivates (David says drools) while the relaxed host snaps twigs for the fire to stoke up just the right heat under the paella. Dinner at David's may seem totally unplanned to his guests, who see little brewing when they arrive. Then, suddenly, an artful Spanish picnic appears out of all that smoke in the kiva fire-place. Although dinner seems an entirely casual affair, this chef is very serious about the quality and preparation of what he serves. His food can be as uncomplicated as a salad of fresh figs, arugula, and ricotta salata cheese, but the flavor is never one-dimensional.

We asked David to give us his instructions for paella on top of the stove. If you want to tackle it in your fireplace, you're on your own, since regulating the heat by adding or raking down the twigs is a tricky business. No matter how you do it, tapas and paella are a sensual and satisfying combination—this is Spanish comfort food.

Both the tapas and dessert assortments on this menu leave a lot of room for personal taste—but try to have an abundance; five is a good number of choices. Feel free to experiment, but hold to the spirit and ethnicity of the meal.

Tapas

In addition to the tapas listed in the menu, most of which require no recipe, here are Tanis's recipes for Steamed Clams with Chorizo and two versions of anchovy sandwiches, along with his marinated green olives. There are so many other simple or no-cook tapas ideas: consider marinated white beans or chickpeas, boiled potatoes in garlic mayonnaise, hard-cooked eggs stuffed with tuna or salmon, mussels vinaigrette, and grilled or cold shrimp with an anchovy, caper, and parsley mayonnaise. Try to find some Manchego (sharp), Iberico (mild), or Mahon (intense blue) Spanish cheese to lend some authenticity to your cheese selection. These delicious imports are available now at good cheese counters.

Steamed Clams with Chorizo

1 cup diced white onion
½ pound Spanish chorizo or Portuguese linguiça, coarsely chopped
½ cup olive oil plus oil for serving
2 pounds Manila clams

½ cup water
4 garlic cloves, minced
1½ teaspoons hot red pepper flakes if you're not using spicy sausage
a good country bread for serving

In a large sauté pan over medium-high heat, sauté the onion and chorizo in the olive oil for a couple of minutes. Add the clams and continue cooking until the onions are lightly browned and the clams are coated, sizzling, and well heated. Then add the water and turn the heat up to high to open up the clam shells. Stir and shake the pan until most of the liquid is gone. Add the garlic and the red pepper flakes if you're using them. Drizzle the clams with additional olive oil and serve with a basket of rustic bread cut into chunks for sopping up the juices.

Catalan Anchovy Sandwiches

*P*aint slices of good rustic bread with olive oil and grill on both sides or toast and paint with oil afterward. Rub with a cut clove of garlic and a good ripe tomato half. (In winter, spread with pounded sun-dried tomato.) Cut the bread into triangles and top with anchovy fillets, freshly ground black pepper, minced parsley, and chives.

Santa Fe Anchovy Sandwiches

*S*pread the toast with garlic mayonnaise (aioli, later in this menu) and top with anchovy fillets, thinly sliced scallions, and minced fresh or pickled jalapeños. Chef Tanis suggests that you try this with pita bread or a small crusty bun.

Marinated Green Olives

*B*athe good green olives in olive oil, toasted cumin seeds, crushed garlic cloves, and hot red pepper flakes. Marinate for at least 2 days.

- *About good anchovies: Finding them is hit or miss. Look for salt-cured anchovies at Italian or Spanish markets or gourmet food shops. Be warned that they come com-*

plete with head and tail and must be rinsed, cleaned, skinned, split, gently deboned, and rinsed again—definitely a fussy task. Each fish yields 2 large, meaty fillets that will make 4 canapés, but you might not be convinced that their superior quality and the free lesson in minifish anatomy is worth the trouble.

- Chef Tanis recommends the salted product imported in jars from Barcelona by Darell Corti—expensive but awesome, he reports.
- If you're stuck with garden-variety anchovies, do what we (and Tanis) do—soak them in milk for a half hour, which not only leaches out the excessive salt but generally mellows the flavor and improves the texture. Salt-cured anchovies benefit equally from the milk bath.

༄

Vegetable Paella

6 cups chicken stock or low-salt canned
   broth
1 large onion, finely diced
¼ cup olive oil
3 cups short-grain rice (Spanish Valencia
   or Italian Arborio, not Asian)
salt
4 cups assorted coarsely chopped
   summer or winter vegetables:

Summer Vegetables:

peas, fava beans, green beans, fennel,
   summer squash, tomatoes (peeled,
   seeded, and chopped), roasted
   sweet peppers, both red and yellow,
   grilled or broiled eggplant

Winter Vegetables:

Pumpkin or winter squash, leeks, cooked
   chickpeas, canned plum tomatoes
   (use sparingly), carrots, turnips,
   mustard greens, or Swiss chard

½ teaspoon powdered Spanish saffron
cayenne pepper to taste
chopped parsley or basil and grilled
   scallions or lemon wedges for
   garnish

Preheat the oven to 350°F. Heat the stock to a slow simmer. Meanwhile, in a 12-inch shallow cazuela, enameled skillet or casserole, or double-handled paella pan over medium-high heat, sauté the onion in the olive oil until it's transparent. Add the rice and a little salt. Stir and cook over medium heat until the onion is soft and the rice is translucent. Add all the hot stock and cook for 5 minutes. Add the vegetables, saffron, and cayenne pepper. Taste before adding more salt. Cook uncovered for 2 minutes, stirring occasionally. Move the casserole to the oven for 20 minutes. Remove and cover with a kitchen towel or foil and let rest for 10 minutes before serving. Garnish with chopped parsley and/or basil, and grilled scallions or lemon wedges. Serve with the traditional aioli sauce, as David sometimes does.

Aioli Sauce

Mash 4 or more garlic cloves through a garlic press into 1 cup of (preferably) homemade mayonnaise.

- *If you have some guests in your group who don't like spicy food, omit the cayenne pepper from the paella and add to only half of the aioli sauce for those of us who crave both garlic and heat.*
- *If you don't want to make mayonnaise, beat 1 yolk and the juice of ½ a lemon into a cup of good store-bought mayonnaise such as Hellmann's.*
- *The garlic mayonnaise can be made as much as 2 days ahead and stored in the refrigerator.*
- *If you didn't have time to fix the clams and chorizo for the tapas table, do them while the paella is in the oven and arrange them on top.*
- *You can also decorate the top of the finished paella with grilled jumbo shrimp, tails on—or ring the edge of the cazuela with steamed mussels in their shells.*
- *Although you can satisfactorily reheat any leftover paella for yourself or your family, we don't recommend making this superb main dish ahead of time for a company dinner.*

John Taylor

&

Charleston

South Carolina

Cuban Roast Pork with Lime

Fresh ham studded with garlic and marinated in fresh lime

*Black Beans and Rice

*Mango Relish

A chunky salsa with oranges, jalapeño and sweet peppers, cilantro, and cumin

Warm Tortillas

*Minted Strawberry and Champagne Sorbet

&

Beverage:
Iced Mexican Beer
Sangria

"*H*oppin' John" Taylor's Charleston culinary bookstore of the same quirky name turns out to be much more than a bookstore, more a kind of informal community center for chefs, visiting celebrities, food writers, and anyone who loves to eat and talk about it. The store stocks an unusual mix of cookbooks, including some out of print, the best country ham, stellar condiments (the hallmark of the southern low-country table), real honest-to-goodness charcoal, and grits ground and milled to Hoppin's exacting specifications. In his spare time John also writes cookbooks, *Hoppin' John's Lowcountry Cooking* and *The New Southern Cook*—passionate, authoritative books on southern cooking.

John's kitchen is lilliputian, which may be one reason he loves to cook outdoors so much. It could be an oyster roast on an uninhabited island off the Carolina coast or—a particular favorite—deep-frying a whole turkey over a giant portable burner (don't ask). Wherever he is, dessert will probably be hand-churned ice cream. And wherever he is, a party is almost inevitable.

We managed to get John indoors for this company menu featuring country fare. Here he's stretched his culinary roots all the way south of the border and even west to the shores of Cuba to come up with this great between-seasons meal. John's Cuban friend Carlos Porro provided his grandmother's traditional recipe for roast pork shot with garlic and drenched in lime juice.

The mango relish is so good you should consider doubling the recipe. It keeps well, and we bet you'll want some with leftover pork or a roast chicken.

John sometimes serves this with a pitcher of his instant sangria: pour a hearty Spanish rioja into a pitcher, cut it with 7Up, and float a little barge of fresh fruit on top.

Cuban Roast Pork with Lime

You need to start this roast at least a day ahead. The longer the better—John says the best this roast ever tasted was when he marinated it for a whole week.

1 4-pound bone-in fresh ham, butt end
1 head of garlic, cloves separated, peeled, and split lengthwise

1 cup fresh lime juice, from about 8 large limes

With the tip of a sharp paring knife, make slits all over the roast. Insert a garlic sliver, pointy end down, in each slit. Place the roast in a nonreactive container and pour the lime juice over the meat, rolling it over a few times to let the juice seep into the slits. Marinate the roast in the refrigerator no less than overnight and up to a week—the longer the better, turning it occasionally.

Preheat the oven to 325°F. Place the roast fat side up on a rack in a roasting pan. Roast for about 3½ hours or until an instant-read thermometer registers 165°F. Set the roast aside to rest for 20 minutes before slicing.

- *You can also use a bone-in shoulder Boston butt, blade roast, or a center-cut pork loin for this recipe, in which case the cooking times might vary by as much as an hour. Use your thermometer to be certain. The center-cut loin roast will not be as succulent and moist as the other cuts, but the carving will be easier.*
- *Any leftover pork makes wonderful sandwiches or burritos served with the Mango Relish or a spicy Mexican salsa.*

Black Beans and Rice

1 cup dried black beans, rinsed and
    picked clean of any debris
5 cups water
1 small onion, chopped, about ¼ cup
1 small dried hot chile
10 garlic cloves, chopped (optional)

1 strip of smoky bacon
1 cup long-grain rice
2 epazote sprigs, preferably fresh
    (optional)
1½ teaspoons salt

You can make this dish ahead and reheat it. Otherwise, start about 4 hours before you plan to serve dinner. Place the beans, water, onion, chile, garlic, and bacon in a heavy saucepan and simmer gently, covered, for 3 hours or until 2 cups of liquid remain. Measure the liquid and make up the difference with water if there isn't enough. Add the rice, salt, and epazote if you've found some. Cover the pan and bring the beans and rice back to a simmer. Cook over low heat for about 20 minutes, never lifting the lid.

Remove the pan from the heat, but do not lift the lid. Allow the rice to steam in the pan for another 10 minutes, then remove the cover and lift out the epazote and the bacon and discard. Fluff the rice with a fork and serve immediately.

- *Epazote is a Mexican herb used to season traditional Mexican black beans. It grows wild all over North America and is considered an antiflatulent. Dried epazote will work, but fresh is better.*
- *The garlic may be optional, but we recommend using it in spite of the quantity of garlic used in the accompanying pork roast.*
- *You can speed up this dish without a noticeable loss of flavor if you're willing to give up a little texture. Using 2 undrained 16-ounce cans of cooked black beans (we like the Goya brand of frijoles negros), sauté the onion, garlic, and chile with the bacon strip until the onion is transparent, about 10 minutes. Bring 2 cups water to a boil and add the rice. Cook as described and fluff the rice with a fork. Heat the beans with the seasoning mixture and fold into the steamed rice.*

Mango Relish

2 ripe mangoes, peeled, pitted, and cut
into large dice

1 navel orange, peeled, sectioned, and
cut into large dice

1 cup chopped scallions, including some
green, about 2 bunches

1 jalapeño chile, seeded, deveined, and
minced

½ cup chopped red or green bell pepper,
about ½ large pepper

¼ cup fresh lime juice, from about 2 to 4
limes

1 teaspoon ground cumin

1 scant teaspoon sugar (optional)

salt

¼ cup chopped cilantro

Combine all ingredients in a nonreactive bowl, using the sugar if the mangoes aren't
quite ripe and sweet, then add salt to taste.

- *Jalapeños can be fiery or very mild—if you like your salsa hot, taste the pepper and
  add more if it seems disappointing.*
- *Finding a ripe mango when you need one can be a real challenge. But mangoes freeze
  beautifully, so when you see lovely ones at the right price, snap them up. All you need
  to do is peel, pit, and dice them and tuck them into freezer bags, being certain to remove all the air before freezing. Defrost them and you can make this relish in a jiffy.*
- *This relish is perfect alongside grilled skinless boneless chicken breasts, marinated
  for a few minutes before cooking in Consorzio's luscious mango-flavored vinegar.*

$\mathcal{CS}$

Minted Strawberry and Champagne Sorbet

Strawberries:

1 pint ripe strawberries, hulled

1 teaspoon balsamic, berry, or red wine
   vinegar

1 teaspoon confectioners' sugar or more
   to taste

Sorbet:

¼ cup lightly packed chopped fresh mint
   leaves

2 cups chilled semidry champagne, Italian
   prosecco, semisecco cava, or
   another sparkling white wine

Prepare the strawberries at least an hour before you plan to make the sorbet. Cut them in half or quarter them if they're large. Toss them around to coat with the vinegar and sugar, cover, and refrigerate for at least an hour.

Place the berries and mint leaves in a blender or food processor and blend until uniformly smooth. There should be no large pieces of mint visible. Add the sparkling wine and continue to blend. Freeze according to the manufacturer's instructions for your ice cream maker. Take the sorbet out of the freezer and leave at room temperature for about 20 minutes before serving.

- *You can make this sorbet with leftover flat champagne.*
- *John likes this sorbet tart, but you can add more confectioners' sugar to taste.*
- *You can use frozen unsweetened strawberries when good fresh ones are unavailable.*
- *If you run out of time to make sorbet, serve the strawberries simply tossed with the balsamic vinegar and sugar or the juice of a couple of blood oranges. Serve some crispy little chocolate-dipped tea cookies with the berries.*
- *If you don't have an ice cream maker, freeze the sorbet in an ice cube tray. Before it's brick hard, aerate it in the food processor and return it to the freezer for a short time before serving. It tastes better slightly slushy.*

Jan Weimer

Los Angeles
California

*Chilled Tomato and Red Pepper Soup with Basil and Shrimp

Baked Salmon with Spinach and Leeks

Lemon Rice with Dill

Fig Kebabs with Raspberry Cabernet Sundaes

Wine:
Sauvignon Blanc

*J*an Weimer has done virtually every job there is to do in the food industry. She's the former executive food editor of *Bon Appétit* magazine, but she's also been a chef, journalist, caterer, cooking teacher, recipe developer, and kitchen design expert. She's cooked with famous French chefs—Roger Vergé, Jean Troisgros, and Simone Beck—and she's also eaten bread cooked over camel dung at the far ends of the earth.

Perhaps what's most unusual about Jan is her uncanny ability to spot trends—probably because she has such a keen sense of how people integrate food into the rest of their lives. We very much hope her own taste is a new trend; it's evolved toward a healthy style that's both elegant and full of pure flavor. Jan believes in eating well, using lots of fresh foods—no nasty substitutes for her, because she thinks people always feel cheated and unsatisfied. There are no "bad" foods, just foods to be used in a reasonable balance. Here we have a shining example—except for the scoop of ice cream in the sundaes, the menu has virtually no fat, and it's packed with vitamins and great fresh flavors.

This menu is also striking on the table. The soup is a velvety rich red punctuated with commas of shrimp and dots of snipped green herbs. The delicate coral salmon against the intense green of the spinach, bordered with the soft green and ivory leeks, is remarkable. Since the soup, the spinach sauce, the leeks, and the dessert sauce can all be made a day ahead, the menu is also a no-fuss champ.

Chilled Tomato and Red Pepper Soup with Basil and Shrimp

2 large slices of white or rye bread

2 pounds fresh Italian plum tomatoes, quartered

3 large red bell peppers, cored, seeded, and chopped

2 tablespoons fresh lemon juice

1 teaspoon salt or to taste

Basil Dressing:

1 tablespoon water

1 tablespoon fresh lemon juice

2 teaspoons olive oil

¾ ounce fresh basil sprigs, about ¾ cup tightly packed leaves

¼ teaspoon salt or to taste

Shrimp and Vegetable Garnish:

⅓ to ½ pound large peeled cooked shrimp, sliced in half lengthwise

2 medium crookneck squash, cut into ¼-inch dice and microwaved on high for 1 minute

1 tablespoon snipped fresh chives

6 fresh basil sprigs (optional)

Soak the bread in a bowl in water to cover for 10 minutes or until softened. Squeeze the bread dry and puree it along with the tomatoes, red peppers, lemon juice, and teaspoon of salt in a food processor. Process, pulsing on and off and scraping down the sides of the container as necessary, until you have a very smooth puree—at least 5 minutes. Strain the soup through a fine sieve into a large bowl. Cover and chill for at least 4 hours or overnight.

Place all the dressing ingredients in a blender. Process until you have a very smooth puree, pulsing on and off and scraping down the sides of the container as necessary.

To serve the soup, divide the chilled soup among 6 small bowls. Toss the shrimp and squash in the basil dressing and arrange in the center of the soup bowls using tongs. Sprinkle the center with chives. Tuck in a basil sprig and serve immediately.

- *Of course you don't need to use shrimp if you don't want to—just the squash and the herbs would be very pretty.*
- *The soup makes a fine main course for brunch or lunch.*

⌒

Baked Salmon with Spinach and Leeks

*T*he several elements in this lovely composition can be prepared ahead and assembled at the last minute. The salmon is baked on a bed of leeks at a very low temperature, which gives it a silky texture and a delectable taste. It sits on a pool of spinach sauce on the plates, bordered by the leeks.

Spinach Sauce:
3 bunches of spinach, about 3 pounds, tough roots removed
⅔ to 1 cup chicken stock or canned broth
salt to taste

Leeks:
about 1 tablespoon olive oil
6 medium leeks, about 2 pounds, white and light green parts only, thinly sliced on the diagonal

2½ tablespoons minced fresh thyme
salt and freshly ground white pepper to taste

Salmon:
6 salmon steaks, about ¾ inch thick
about 1 tablespoon olive oil
salt and freshly ground white pepper to taste

Wash the spinach and shake dry. Gradually stir the spinach into a large pan over medium-high heat. Cover, reduce the heat, and cook until wilted, about 3 minutes, stirring occasionally. Drain the spinach. Transfer to a food processor and chop finely, pulsing on and off. With the machine running, gradually pour ⅓ cup stock through the feed tube. Process until smoothly pureed, stopping occasionally to scrape down the sides of the container. Thin with additional stock if necessary so that you have a saucelike consistency. Season with salt.

Film a large heavy skillet with olive oil and set it over medium-low heat. Add the leeks and thyme, cover, and cook until almost tender, about 15 minutes, stirring occasionally. Season with salt and pepper. Transfer to a large baking sheet and make 6 piles large enough to hold the salmon steaks. (Unless you're cooking the leeks well ahead of time, you can use the same skillet for the salmon, so don't wash it.)

Preheat the oven to 225°F. Wash the salmon and pat dry. Film the skillet you used for the leeks with olive oil and set it over medium-high heat. Brown the salmon well on one side, in batches if necessary. Arrange the salmon on top of the leeks, brown side down. Season with salt and pepper. Bake for 20 to 25 minutes or until the salmon is just firm.

To serve, reheat the spinach sauce, if necessary, in the microwave or by stirring it quickly over medium-high heat. Ladle the sauce into the center of 6 warm plates. Tilt each plate to cover with sauce. Arrange the salmon in the center of the plate. Spoon the leeks around the rim of the plate. Serve immediately.

- *Using hydroponic or already-washed packaged fresh spinach will save you many minutes at the sink.*
- *Make both the spinach and the leeks earlier in the day or even the day before, and you'll be ready to cook the salmon and assemble the plates in short order.*
- *It's essential that the salmon steaks be the same thickness, or they won't cook in the same time. Cooking salmon at low heat keeps it moist and tender. The interior doesn't turn pink, though it will be done and will taste done.*
- *You can also broil the salmon on one side instead of sautéing it.*

Lemon Rice with Dill

1½ cups long-grain rice
3 cups water
1 tablespoon fresh lemon juice
grated zest of 1 lemon

1 tablespoon butter
salt to taste
1 tablespoon minced fresh dill

Combine all ingredients except the dill in a 2-quart saucepan with a tight-fitting lid and bring to a boil. Cover the pot and cook over the lowest heat for 17 minutes or until the liquid is absorbed and there are little craters in the rice. Turn off the heat and let the rice sit, covered, for 5 minutes. Fluff the rice with a fork, stir in the dill, and serve.

• *Since the entire plate is taken over by the salmon and its sauce, you'll need to serve the rice on a small side dish.*

Fig Kebabs with Raspberry Cabernet Sundaes

Raspberry Cabernet Sauce:
1 cup sugar
1 cup cabernet sauvignon or other dry
   red wine
2 teaspoons fresh lemon juice
1½ cups fresh raspberries

Sundaes:
12 fresh figs threaded on 6 small metal
   skewers
1 quart vanilla ice cream
1 cup raspberries

Heat the sugar and wine in a medium heavy saucepan over low heat until the sugar dissolves, swirling the pan occasionally. Bring to a boil, stir in the lemon juice and raspberries, and immediately remove from the heat. Puree the mixture in a blender and strain through a fine sieve. Refrigerate for several hours or until chilled.

If you're going to barbecue the fig kebabs, preheat the grill until the coals are medium-hot. If you're going to broil them, preheat the broiler and put the fig kebabs on a broiler rack. Turn the fruit occasionally as it cooks, until it's browned on all sides, 10 to 15 minutes on the barbecue, less than 10 minutes in the broiler.

Push the figs off the skewers, split them in half, and place 4 halves in the bottom of each ice cream dish. Scoop in the ice cream, drizzle on the raspberry sauce, and sprinkle the sundae with berries.

- *You can make the sauce up to 2 days ahead.*
- *If you can't find the figs, the sauce makes a good raspberry sundae on its own.*
- *You can also serve just the figs, cooked or uncooked, with the sauce.*
- *You can use peaches, plums, pears, apricots, and/or nectarines instead of figs.*
- *If you sprinkle a little sugar over the figs before you cook them, they'll caramelize slightly.*

Eileen Weinberg

New York

New York

*Haricots Verts on Baby Greens with Shaved
Goat Cheese

Smoked Duck with Lavender and Lime Honey
Glaze

Roasted Sweet Potatoes with Red Onion

Raspberry Shortcake

Wine:
1993 Côtes-du-Rhône, Guigal

$\mathcal{E}$ileen Weinberg started out as a dancer—modern dance, not fans and feathers—but found herself irresistibly attracted to the world of fine food. She's one of those great self-taught cooks who began with nothing but curiosity and a remarkably sensitive palate—a breed of cat we especially admire. After years of catering, she and a partner opened Word of Mouth on Manhattan's Upper East Side—a wildly successful take-out shop that rivaled The Silver Palate. A restaurant seemed inevitable, and she left Word of Mouth to open Carolina, a southern barbecue restaurant in the theater district that served memorable feasts for many years. Now Carolina's gone and Eileen is back to her old loves, take-out food and catering, at Good & Plenty to Go, a tiny shop off Times Square bursting with wonderful things to eat. And Eileen is still catering—for a select list of famous designers, rock stars, actors, and journalists. Good & Plenty also has a big heart; Eileen has been honored for her work with AIDS patients.

Because she has a small apartment with a big terrace, Eileen's entertaining is seasonal—spring, summer, and early fall. There are two cats that help cook and two dogs that help with the cleaning up. The barbecue comes out, and everything is very informal among the palm trees and Eileen's burgeoning birdhouse collection. Ten floors above the city streets, the unmistakable aromas of barbecue begin to float away on the wind as the guests hoist glasses of sparkling wine, beer, homemade lemonade, or mint tea. Sometimes, says Eileen, a really good bottle of champagne will find its way onto the terrace—and "it doesn't get any better than that on a warm day."

This dinner begins with a beans-and-greens salad, with a bit of cream in the lemony dressing and a taste of goat cheese on top. It ends with a raspberry shortcake that is simply sensational—the biscuits are classic, and yet using raspberries instead of strawberries makes the whole idea seem fresh and new.

℞

Haricots Verts on Baby Greens with Shaved Goat Cheese

*H*aricots verts are those skinny little beans imported from France that cost a fortune—at least a fortune in beans. If you have access to garden green beans, by all means use them instead. The mesclun is pricey too, but this amount is minimal, and it saves you time since all you have to do is put it on the plates.

1½ pounds haricots verts
⅓ pound mixed baby greens (mesclun)
¼ pound hard goat cheese

Creamy Lemon Vinaigrette:
6 tablespoons canola oil
2 tablespoons fresh lemon juice
salt and freshly ground pepper to taste
1 shallot, minced
1 to 2 tablespoons heavy cream

Top the beans and plunge them into a large pot of boiling salted water. Let them cook for just a couple of minutes, then turn them into a colander in the sink to drain. Pour cold water over them to stop the cooking and dry them thoroughly with a kitchen towel.

Put the vinaigrette ingredients, except the cream, in a small screw-top jar and shake well. Just before serving, divide the salad greens among the plates and top with the beans. Shake the dressing well again and add a spoonful of cream. Beat the cream in with a fork, taste for seasoning, and pour evenly over each salad plate. Top the salads with a few shavings of the goat cheese.

℃

Smoked Duck with Lavender and Lime Honey Glaze

*I*f you cook the duck in a lidded barbecue, it will be smoked; in the oven it won't be smoked, of course, but it will still be delicious. You can mix duck breasts and legs if you like or use half a duck per person. Just be sure to take note of their different cooking times and allow for it. The duck should be marinated at least two hours and up to twenty-four hours ahead.

12 duck legs with thighs attached or 12
duck breasts
salt and freshly ground pepper

Marinade:

½ pound light brown sugar
1 cup cider vinegar
1 cup apple juice
⅓ cup paprika
2 teaspoons salt

Glaze:

½ cup (1 stick) butter
1 cup honey
¼ cup fresh lime or lemon juice
several fresh lemon thyme branches
2 tablespoons dried lavender (optional)

Garnish:

1 red bell pepper, cored, seeded, and cut
into rings
1 yellow bell pepper, cored, seeded, and
cut into rings
fresh chervil or parsley sprigs

Trim the duck of any excess fat. Combine the marinade ingredients in a large nonreactive bowl. Add the duck pieces and coat them thoroughly with the marinade. Let them rest in the refrigerator for at least 2 hours.

Meanwhile, prepare the glaze. In a saucepan, melt the butter with the honey, lime juice, and thyme. Turn up the heat and bring the mixture to a boil, then simmer for 10 to 15 minutes. Set aside.

Prepare the barbecue for grilling. Remove the duck pieces from the marinade, wipe them dry with paper towels, and let them come to room temperature. Lightly prick the duck pieces all over with the tines of a cooking fork. Season with salt and pepper to taste.

When the fire is ready—the coals are glowing red and covered with white ash—add the duck. Legs will take about 45 minutes, breasts only about 5. If your barbecue has a lid and you want the smoky taste, use the lid, slightly ajar, once the duck pieces are nicely browned.

Check the duck to be sure it's cooked—it should be just a little rosy—then take it off the fire. Bring the glaze mixture back to a boil and add the lavender. Dip the duck pieces in the glaze and serve garnished with the pepper rings and herbs.

- *If you need to, you can also cook the duck in the oven at 375°F. Put the legs on a rack in the oven and roast for 1½ to 2 hours, until tender and a dark golden brown. Baste every 20 minutes with the marinade. Breasts will take only about 15 minutes.*

Roasted Sweet Potatoes with Red Onion

6 sweet potatoes, peeled and sliced into
   ½-inch rounds
3 garlic cloves, chopped

salt and freshly ground pepper
¼ cup olive oil
3 to 4 red onions to taste, sliced

Preheat the oven to 350°F. Toss the sweet potatoes with the garlic, salt, pepper, and oil. Spread on a cookie sheet and bake for 30 to 40 minutes or until fork-tender. The potatoes should be slightly caramelized. Top the potatoes with the red onions and return to the oven for 5 minutes. Toss together and serve hot or at room temperature.

Raspberry Shortcake

This would also be great with blueberries, especially wild blueberries, and of course strawberries are classic.

4 cups flour	1½ cups heavy cream
6 tablespoons sugar	6 tablespoons butter, melted
5 teaspoons baking powder	6 cups raspberries
2 teaspoons salt	a little sugar for the berries
12 tablespoons (1½ sticks) cold unsalted butter, cut into small pieces	1 cup heavy cream, whipped

Preheat the oven to 450°F. Sift the dry ingredients together in a large bowl. Add the butter pieces and blend with your fingers until it resembles coarse meal. Add the cream and mix until you have a soft dough. Gather the dough on a floured board and knead just for a minute or two. Roll the dough out 1 inch thick and cut out 6 rounds using a 4-inch cookie cutter or glass. Place the rounds on a buttered cookie sheet and brush them with the melted butter. Bake for 12 to 15 minutes. Cool the biscuits on a rack.

Mix two thirds of the raspberries with a little sugar in a bowl. When you're ready to serve, split the biscuits on each plate and spoon some of the sugared raspberries over the bottom biscuit. Mound with whipped cream and top with the other biscuit half. Drizzle more of the sugared raspberries on top, add a little more whipped cream, and garnish with the remaining third of the raspberries.

- *You could add a little vanilla and a little sugar to the whipped cream.*
- *If you want to whip the cream ahead, place it in a sieve inside a larger bowl and re-frigerate it. A little liquid will drip into the bowl, but the cream will stay whipped.*
- *You can skip the biscuits and just make the shortcake with very good store-bought pound cake. To gild the lily, brush the slices with melted butter and run them under the broiler before adding the berries and cream.*

EILEEN WEINBERG

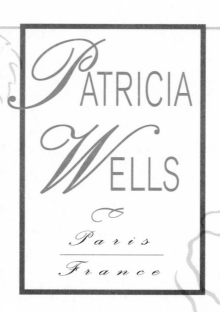

PATRICIA WELLS

Paris

France

*Mixed French Olives, Country Sourdough Bread,
and Salami

Grilled Quail with Sherry-Shallot Vinaigrette

*Provençal Couscous Salad

Mixed Green Salad

*French Cheese Board: Fresh and Aged Chèvre,
Roquefort, and Gruyère

*Modeste: A Modest Berry Dessert

Wine:
Côtes-du-Rhône

*A*lthough she'd written two highly respected books on French food, it seemed astounding when Patricia Wells, the first foreigner and the only woman, was appointed restaurant critic for *L'Express,* the French newsweekly. But it turns out the French are delighted to be told where and what to eat by an American, at least one so knowledgeable and spirited as Ms. Wells. And in this country, Patricia Wells has been almost single-handedly responsible for our renewed love affair with traditional French bistro food. It's because of the success of that mission that she and her husband—news editor of the *International Herald Tribune*—have spent an enviable fifteen years in Paris instead of the two or three years they had planned. "Since we left New York," Walter Wells groans, "I've been chewing just as fast as I can."

But even in France one can't eat out all the time, and fortunately Patricia loves to cook as much as she loves to write about food. The kitchen where she does most of her cooking is in her 250-year-old renovated farmhouse perched on a hillside in Provence, where you can easily grow woozy with the intense fragrance of lavender and rosemary. The markets are equally dizzying, bursting with extraordinary produce, cheese, bread, and charcuterie.

This insouciant summer meal, which begs to be eaten outdoors, comes right out of the market. It's a good example of Patricia's inspired improvisational cooking—like everyone else, she says, she finds her meals just get simpler and simpler. To start, for instance, there might be just olives (the Wellses cure their own), or olives and bread, or olives and bread and a little salami from M. Henny, their legendary Provençal butcher. Quail is a longtime favorite of the Wellses', partly because Walter's family comes from Virginia, where the little birds are farmed. The sweet quail stay succulent with a simple vinaigrette and can be cooked indoors or out. The zingy couscous tabbouleh has been a rage in Provence since the 1980s; it's plumped with just the juices in the vegetables themselves, not the usual boiling water or broth. It's a snap to make in the food processor, and it's both light and intensely flavored. Tabasco is the surprise here; not your typical French ingredient, but the Provençal markets are full of spicy pepper sauces from North Africa. The *modeste* or "modest" dish of berries lies somewhere between a clafouti and a cobbler—it's made in moments and begins to be addictive; Patricia has made this dish more than a hundred times, varying the fruits and the flavorings. If even the *modeste* seems like too much trouble, you can simply serve the cheese plate along with some country bread and grapes.

∽

Grilled Quail with Sherry-Shallot Vinaigrette

*P*atricia says: "When it comes to quick, easy entertaining, I can't imagine anything more appealing than grilled poultry. It tastes good cold or hot, pleases most everyone, and doesn't break the budget. This recipe was inspired by Pierre Kauffmann, whose London restaurant, La Tante Claire, is one of the best in the city. Once the poultry is grilled, it's covered with an intense vinaigrette, making for a lovely, warm, saladlike poultry dish." You can also use split pigeon, Cornish hens, or chicken, adjusting the grill times according to the size of the bird.

Quail usually come packed in fours, frozen or deep-chilled. Check with your butcher ahead of time to be sure they'll be available. The breastbones will probably have been removed; if not, ask the butcher to do it. We've suggested using eight quail here and having the quail cold the next day.

This prep directions may seem complicated, but don't be daunted; it's very simple and so good you'll serve these elegant tiny birds often.

8 quail, breastbones removed
sea salt

Sherry-Shallot Vinaigrette:
6 shallots, minced
2 tablespoons sherry vinegar
sea salt
½ cup extra-virgin olive oil
1 cup minced flat-leaf parsley leaves

Preheat the broiler or prepare a grill—the fire is ready when the coals glow red and are covered with ash.

To get the birds as flat as possible, place them breast side down on a flat surface. Using poultry shears or a sharp knife, split the bird lengthwise along the backbone and open it flat. Press down with the heel of your hand to flatten it completely. Turn the quail skin side up, then press down once more to flatten. With a sharp knife, make tiny slits in the skin near the tip of each drumstick. Tuck the opposite drumstick through the slit to cross the bird's legs. The bird should be as flat as possible to ensure even cooking. Set aside.

Season the quail generously with salt. With the skin side toward the heat, place beneath the broiler or on the grill about 5 inches from the heat so that the poultry cooks evenly without burning. Cook until the skin is browned evenly, about 5 minutes. Using tongs so you don't pierce the flesh, turn and cook the other side, about 5 minutes more. Continue cooking and turning until the juices run clear when the thigh is pierced with a skewer, about 15 minutes altogether.

While the quail is cooking, prepare the vinaigrette. In a small bowl, combine the shallots, vinegar, and salt to taste. Mix with a fork to blend. Stir in the oil and taste for seasoning. Set aside.

Remove the quail from the heat and season once more with salt. Place the birds side by side on a deep platter, drizzle with the vinaigrette, and cover loosely with foil. Let rest for at least 5 minutes.

To serve, arrange a whole quail on each warmed plate and sprinkle with minced parsley. Be sure to provide sharp knives—good steak knives are perfect—with the poultry and offer finger bowls so your guests can eat with their fingers.

PATRICIA WELLS

Provençal Couscous Salad

This crunchy, tangy salad needs to be made with small, firm tomatoes, such as cherry tomatoes or the baby ones imported from Israel. If you use giant ripe juicy tomatoes, all the juice will dilute the salad and make it bland and tasteless. Be sure the fresh herbs are perfectly dried, or you'll end up with mush.

1 cup couscous

¾ teaspoon fine sea salt or more to taste

2 tablespoons extra-virgin olive oil

1 cup loosely packed fresh mint, including stems, washed and dried

1 cup loosely packed flat-leaf parsley, including stems, washed and dried

1 pound small ripe firm tomatoes

3 tablespoons fresh lemon juice

several drops of Tabasco sauce to taste

tomato wedges and diced seeded cucumber for garnish (optional)

In a large bowl, combine the couscous and salt and toss with a fork to blend. Add the oil and fluff the grains with a fork until they're separated and coated evenly with oil. Set aside.

In the bowl of a food processor, combine the mint and parsley and mince. Add the remaining ingredients and process until liquefied—you should have about 2 cups of liquid. If necessary, add tomato juice, broth, or water to make 2 cups. If you have more than 2 cups, discard the excess.

Pour the liquid over the couscous and stir to blend. Cover and refrigerate at least 30 minutes before serving. Stir the salad and taste for seasoning at serving time. Fluff with a fork and serve garnished with the tomatoes and cucumber. You can also use the salad to stuff tomatoes or other vegetables.

Modeste: A Modest Berry Dessert

*T*his *modeste* is indeed a modest dish, sort of like a glamorous tart without the crust. Yet it has a sophistication that more rustic desserts usually don't—it's the eau-de-vie, an essence of pure fruit brandy that can be pear (poire), raspberry (framboise), cherry (kirsch), etc. This version has an intense berry taste that seems to capture the intensity of summer fruit.

butter for the baking dish

2 pints raspberries, blackberries,
      blueberries, or a mix

1 tablespoon eau-de-vie (kirsch,
      framboise, etc.)

½ cup water

½ cup confectioners' sugar plus more for
      dusting the top (optional)

½ cup flour

½ teaspoon vanilla extract

¼ teaspoon almond extract

2 to 3 tablespoons unsalted butter,
      chilled, in chips

Preheat the oven to 400°F. Generously butter the bottom and sides of a 10-inch round porcelain or glass baking dish. Place the berries in the dish in a single layer. Sprinkle the fruit with the eau-de-vie.

In a food processor, mix everything but the butter chips. Spoon the batter around the fruit, dot the top with butter, and put in the oven for 35 to 40 minutes, until the top is golden.

Let cool to room temperature, dust with confectioners' sugar if desired, and serve with whipped cream, lightly sweetened, with a little eau-de-vie added. That's the French approach; for a more American version, add a scoop of vanilla ice cream to each plate.

• *You can make the* modeste *with almost any kind of fruit, but if it's very juicy, you may have trouble getting the slices out of the baking dish in good form—in which case, serve it in bowls, with ice cream.*

- *The original* modeste *is made with cherries, which aren't no-fuss since they have to be pitted. But try using defrosted frozen ones or the very good canned tart ones from Oregon (use two 1-pound cans). Drain them very well first. Tart cherries will need more sugar, up to twice as much (use regular sugar for the extra amount and mix it with the fruit), and try using Amaretto for the eau-de-vie.*
- *We like the* modeste *with a little crunch: add to the batter ¼ cup blanched almonds, finely chopped in a food processor. The crumbs of about 4 amaretti cookies will have the same effect.*

Mix-and-Match Menus

FISH BUT NOT FISHY

Select the freshest, most flexible white fish fillets and slit them down the center at the backbone groove. Starting at the thick end, roll them up with the thin tail on the outside and fasten with a toothpick. Put them side by side in a flat glass gratin dish and pour in a puddle of bottled clam juice or white wine about ⅛ inch deep. Cover tightly with plastic wrap and store in the refrigerator. Prepare some lightly creamed spinach with a dash of cayenne. You can make the spinach ahead and reheat it. Start Paula Wolfert's Fried Rice with Nutmeg about 25 minutes before serving.

Poach the fish roulades in the microwave, pulsing the microwave in increments of 3, 2, and 1 minutes just until the fish is opaque and feels medium firm. The very center will continue to cook as it stands for 5 minutes. While the fish is cooking, quickly sauté 1 or 2 cherry tomatoes for each guest in a little oil or butter only until the skin starts to split. Put the reheated creamed spinach in the center of the plate and top with 1 or 2 roulades and a sautéed cherry tomato. Ring the plate with nutmeg rice.

FAITH HELLER WILLINGER

Florence

Italy

Fettunta with Caviar
Toasted country bread with caviar

Spaghetti alla Carrettiera

*Tonno di Pollo
Poached chicken in the style of tuna

*White Beans with Garlic, Oregano, and Tomato

*Minimalist Cheesecake

Wine:
Chianti, Castello di Ama
Carmignano, Tenuta di Capezzana

With dessert: Vin Santo

*F*aith Willinger is one of those expatriate Americans in Italy who seem to live a charmed life. She's the author of what many knowledgeable critics consider the best guide to eating in Italy, and in fact her home in Florence has become a legendary stopoff for American food writers, who bring home tales of amazing roasts cooked over the spit in her fireplace. Faith is also a walking information center (always in red shoes) for young American chefs who want to learn about real Italian cooking—and she's placed a few choice Italian chefs in American restaurant kitchens. For the lucky ones who've been on her regional tours for food professionals, she gets as high marks for her wit as for her uncanny ability to ferret out the secret addresses of the best producers, cooks, bakers, and vintners.

Of course, in Italy it's a snap to put together a no-fuss meal; even the convenience foods have extraordinary quality. Still, an American supermarket can produce almost everything you need for this simple but unusual meal. Making this dinner doesn't even seem like cooking—it's more like playing in the kitchen.

Fettunta is the Tuscan version of bruschetta, dressed up here with caviar. The pasta is a snap to make, and the chicken, which can also be made with rabbit, can be made days ahead. The chicken is a very Italian concept: the idea is that you're making chicken to taste like canned tuna by gently poaching it in delicate broth and then letting it sit bathed in olive oil, garlic, and sage for at least 24 hours. You'll understand this concept only if you've tasted the superb canned Italian tuna. But never mind; the chicken is extraordinary: velvety, delicate, memorable.

Faith usually doesn't serve dessert—another Italian concept—because she prefers to spend her calories on wine. So she might just have the Vin Santo, an addictive after-dinner wine, and perhaps a biscotto to dip in it.

It goes without saying that Faith's white beans don't come from a can—but ours do, and she's forgiven us. The organic ones are the best, from the natural foods store.

Fettunta with Caviar

country-style bread sliced ¾ inch thick
1 shallot, sliced in half
caviar

extra-virgin olive oil, preferably Ligurian
    (i.e., delicate)

For each person, use I slice of bread and toast just before serving—the toaster oven is fine. Rub the hot toast with the shallot, spread a spoonful of caviar on top, and drizzle with olive oil.

• *Try the excellent American caviar from Walter's Caviar in Georgia. For information, call (912) 437-6560.*

Spaghetti alla Carrettiera

The carrettiera are Italian teamsters.

1 garlic clove, chopped
1 small fresh green chile, chopped
¼ cup extra-virgin olive oil
2 cups chopped, seeded (peeled if you
    want) tomatoes

salt to taste
2 tablespoons chopped parsley
¾ pound spaghetti, preferably Latini
    brand

For the sauce, place the garlic and chile in a 12-inch nonstick skillet, pour in half of the olive oil, and stir with a wooden spoon or fork to coat. Turn the heat to high and, when the garlic just begins to color, add the tomatoes. Cook for 5 minutes to evaporate excess water. Add salt to taste and the parsley.

Cook the pasta in a huge pot of salted boiling water until it's still quite firm. Drain, keeping 1 cup of the cooking water. Put the pasta into the sauce skillet, turn the heat to high, and add ½ cup of the pasta water. Cook the sauce into the pasta—it will reduce a little—for a few minutes, until the sauce thickens and the pasta is done. Add more starchy pasta water if necessary to loosen the sauce. Remove from the heat and toss with an enrichment of 2 tablespoons more olive oil before serving. (No cheese with this.)

• *You can used canned, diced Muir Glen organic tomatoes here.*

Tonno di Pollo

*S*tart this dish at least one and up to three days ahead.

1 large chicken, about 5 pounds	2 stems of parsley
1 carrot	salt and freshly ground pepper
1 medium onion	about 30 small fresh sage leaves
5 to 8 garlic cloves to taste	extra-virgin olive oil
1 leek	mixed salad greens

At least a day ahead, poach the chicken: Put it in a large heavy pot with a lid, add the carrot, onion, 2 garlic cloves, the leek, parsley, and salt to taste, then add water almost to cover the chicken. Bring it to a boil, spoon off any scum that rises to the surface, lower the heat to medium-low—the chicken shouldn't even simmer—and cover. Cook it for about 3 hours or until the meat is falling off the bones.

Let the chicken cool in the broth. Remove and discard the skin. Remove the meat from the bones and chop it into chunks. In a terrine, layer the chicken chunks in at least 3 layers. Salt and pepper each layer, adding about 10 sage leaves and a garlic clove or two to each layer, drizzling each time with olive oil. Cover the final layer with olive oil and set aside to marinate for a couple of hours. Cover with plastic wrap and refrigerate for at least 1 day and up to 3 days. Remove the chicken terrine from the refrigerator about 3 hours before serving to bring to room temperature.

Spoon a little of the olive oil marinade from the terrine over the greens and toss to dress them. Serve the chicken on top of the greens.

• *Your guests may want a little lemon to squeeze over the greens, though the Italians wouldn't.*

℘

White Beans with Garlic, Oregano, and Tomato

1 32-ounce can cannellini beans	pinch of dried oregano
2 tablespoons extra-virgin olive oil	freshly ground pepper
1 garlic clove, pressed or minced	1 tablespoon imported tomato paste

Drain the beans and rinse them in a colander. In a small saucepan, heat the olive oil over medium-high heat and add the garlic, mixing with a wooden spoon until it just begins to turn golden. Add the remaining ingredients, stir well, and add the beans. Cook briefly, cover, and turn off the heat—let the beans sit for a few minutes to heat through.

Minimalist Cheesecake

1 pint whole-milk ricotta

For the sauce,
one of the following:
diluted bitter orange marmalade

chestnut honey
candied chestnuts and their syrup,
    preferably Agrimontana
candied sour cherries and their syrup,
    preferably Agrimontana

Drain the ricotta for several hours in a sieve to remove excess moisture. Using a basket small enough to mold the ricotta into a little cake, line it with plastic wrap and press the drained ricotta into the basket. Fold the plastic wrap over the cheese and refrigerate until serving. Unmold the cheesecake onto a platter. To serve, slice into wedges and sauce.

• *American ricotta is usually a far cry from the superb Italian product. We suggest you add a little cream or some Italian mascarpone and a little confectioners' sugar to taste and a bit of vanilla—start with ½ teaspoon and taste. Give the draining ricotta a stir with a wooden spoon from time to time to help it along.*

More Menu Ideas

COUNTRY DINNER

Buy well-marbled thick rib pork chops, grind some pepper over them (really, that's all), then stand them in a roasting pan on their bones. Put them in a preheated 325°F oven and roast for 30 minutes. Turn the oven up to 350°F and roast for another 30 minutes or until they are soft and golden. Salt the chops and serve them with sweet potatoes mashed with cream and salt and spiked with grated horseradish. If you use bottled horseradish, heat it in the cream for a few minutes to sweeten and diffuse the vinegar. Charred white onions go alongside: halve the onions, then quarter them and separate the layers. In a hot skillet or wok with a little garlic oil, shake and toss them over high heat until tender but not soft. They will have little caramelized brown and black spots. Shake in a few drops of natural liquid smoke seasoning halfway through the sautéing. For dessert, soak a thick piece of pound cake with Jack Daniel's, then mound slightly softened vanilla or butter pecan ice cream over the cake, spreading it out even with the edges. Cover the top and sides with chopped toasted pecans.

Paula Wolfert

Newtown Connecticut

*Pulled Parsley Salad with Black Olives and Pecorino

Fillet of White Fish with Mixed Nuts and Raisins

Fried Rice with Nutmeg

Mixed Green Salad

*Sicilian Ricotta Ice Cream

Wine:
White Graves

*P*aula Wolfert's cookbooks give you everything: romance, adventure, stories from faraway places, and extraordinary recipes. For several decades now her passion for the great little-known dishes of the world has taken her on culinary adventures around the Mediterranean—France, Italy, Greece, Spain, and North Africa. The result is five classic cookbooks—*Couscous and Other Good Food from Morocco, Mediterranean Cooking, The Cooking of South-West France, Paula Wolfert's World of Food,* and *The Cooking of the Eastern Mediterranean*—full of not only wonderful recipes but also a wealth of kitchen savvy available nowhere else.

Above all Paula looks for what she calls the Big Taste—although she enjoys simple grilled food as much as the rest of us, the Big Taste is on another level, deeply satisfying food that appeals to all the senses. Complex flavors that linger, aromas you can't forget, a fully rounded quality are what she strives to create. These are the reasons she's drawn to traditional food, dishes that have slowly built up layers of flavor by being cooked many thousands of times over the centuries. And if there's one especially brilliant cook in a remote place where a famous dish is made, Paula will find her—this is women's food, after all—and pry loose the secrets of the dish. Then she'll refine it even further, another Wolfert trademark.

When she entertains at home, Paula likes to keep things informal. In summer, drinks are served in the gorgeous gardens of her country house, with bottles of wine and sparkling water cooling in a wheelbarrow filled with ice. In chilly weather, tables are set in front of the huge stone fireplace in the dining room. To begin, there might be a *meze*, a spread of salads and side dishes served at room temperature. Then, as the meal progresses, the main dish is just added to the buffet table and guests continue to help themselves. Dinner plate–size Middle Eastern flatbreads are bundled in groups of three, folded over, and simply set out on the table for guests to tear off pieces as they're needed. In the Mediterranean style, dessert is usually fruit and cheese and perhaps a pastry.

Although this particular menu doesn't follow that formula, it's both rustic and Pan-Mediterranean; the main dish is a famous one from Barcelona, the parsley salad has elements from everywhere, and the dessert is a Sicilian specialty. Although the fish has to be done at the last minute, the sauce can be prepared ahead. Everything here has Paula's Big Taste.

ɔ

Pulled Parsley Salad with Black Olives and Pecorino

2 to 3 large bunches of garden-fresh
    curly parsley, stems removed
24 Kalamata olives, pitted
3 tablespoons minced shallots
½ teaspoon Worcestershire sauce

3 tablespoons extra-virgin olive oil
4 teaspoons mild vinegar, preferably cider
salt and freshly ground pepper to taste
3 tablespoons freshly grated pecorino
    cheese

Wash and spin-dry the parsley. Tear each parsley tuft into tiny bits or use a small pair of scissors. You should have about 3 cups of fluffy parsley flakes. Sliver the olives.

To serve, gently toss all ingredients except the cheese in a mixing bowl. Pile the salad into a mound on a serving plate and sprinkle the cheese on top.

• *To pit olives, put them on a work surface and press down on them with your thumb until the pit pops out.*

Fillet of White Fish with Mixed Nuts and Raisins

*N*uts and raisins may seem like unlikely partners for fish, but this combination is one of the great dishes of Barcelona. The secret, says Paula, is the lemon butter that pulls it all together, keeps the fish moist, and accentuates all the flavors and fragrances.

The classic dish is made with flounder or sole, but since we're cooking for six and it's hard to keep three big skillets going to accommodate the thin fillets, we've changed the original fillets to other mild fish, such as grouper or snapper. This way the fish can be finished in the oven without overcooking. Tilapia would also work here.

If you're making the dish just for two, use flounder and cook it entirely on top of the stove—it will take only four minutes from start to finish.

6 tablespoons raisins

6 tablespoons cognac

6 small fillets of grouper, snapper, or tilapia

salt and freshly ground pepper to taste

flour for dusting fish

5 tablespoons unsalted butter

1 tablespoon olive oil

¾ teaspoon grated lemon zest

1 tablespoon fresh lemon juice

6 tablespoons pine nuts, toasted* and coarsely chopped

6 tablespoons each toasted, skinned, and coarsely chopped almonds and hazelnuts (page 126)

3 plum tomatoes, peeled, seeded, and cubed, for garnish

Soak the raisins in cognac for 10 minutes. Preheat the oven to 350°F. Rinse and dry the fish. Season it with salt and pepper and dust with flour, shaking off any excess. Using 2 skillets or working in batches, put 2 tablespoons of the butter, the olive oil, and a pinch of salt in a large nonstick skillet. Heat the fat until it sizzles and just begins to brown. Add as many fillets as the pan will accommodate and sauté them until golden, turning once, about 1 to 2 minutes on each side. Transfer the fish to a baking sheet. Mix

*Toast nuts in a dry skillet over medium heat, shaking the pan often—watch carefully; they burn easily.

the remaining butter with the lemon zest and juice and dot the fish with half the lemon butter. Bake the fish for 6 to 8 minutes. When it's done, the fish will give off a delicious aroma and will just barely flake. Transfer it to a serving platter and cover to keep warm.

Meanwhile, add the mixed nuts to the skillet and brown them lightly. Stir in the raisins with the cognac and bring it to a boil. Ignite the cognac; when the flames die, swirl in the remaining lemon butter and pour it over the fish. Decorate the fish with tomato cubes and serve at once.

◌

Fried Rice with Nutmeg

Fry 1 cup of long-grain rice in 2 tablespoons olive oil in a 10-inch skillet, stirring until all the grains are coated and lightly fried, about 9 minutes. Add enough chicken broth to cover by 1 inch. Add salt, nutmeg, and white pepper to taste. Stir once. Cook the rice, uncovered, over brisk heat until the liquid is absorbed and the rice is tender, about 20 minutes. Rotate and shake the skillet from to time to cook the rice evenly.

◌

Sicilian Ricotta Ice Cream

This isn't a classic gelato since it has no eggs, but it's subtly delicious. You should start the mixture two or three days ahead so the ricotta will have a chance to ripen. You might want to decorate it with candied fruit or shaved chocolate.

2 15-ounce containers part-skim ricotta
    cheese
1 scant cup confectioners' sugar
1 cup cold water

¾ cup well-chilled whipping cream
1 tablespoon pure vanilla extract
2 tablespoons dark rum

Drain the ricotta in a sieve for several hours, then beat it until fluffy using an electric mixer. Gradually beat in the confectioners' sugar. Place in a bowl, cover the ricotta, and refrigerate for 2 days to ripen in flavor.

Whisk the cold water into the cheese. Beat the cream in another bowl until soft peaks form. Flavor with vanilla and rum. Fold the whipped cream into the cheese and refrigerate until the mixture is well chilled. Process the mixture in an ice cream maker according to the manufacturer's directions. Keep the ice cream frozen for several hours to mellow the flavors. If it's frozen too hard to serve, soften it slightly in the microwave—20 seconds on high.

Frying Without Tears

Somewhere between health concerns, panic over kitchen fires, and a reluctance to deal with the messiness of it, most home cooks have gotten out of the habit of frying. But of course we all love to eat anything fried, and a home-fried tidbit is a great treat for your guests. Take heart: if you have the fat at the right temperature, the food will absorb almost none of it. There are several ways to do it.

Most foods can be shallow-fried in a wok or a deep skillet with just an inch or two of oil. Unless you have a thermostatically controlled electric wok or a deep-fat thermometer (which we recommend in any case), it's tricky to keep the oil at a constant temperature. And it's the top-of-the-stove deep-fat frying that can be dangerous.

The easiest way of all to fry is to get an inexpensive bucket-style electric fryer in which you can store the oil between uses. Then you just plug it in, let it heat for about 10 minutes, and you're all set. Here's what you need to know.

• The right temperature is 375°F. The electric fryers are set to maintain that temperature, but be careful not to overload them; otherwise the temperature will drop too much and the food will begin to absorb the fat and won't be crisp. Use a thermometer. When you're frying in batches, wait a few minutes between them for the oil to return to 375°F; otherwise the food will absorb oil and become soggy.

- The tastiest oil for frying is peanut oil, but you can use any vegetable oil, including an inexpensive olive oil. Check the labels and avoid partially hydrogenated fats for health reasons.

- You'll need a slotted spoon or mesh skimmer to remove the fried food, a spatter screen for stovetop frying, and a baking sheet with either a rack or layers of paper towels for draining the fried food.

- If you have no thermometer, the oil will be ready to fry when it has a faint blue haze rising from it. Drop in a little piece of bread; if the oil bubbles and the bread turns golden immediately, you're ready to fry.

- The food needs to be really dry when it goes into the fryer, so make sure that wetter items like potatoes and onions are completely dried first (for french fries: soak the potato slices in cold water with a little vinegar for a half hour before frying for particularly delicious fries).

- Always avert your face when you add the food to the fryer.

- A quick batter for coating vegetables or fish: mix equal parts of tonic or beer with flour—whisk together and let sit for 30 minutes. Whisk again; if the batter doesn't make a thin coating for the food, adjust the water or flour accordingly.

- Batter-dipped side-dish vegetables: asparagus, baked beet slices, broccoli or cauliflower florets, red pepper strips, zucchini or eggplant fingers.

- Quick garnishes for the plate that require no coating: thinly sliced carrots, parsnips, sweet potato, and taro—all cut lengthwise to get the longest strips; kale cut into ribbons; whole stemmed spinach leaves; fresh herb sprigs—parsley, basil, tarragon, and oregano.

- Salt the fried food just before you serve it or let the guests salt their own to avoid sogginess.

- Drain the fried food well, on paper towels or on racks.

- Discard the oil after two or three uses; it begins to break down, and the food will not be as crisp. Filter used oil through a coffee filter or paper towel in a sieve before storing it. When you use it again, refresh it by tossing in a peeled half potato, a lemon, or a cinnamon stick while the oil is heating.

Diane Rossen Worthington

Sherman Oaks
California

*Smoked Trout Mousse

*Beef Stew with Sun-Dried Tomatoes and
Butternut Squash

Salad of Winter Greens

Corn Muffins

Apple Crisp with Dried Fruit

Beverage:

With the mousse: Sauvignon Blanc or Sparkling Wine

With the stew: Merlot, Zinfandel, or Full-Bodied Beer

$\mathcal{D}$iane was one of those few kids who think a lot about what they eat—and there can't have been too many teenagers who read themselves to sleep with Escoffier every night, but Diane did. Although she's certified to counsel the severely disabled—great training, she jokes, for her job as host of *California Food*, her Los Angeles radio show—somehow she kept thinking about food more than anything else. Finally she went to London to get a diploma at the Cordon Bleu and cooked up a storm in Paris, where she also studied. By the time she got back to California in the early 1970s, something was definitely cooking there: the California cuisine was in its infancy, and Diane jumped right in.

Her cookbook on the subject, *The Cuisine of California*, has become a classic. Diane saw clearly that the elements of this recent emphasis on pristine produce, a Mediterranean bias that suits the climate, contributions from the unique ethnic mix, and the adventurous appetite for the new that has always characterized the Golden State would combine into a lasting culinary influence. Since that time, of course, California's food has become everyone else's too, the darling of chefs all across the country. Diane's research for her latest book, *The California Cook*, turned up a few surprises: even trendy focaccia wasn't born yesterday; it was sold in San Francisco bakeries in the 1940s.

The mission Diane set herself was to adapt the cuisine from the chefs' kitchens to the home kitchen. She's done it so successfully that for a huge number of Californians Diane's three major books are the ones they turn to again and again when they want something really delicious that's also a little sophisticated. The key to her style is that it has integrity, because each dish is grounded in a classic combination—but updated, given a little twist.

Like so many southern Californians, Diane is overjoyed to see a dismal day. A little rain or cold weather means a fire in the fireplace and a wonderful stew like this one. It's perfect for fall, and of course it only improves if you can make it a day or two ahead. It's important to make the mousse ahead, even several days ahead. The muffins and the crisp won't keep, but you can assemble elements of each recipe and then just toss them together at the last minute.

Smoked Trout Mousse

Remember to make this at least a day ahead and add the lemon juice a little at a time—too much and the smoked fish will taste too salty.

1 small shallot
½ pound lean smoked trout, all bones
    and skin removed
3 tablespoons mayonnaise
3 tablespoons cream cheese

1 to 2 tablespoons fresh lemon juice
pinch of freshly ground white pepper
pinch of cayenne pepper
1 tablespoon finely chopped parsley
parsley sprigs for garnish

In a food processor with the motor running, mince the shallot. Combine all remaining ingredients and process until pureed. Taste for seasoning—it might taste a little too salty, but the flavor will balance out as it sits. Spoon into a crock, cover well, and refrigerate. Serve slightly chilled, garnished with parsley sprigs, with crackers or crisp toasts.

DIANE ROSSEN WORTHINGTON

Beef Stew with Sun-Dried Tomatoes and Butternut Squash

*D*o make this a day ahead if you possibly can. Let the stew come to room temperature and then refrigerate it. There are two virtues here aside from the obvious one of saving yourself time on the day your guests come: you improve the flavor, and you can remove any excess fat before you reheat it.

10 sun-dried tomatoes, soaked in boiling
    water for 20 minutes
½ cup flour
3 pounds boneless beef chuck, cut into
    1½-inch cubes
5 tablespoons olive oil
2 large yellow onions, sliced
2 medium carrots, thinly sliced
¼ cup balsamic vinegar
3 cups beef stock or canned broth
1 cup red wine

¼ cup tomato paste
3 garlic cloves, minced
4 parsley sprigs
2 fresh thyme sprigs or 1/2 teaspoon
    dried
4 cups ¾-inch chunks peeled butternut
    squash, about 1½ pounds
½ teaspoon salt
¼ teaspoon freshly ground black pepper
2 tablespoons finely chopped parsley

When the tomatoes are finished soaking, quarter them. Reserve the soaking liquid.

Spread the flour on a large plate and dredge the beef thoroughly, shaking off any excess flour.

In a large nonstick casserole, heat 3 tablespoons of the olive oil over medium-high heat. Add the dredged beef pieces in batches and brown them, turning with kitchen tongs to be sure they brown evenly on all sides, about 5 to 7 minutes per batch. Drain the beef pieces and reserve.

Add the remaining oil to the pan and sauté the onions for about 15 minutes, stirring occasionally until nicely browned and lightly caramelized. Add the carrots and sauté for about 3 minutes or until slightly tender. Add the vinegar and deglaze the pan by scraping up all the brown bits. Add the stock, wine, tomato paste, garlic, parsley, thyme, and sun-dried tomatoes. Cover the casserole and simmer, covered, on low heat for about 1½ to 1¾ hours, stirring occasionally, until the meat is almost tender.

Add the butternut squash, turning up the heat to medium, and simmer for about 15 minutes or until the squash and meat are fork-tender. If the liquid is getting too thick, add some of the reserved tomato-soaking liquid. Add salt, pepper, and 1 table-spoon of parsley and mix to combine. Remove the cooked parsley sprigs. Taste for sea-soning and serve in shallow soup plates garnished with the remaining parsley.

• *You can save a little time here by skipping the caramelizing of the onions and pre-cooking of the carrots. Just add them in with everything else.*

∽

Corn Muffins

MAKES 12 MUFFINS

2 cups flour

1 cup yellow cornmeal

1 tablespoon baking powder

½ teaspoon salt

¼ cup firmly packed light brown sugar

2 large eggs

6 tablespoons unsalted butter, melted

1 cup milk

½ cup corn kernels, fresh or defrosted frozen

Preheat the oven to 350°F. Grease a 12-cup muffin tin.

Combine the flour, cornmeal, baking powder, and salt in a large bowl.

In a medium mixing bowl, whisk the brown sugar into the eggs until well blended. Add the melted butter and milk and whisk until well combined.

Pour the liquid over the dry ingredients and fold them together with a rubber spatula until the dry ingredients are completely blended. Add the corn kernels and mix to combine.

Spoon the batter into the muffin cups two thirds of the way up. Bake for 25 to 30 minutes or until the tops are golden brown and the center comes out dry when tested with a toothpick. Cool the muffins in the pan for 15 minutes. Serve immediately.

- *To make 48 minimuffins, bake for 20 minutes. These are great for breakfast. You might want to add ⅓ cup maple syrup along with the melted butter. Very good with orange butter: just flavor softened butter with a little orange juice and minced orange zest.*

Apple Crisp with Dried Fruit

*T*his recipe has all the elements everyone loves so much about this homey dessert, but it also has dried cherries or cranberries. It begs to be served with French vanilla ice cream or frozen yogurt.

Topping:
1 cup coarsely chopped pecans
¾ cup flour
½ teaspoon ground cinnamon
¼ teaspoon ground nutmeg
¼ teaspoon ground allspice
⅛ teaspoon ground cloves
pinch of salt
¾ cup rolled oats
½ cup sugar

½ cup firmly packed light brown sugar
12 tablespoons (1½ sticks) cold unsalted
    butter, cut into small pieces

Fruit:
8 medium cooking apples, about 2½
    pounds
3 tablespoons fresh lemon juice
½ cup dried cranberries or cherries

Preheat the oven to 350°F. Butter a 9- by 12-inch oblong or oval pan and set aside. Spread the pecans evenly on a baking sheet and toast in the oven for 5 to 7 minutes, watching carefully to be sure they don't burn. Pour onto a plate to cool.

Make the topping: In a medium mixing bowl, stir together the flour, cinnamon, nutmeg, allspice, cloves, and salt. Add the toasted nuts and the remaining topping ingredients. Rub the mixture between your fingertips until it's crumbly and resembles coarse bread crumbs. Set aside.

Prepare the fruit: Peel and core the apples, then cut them into ½-inch slices. Place the apples in a bowl and toss immediately with the lemon juice and dried cranberries or cherries. Pour the fruit into the buttered pan, sprinkling the topping evenly over the fruit, pressing the topping down lightly and leaving about ¼-inch space between the topping and the sides of the pan. Bake the dish for 40 to 45 minutes or until the topping is golden brown and bubbling, covering the top with foil if the crust begins to over-brown. Allow the dish to cool for 15 minutes before serving.

Bright Ideas

DESSERTS

Coconut Steamed Bananas: This unusual recipe of Michael Min Khin's sounds—well, bananas. But it's wonderful, a perfect ending to an Asian meal. Cut 4 big bananas into thin slices, put them in a microwave-safe baking dish, and cover with unsweetened coconut milk (two 12-ounce cans will do it). Cover the dish with plastic wrap and microwave on high for 10 minutes. Put the covered dish in the refrigerator until the liquid thickens to a soft custard, at least several hours. Serve with grated fresh coconut and a sprinkle of cinnamon or nutmeg.

Dressed-Up Strawberries: Extra-large strawberries with stems are what you need here. Crush several chocolate-hazelnut biscotti in the food processor and spread the crumbs on wax paper. Melt semisweet chocolate in a measuring cup in the microwave. Dip the strawberries in the chocolate and then in the crumbs and leave them to dry on the wax paper.

Instant Exotic Ices: Use the canned tropical juices (Goya, for instance) and pour the juice into ice trays to freeze. Just before serving, whirl the ice in a food processor and add some fresh lime juice to taste.

Gorgonzola with Honey: That's it. This is a classic Italian dessert, a sensational combination. Just drizzle the honey—a sage honey would be particularly good—over the slice of room-temperature cheese. We like this combination with Carr's wheatmeal biscuits.

Nut Cookies: Preheat the oven to 275°F. Mix 2 cups flour with 1 cup softened butter with your hands until it's smooth and shiny. Add ¼ cup sugar, 2 teaspoons vanilla, 1/4 teaspoon salt, and 1 ½ cups chopped nuts—pecans, walnuts, pistachios. Make little balls of dough and put them on a cookie sheet lined with aluminum foil. Bake for 20 minutes, then raise the heat to 325°F and bake for 10 minutes longer. Roll the cookies in confectioners' sugar as soon as they're out of the oven—use spoons so you don't get burned—and let them cool on a plate.

Dessert Wine with Cheese: Quady makes a wonderful California muscat called Elysium, which is great with Gorgonzola. Serve with not-too-sweet cookies or biscuits.

Venetian Lemon Sorbet Aperitif: Actually you can serve this at the beginning of the meal as well as at the end. It's a classic Venetian specialty, the perfect end to a hot-weather meal, along with a plate of biscotti. Mix in the blender in 2 batches if necessary: 1 cup lemon sorbet, ½ cup heavy cream, 2½ cups prosecco (Italian sparkling wine), and 4 ice cubes. Blend for 30 to 40 seconds, being careful not to overprocess it. Serve immediately in champagne flutes.

Pomegranates with Orange Flower Water: A great fall dessert. You need 3 pomegranates, 1 tablespoon plus 1 teaspoon orange flower water or rose water with a little lemon juice, and 3 tablespoons sugar. To get the seeds out, remove the blossom stem and cut the pomegranate in half lengthwise. Mix the seeds, perfumed water, and sugar and let stand in the refrigerator for an hour before serving in glass bowls.

Apricot Soufflé: A great winter dessert, an update of an old recipe from classic British food writer Elizabeth David. Don't be scared because it's a soufflé; it's a snap. Preheat the oven to 375°F. Butter and sugar a medium soufflé dish. Plump ½ pound dried apricots in the microwave for 12 minutes in water to cover. When they're soft, drain them and puree in a food processor. Add 2 tablespoons almond paste and 1 teaspoon almond extract. Beat 4 egg whites until stiff and fold in the apricot mixture. Bake in the soufflé dish for 15 to 20 minutes, until the top is lightly browned.

Stilton and Apple Napoleons: Bake 4½- by 2-inch rectangles of frozen puff pastry—2 per serving. After they cool and not too long before serving, spread the first layer thinly with a little whipped cream cheese to act as glue for the crumbled Stilton scattered over it. Top with the second pastry layer and arrange caramelized apple slices on top. Caramelize the apples in a skillet with brown sugar (add a little butter if you like) and a splash of Calvados. This makes a great holiday dessert. You could drizzle warm Calvados or brandy over the apples, light it, and bring it to the table flaming.

Filled Panettone: Buy an imported panettone—but not too tall; a giant pandoro will collapse given this treatment—and slice it through just above the base, so you can remove some of the interior. Sprinkle the cavity with rum or brandy and spread some Nutella, the chocolate-hazelnut spread, all over the inside. Now mix up whipped cream cheese blended with some mascarpone, adding a little vanilla, a little sugar, some chopped chocolate, and a few raisins or chopped dried apricots you've soaked in rum or brandy for 20 minutes. Add the crumbled panettone pieces and pack the cream mixture back into the panettone. Cover the base with more Nutella, put it on the panettone, and invert the whole thing onto a platter so it's right side up. Dust with confectioners' sugar and decorate with candied orange peel around the base.

SOME GREAT SINGLE DISHES

Here are some single dishes we think are good enough to build a meal around—some from contributors to this book, some from other sources. All of them are simple, though some take a little longer, like Diana Kennedy's gingerbread, but it should be made days ahead of serving. Sometimes we're so rushed that we can focus on cooking just one dish—when you're in that fix, check these recipes and fill in the missing blanks on the menu with salads, high-quality take-out food, or suggestions from the "Bright Ideas" boxes that appear throughout.

ↄ

Lemon Chicken Black Bean Salad with Corn

BRUCE AIDELLS

SERVES 4

This delicious salad uses Bruce's superb lemon chicken sausage—which doesn't always appear even at markets well stocked with Aidells sausages. It's worth demanding. If you can't find it, use Aidells New Mexico sausage.

4 links of Aidells lemon chicken sausage

3 cups canned black beans, drained, about 2 large cans

1½ cups whole corn kernels, fresh or defrosted frozen

1 cup chopped red bell pepper

1 cup peeled, pitted, and chopped avocado

¼ cup chopped cilantro

½ teaspoon salt

Dressing:

2 tablespoons fresh lemon juice

1 tablespoon red wine vinegar

½ cup safflower, canola, or extra-virgin olive oil

tomato wedges for garnish

Grill or broil the sausage for 5 to 7 minutes, until throughly heated, and set aside.

Combine the remaining salad ingredients in a large bowl and toss gently. Whisk together the dressing ingredients. Slice the sausage and add it to the beans. Pour the dressing over the salad and mix gently. Serve on a platter garnished with tomato wedges.

⌒

Lentil Soup with Prosciutto

MICHEL RICHARD

SERVES 6

The maestro of the incandescent Citrus restaurant in Los Angeles—and its many off-shoots throughout the country—makes a sophisticated, rich, but still homey lentil soup. The surprise is that it's a *cold* lentil soup, but still smoky and delicious. You can make it a day ahead and keep it refrigerated until ready to serve.

1 thick ¼-inch slice of smoked bacon	1 cup heavy cream
1 medium onion, diced	balsamic vinegar
2 quarts chicken stock or unsalted canned broth	salt and freshly ground pepper
	6 thin slices of prosciutto
¾ pound lentils, 1¾ cups	croutons (optional)
1 bouquet garni (see note below)	a few parsley sprigs, finely chopped

In a 4- to 6-quart soup pot over medium heat, sauté the bacon until it starts to color. Add the onion and stir until golden brown. Add the stock, lentils, and bouquet garni, bringing the liquid to a boil. Reduce the heat and simmer about 45 minutes, until the lentils are tender but still hold their shape. Remove the bacon and the bouquet garni. Add the cream and bring the soup to a gentle boil.

Remove the soup from the heat. Cool slightly. Puree in a food processor or blender and pass through a medium sieve if you'd like a finer texture. Add a splash of balsamic vinegar. Season with salt and pepper. Cool quickly and store.

To serve, ladle the cold soup into 6 bowls. Ruffle a thin slice of prociutto on top and add croutons if desired. Then sprinkle some finely chopped parsley over all.

· *To cope without a bouquet garni, just add a bay leaf, several stemmed parsley sprigs, and a teaspoon of dried thyme to the pot. Remove the parsley and the bay leaf once the soup is cooked.*

- *Of course, you can serve the soup hot if you prefer. If you do, cut a ¼-inch thick slice of prosciutto into slivers and heat it in the soup. Finish with the croutons and minced parsley.*

❧

Butternut Squash Soup with Crayfish

CHARLES DALE

SERVES 6

Possibly because his restaurant, Renaissance, is in Aspen, Charles Dale makes a specialty of soups. Crayfish tails, aka crawfish tails (which come to the market cooked and peeled), are increasingly available in seafood markets, but you can also use crab and/or cooked shrimp if you can't find them.

2 tablespoons unsalted butter	1 quart water
¼ cup extra-virgin olive oil	1 cinnamon stick
2 medium onions, sliced	1/8 teaspoon cayenne pepper
2 large butternut squash, peeled and cut into 2-inch dice	1 teaspoon salt
	1 pound cooked peeled crayfish tails
1 garlic clove, roughly chopped	¼ cup chopped fresh chives
1 quart homemade chicken stock or 2 16-ounce cans unsalted broth	

Melt the butter and oil in a 6-quart saucepan. Add the onions and cook over medium heat until translucent but not brown. Add the squash and garlic and cook for 10 minutes, stirring periodically. Add the stock, water, and cinnamon stick. Bring it to a boil, reduce the heat, and simmer for 30 minutes or until the squash is soft to a probing knife. Season with cayenne and salt. Strain half the liquid and reserve.

Remove the cinnamon stick and puree the soup with a hand-held or regular blender. Add the reserved liquid as necessary to obtain a smooth, silky consistency. Adjust the seasonings to taste.

To serve, warm the crayfish in the soup, sprinkle with chives, and serve immediately.

℃

Warm Bird Salad with Wild Mushrooms and Crisp Potatoes

CATHERINE BRANDEL

Now Catherine is a chef's chef, teaching at the Culinary Institute in the Napa Valley. But she made her reputation at Chez Panisse in Berkeley, for her elegantly simple, intensely flavorful food—exhilarating ideas like thinly sliced artichokes, fennel, and lemons, soaked in buttermilk, fried, and served with a spiced orange mayonnaise. At home she's ready to improvise with a number of favorite salads: fennel, blood oranges, and olives or wilted greens (escarole, beet, chards, etc.) with garlic toast and olives. The bird for this salad can be duck or chicken breasts or duck leg confit; the greens can be just about anything substantial; the mushrooms can be portobellos or something more exotic—or forget the mushrooms and use torn bread croutons instead. What pulls it all together is the vinaigrette.

The Bird

Grill or sauté whatever bird you're using (or warm a cooked bird)—save any cooking juices to add to the vinaigrette. You can also use a take-out roast chicken and simply slice it over the greens.

The Mushrooms

Slice some mushrooms and sauté them in a little olive oil with salt and pepper. Or salt and pepper them, put them in a covered dish, and roast them whole in the oven along with the potatoes. Be sure to save any juices to add to the vinaigrette.

The Potatoes

Preheat the oven to 375°F. Use small Red Bliss or Yukon Gold potatoes, 2 for each guest. Scrub them, oil them with a little olive oil, salt them, and put them in a baking dish with a little water in the bottom to keep the skins soft. Roast them for about 40 minutes or until fork-tender. When the potatoes are done, cut them in half and fry the cut side in a little olive oil with thyme and garlic until they're crispy on that side, still soft on the skin side.

The Vinaigrette

Meanwhile, make the vinaigrette. Use at least 2 tablespoons minced shallot; put it in a small bowl with 2 tablespoons sherry vinegar, a dash of balsamic vinegar, and salt to taste—start with 2 large pinches of sea salt. Mash the salt into the shallot with a fork and let mellow in the vinegar for 30 minutes or so while the vegetables cook. Then add ½ cup olive oil and pepper to taste, whisk, and adjust the seasonings to taste, adding any cooking juices from the mushrooms and poultry.

Assembling the Salad

Dress the greens and arrange them on the serving plates, adding a few shavings of Parmesan to each salad. Slice the mushrooms and add them too. Arrange the warm poultry and the crisp potatoes on the plates and serve immediately.

ᆼ

Fresh Mint Chutney
MICHELLE MUTRUX

This splendid chutney is served at the Wappo Bar and Bistro in Calistoga, California, where Michelle Mutrux is the chef. It's incredibly zesty and complicated-tasting but equally easy to make. This makes a plain grilled fish, chicken, or kebab into something really special. Keeps for two days, refrigerated.

2 cups packed fresh mint leaves

¼ cup unsweetened shredded coconut

4 dates, pitted

2 jalapeño chiles, seeded

juice of 1 orange

juice of 2 limes

¼ to ½ cup water

salt to taste

Put everything but the water and salt into a blender and blend until you have a smooth paste with a little texture. Add water gradually until you have a spoonable sauce. Salt to taste.

Roasted Habañero Salsa

REED HEARON

This fiery sauce is the perfect counterpoint for Hearon's Yucatán chicken (page 89) and just about any other grilled main dish that needs a jolt.

4 Italian plum or Roma tomatoes

2 habañero peppers

1 small white onion, thickly sliced

2 garlic cloves

¼ teaspoon dried Mexican oregano,
      toasted briefly in a skillet

½ cup water

salt to taste

In a dry skillet over high heat, pan-roast the tomatoes and habañeros until they're charred and blistered all over, turning them frequently. In a small dry skillet, pan-roast the onion and garlic over medium-high heat until they're brown and soft. Chop everything together in a food processor or with a knife until you have a coarsely textured salsa. Add the oregano, thin with the water to get a consistency you like, and add salt to taste.

The salsa will keep for several days in the refrigerator.

• *Habañeros are sometimes found nestled next to jalapeños and other hot peppers in the produce section of the supermarket. Watch out; these innocent-looking balls of fire come in both orange and yellow, and they're thin-skinned. Use gloves or stick your hands inside plastic bags when you're dealing with them directly.*

- *If you have a stovetop grill, use it to roast the tomatoes and peppers.*

℃

New Orleans Shrimp Rémoulade on Fried Green Tomatoes

JoAnn Clevenger

This sensational appetizer or lunch dish pairs two classics—it's a big hit at JoAnn's up-town New Orleans restaurant, Upperline. The tomatoes are also wonderful on their own, for breakfast or with any pork dish. The boiled shrimp is wonderful on its own too, with ears of corn and little red potatoes cooked in the same broth. It makes an exuberantly messy backyard supper served on newspaper—simplicity itself, and the guests do all the hard work of peeling the shrimp.

SERVES 4

New Orleans Rémoulade Sauce:

Arnaud's rémoulade sauce (the best of the store-bought, according to JoAnn) or mayonnaise mixed with a little horseradish, Creole mustard, paprika, Louisiana hot sauce, white pepper, minced scallion greens, pressed garlic, and a bit of ketchup

Shrimp Boil:

2 quarts water

⅛ cup salt

½ 3-ounce bag of crab boil spices, preferably Zatarain's,* about ¼ cup

1 whole head of garlic, the top third sliced off

1 lemon, sliced

1 pound large shrimp in their shells

*Or make your own: use pickling spice as the base and add mustard seeds, celery seeds, peppercorns, bay leaves, oregano, red pepper flakes, and salt.

3 hard green tomatoes

buttermilk for dipping the tomatoes

corn flour or yellow cornmeal seasoned
*   with salt and freshly ground pepper,*
*   preferably white, for coating the*
*   slices*

a little bacon fat or oil for sautéing

If you're making the sauce, mix the ingredients and refrigerate until serving time. Bring to room temperature before serving.

For the shrimp boil, combine everything but the shrimp in a very large pot and bring to a rolling boil. When it's boiling, drop in the shrimp and cook for just a couple of minutes, until the shrimp curl up and turn bright pink. Turn the heat off and let the shrimp sit in the broth for another 5 minutes to absorb more flavor. Drain and cool them.

When the shrimp are cool, peel them and refrigerate to chill.

Right before serving, slice the tomatoes crosswise about ¼ inch thick. Dip them in buttermilk, then in the seasoned corn flour or cornmeal. Heat the bacon fat in a large skillet until it's very hot but not smoking. Put the tomato slices in the skillet—don't crowd them—and sauté uncovered until they're nice and crisp on both sides but not mushy in the middle, about 5 minutes per side.

Serve on individual plates—4 or 5 cold shrimp over 2 hot tomato slices with a dollop of rémoulade on top. If you're tempted to add a lemon slice or two, don't; the tomatoes are acidic enough.

- *To serve the shrimp boil as a main course, double the recipe and add one ear of shucked corn and a handful of small (2-inch-diameter) red-skinned potatoes per person. When the stock comes to a rolling boil, drop in the potatoes. Eighteen minutes later, add the corn and shrimp. Two minutes later, turn off the heat and let everything sit for 5 minutes. Drain and serve in one giant bowl or in separate serving dishes. Be sure to include the garlic, which will be delicious.*
- *This should be an intense broth; to be sure it's flavorful enough, drop in a potato slice,*

cook, and taste it, adjusting seasonings as needed, before you start cooking. You may want to add some hot red pepper flakes.

- *Commercial crab boil is a good thing to have on hand, not only for cooking shrimp, but also for rice—just drop the bag into the boiling water along with the rice.*

≈

Pickapeppa Chicken

NORMA SHIRLEY

This wonderfully simple chicken has the taste of Jamaica, where Norma Shirley has her two famous restaurants: Norma, and Norma at the Wharfhouse. The Jamaican taste comes right out of the Pickapeppa bottle, available in most supermarkets—it's savory, spicy, and haunting, with a little sweetness to mellow things out. The other essential Jamaican element here is the scotch bonnet pepper—just a touch; it's the hottest pepper in the world. If you can't find scotch bonnet pepper or you can't face it, use a couple of pinches of cayenne instead.

Norma cooks the chicken in a covered skillet on top of the stove—we've modified it slightly to cook it in the oven. She serves the chicken with parsleyed rice. You might even speckle the rice with a few black beans for contrast.

2½ pounds chicken thighs, skinned
2 garlic cloves, minced
1 tablespoon chopped parsley
pinch of scotch bonnet chile pepper or
    cayenne
1 tablespoon chopped fresh thyme leaves

1 large onion, sliced
1 cup chicken stock or canned broth
1 bottle Pickapeppa sauce
ripe mango and/or pineapple slices,
    soaked in rum, for garnish

Wash the chicken pieces and pat them dry. Put the chicken in a large baking dish and toss in the garlic, parsley, chile, thyme leaves, and onion, moving the chicken around with a wooden spoon to distribute the seasonings evenly. Set aside for 1 to 2 hours to bring the chicken to room temperature.

Preheat the oven to 375°F. Add the stock and Pickapeppa sauce to the pan. Cover with foil or a lid and bake for 50 minutes, basting the chicken from time to time.

Transfer the chicken to a serving platter and keep warm. Pour the pan juices into a saucepan and reduce over high heat until the sauce thickens. Adjust the seasonings to taste and pour the sauce over the chicken. Garnish with the rum-soaked fruit and ignite at the table.

- *If you'd like to forgo the drama of flaming the fruit, skip the garnish and serve the chicken with the Mango Relish on page 185.*
- *For a different but very good and crispy version of this dish, leave the chicken skin on, bake it uncovered, and skip the chicken stock.*
- *To make the chicken on top of the stove, put it—together with the sauce and the Pickapeppa sauce—in a large skillet with a lid. Bring to a boil, cover, and simmer slowly until the chicken is tender, about 30 to 40 minutes.*

ℭ

Tuna and Fennel Seeds
CARLO MIDDIONE

SERVES 4

Here's one of the world's simplest recipes, a southern Italian specialty to serve four. It's also versatile—you can deglaze the pan with a little white wine to make a sauce of the pan juices or just drizzle the pan juices over the fish. And you can make the same dish with a pound of shelled shrimp instead of tuna.

4 tuna steaks, about ½ inch thick, or
    1 pound shrimp, peeled
¼ cup extra-virgin olive oil
¼ cup fennel seeds

½ teaspoon salt or to taste
freshly ground black pepper
a splash of dry white wine (optional)

Carefully dry the tuna steaks. Put the olive oil and fennel seeds in a large frying pan over medium heat. When the seeds begin to sizzle, put the slices of tuna on top of them and sprinkle on some salt and a few grinds of pepper. In about 5 minutes, carefully turn the tuna slices over and salt and pepper again. After about another 3 minutes the tuna steaks should be done—be sure they're not raw in the middle.

Put the tuna on a heated serving dish. If you're using the wine, put it in the pan with the juices and the seeds remaining in the pan. Cook the juices and wine over very high heat long enough to cook off the alcohol and reduce the pan juices, just a couple of minutes. Drizzle the juices on the pieces of fish and serve immediately.

If you're not using the wine, just drizzle the pan juices and seeds over the tuna.

• *If you're using the shrimp, they'll be done in just a few minutes, when they're pink.*

⚬

Potatoes Baked in Sea Salt
PAULA WOLFERT

SERVES 6

This old French recipe is traditionally cooked in a clay pot, with the potatoes inside a nest of sea salt. In effect the potatoes are steamed with sea water, which makes them particularly moist and flavorful. You can also use half kosher salt or all kosher salt for that matter—and you can keep the salt in a jar to use again.

We're assuming you don't have the traditional clay pot (don't use a Romertopf), so use an enameled cast-iron one instead.

2 pounds creamers (little new potatoes)   *2 cups sea salt or kosher salt or a mixture*

Preheat the oven to 450°F. Wash and dry the potatoes. Spread the salt in an even layer on the bottom of the enameled cast-iron pot and arrange the potatoes on top side by side. Cover and bake for 45 minutes to 1 hour, depending on the size of the potatoes.

Remove the pot from the oven, set the cover askew, and let the pot stand for 5 minutes. Remove the potatoes and brush off the salt. Serve hot with butter or butter mixed with roasted garlic (page 15).

Gingerbread

DIANA KENNEDY

SERVES 8

This is a gingerbread like no other—it originated in Scotland, and Diana Kennedy has taken it to Mexico and almost everywhere else in the world she's been. It's wickedly rich and sticky, not at all like the usual spongy gingerbread, which Diana says has far too much baking soda.

The batter rises up dramatically, so you need to use a pan at least three inches deep, and even then you may have a little overflow. If you can find it, the West Indian molasses is particularly wonderful here.

The gingerbread is perfect for company, because it's at its best two days after baking—or so Diana says; we wouldn't know since we've never been able to keep our hands off it that long.

½ pound unbleached flour, about
    2 cups
2 tablespoons ground ginger
1 tablespoon ground cinnamon
3 ounces sultanas or golden raisins,
    about ½ cup, rounded
1 cup (2 sticks) unsalted butter, plus
    extra for greasing the pan

½ pound dark brown sugar, about 1¼
    cups, firmly packed
½ pound dark molasses, about ¾ cup
2 eggs, lightly beaten
1 teaspoon baking soda
⅓ cup warm whole milk
several slices of preserved ginger to
    decorate the top (optional)

Preheat the oven to 325°F and place a baking sheet on the middle rack. Lightly grease a 9-inch square cake pan at least 3 inches deep, measuring the bottom of the pan, not the top.

243

SOME GREAT SINGLE DISHES

Put the flour, ginger, cinnamon, and raisins into a plastic bag and shake them around thoroughly. Cream the butter with the sugar until fluffy. Gradually beat in the molasses, followed by the eggs and then the flour mixture. The batter will be soft and sticky. Dissolve the baking soda in the warm milk, stir briefly, and add to the mixture. Stir until all the ingredients are thoroughly blended. The batter will now be very loose.

Pour the batter into the prepared pan and bake for about 1½ hours. (If you're decorating the top with the preserved ginger, put it on after about an hour of baking; otherwise it will disappear.) The gingerbread will be cooked when a slight crust has formed around the edge, which has pulled away from the sides of the pan. Set aside to cool completely before attempting to unmold. With a spatula, carefully loosen the sides and as much of the bottom of the gingerbread as you can without breaking it and then unmold. Wrap the gingerbread in wax paper and then foil and store for 2 days in an airtight tin—of course you can eat it right away, but it gathers flavor with keeping.

ᗡ

Syrian Nutmeg Cake

LAURIE COLWIN

The late Laurie Colwin was best known as a novelist, but she was also a passionate cook who liked to search out unusual recipes and write little essays about them. This cake is one that she never wrote about but passed along to a nonbaking friend. "This is going to be your cake, your specialty. It's easy. You can do it." We all can, and in fact it *is* special, with its shortbread base and its fragrant spices. Once you make this cake it will become part of your repertoire.

½ cup (1 stick) cold butter

2 cups flour

2 cups packed dark brown sugar

1 egg, beaten

1 cup yogurt

4 teaspoons ground nutmeg

1 teaspoon ground cinnamon

1 teaspoon ground cloves or less to taste

1 teaspoon baking soda

½ cup chopped walnuts

Preheat the oven to 350°F. Butter the sides only of a 10-inch springform pan. In a large mixing bowl, cut the butter into the flour and sugar until the mixture resembles fine meal. Firmly press half of this mixture into the prepared pan. Stir the egg and yogurt together to mix well, then stir into the remaining half of the flour mixture. Stir in the spices, then the baking soda. Pour this batter over the mixture in the pan. Scatter the walnuts on top. Bake for 40 minutes. Cool on a cake rack before removing the rim of the pan. To serve, cut down hard through the shortbread bottom.

- *Speed this along by slicing the butter into the work bowl of a food processor, then process it with the brown sugar and flour.*
- *Unless you're crazy about cloves, ½ teaspoon is a more harmonious amount. For the best cake of all, take an extra couple of minutes for freshly grated fresh nutmeg. You might want to replace 1 teaspoon nutmeg with a teaspoon of mace.*
- *You can use a regular 10-inch pan here if you don't have a springform. Grease the bottom and sides with vegetable shortening.*

Giant Almond Cookie

JO BETTOJA

This traditional Italian dessert, *torta fregolatta*, is like a crumbly shortbread, always broken up with the fingers. It's served with ice cream or a dessert wine like Vin Santo. Best of all, it's better made at least a day ahead, and it will keep for a very long time wrapped in aluminum foil.

2⅔ cups all-purpose flour

1¼ cups finely chopped almonds

pinch of coarse salt

1 cup plus 1 tablespoon unsalted butter, in small pieces

1 cup sugar

2 tablespoons grappa or cognac

grated zest of 1 lemon

2 tablespoons fresh lemon juice

Preheat the oven to 350°F. Butter a round 12-inch pie pan with low sides, then flour lightly, shaking out excess flour.

Mix all the ingredients together with a large spoon until they're crumbly. If you're using an electric mixer, put all the ingredients in a large mixer bowl. Using either the dough hook or the paddle, mix until the dough masses. Wrap a kitchen towel around and over the top of the mixer and bowl to keep the flour from scattering. The mixture should be crumbly, not smooth.

Transfer the mixture into the prepared pan, smoothing the top with a spatula or with your hands. Bake for about 1 hour. Check after 50 minutes: it should be lightly browned, darker around the edges.

Place on a rack and remove from the pan before completely cooled, after about 10 minutes. Replace on the rack to cool completely.

• *If you're using supermarket almonds, you might want to add ½ teaspoon almond extract to perk up the almond flavor.*

Mix-and-Match Menus

SUPER SOUP

Start with Diane Worthington's Smoked Trout Mousse, then bring out a tureen filled with Michel Richard's hot Lentil Soup with Prosciutto (page 233) and a basket of Diane's Corn Muffins. Serve a red leaf lettuce and arugula salad with lemon vinaigrette and a dusting of grated Parmesan. Dessert: Jeffrey Buben's Lemon Chess Pie.

Simple Wines for Simple Meals

Great wines for casual entertaining are not necessarily "great wines"—at least not in the sense of exceptional vintage wines from prestigious houses bearing immodest price tags. Instead these wines are best chosen to match the events they serve: simple, straightforward, pleasant, and versatile with a touch of elegance. Easy-to-drink wines that encourage conviviality are the ones to look for, and today's market offers many good choices.

Dinner in the garden on a warm summer evening naturally suggests a different wine from the one you'd serve indoors next to a roaring fire. Depending on the food, of course, the summer wine might be a light, fruity dry rosé or a crisp, grassy sauvignon blanc or a zesty dry French muscadet. There are many options, but the choice should go in the direction of a wine that's clean tasting and low in alcohol. If you're fond of a dry superchilled rosé in the summer but find most of them too sweet, stick with the ones from Provence or southwestern France (Fortant de France) and avoid the Portuguese or the French Anjou rosé. Etude makes a wonderful California one. The winter wine could be a robust red Côtes-du-Rhône (Guigal) or a zinfandel (Ravenswood, California)—both of which have a warm spicy character very welcome on chilly evenings.

Not only is weather a consideration, but there's also the question of mood. Is this event a celebration? Naturally, the most festive wines are the sparklers. True champagne can be prohibitively expensive, but there are many excellent sparkling alternatives at less than half the price. The delicious little-known dry crémants of Alsace—made by the "Champagne method"—will impress your guests and not your pocketbook. Pierre Sparr is a good example. There are also very high quality American sparkling wines to fit any budget. Try Scharffenberger's or Schramsberg's Blanc de Blanc. For something a little unusual, try the slightly creamy Gruet from New Mexico, a best buy.

Is the occasion a small romantic dinner? No wine in the world is as seductive as a great red burgundy from the Côte de Beaune, such as a Volnay or a Corton. These are pricey, but careful shopping will uncover superb and reasonable alternatives from the adjoining areas of Ladoix, Pernard-Vergelesses, Monthelie, or Saint-Romain.

247

SIMPLE WINES FOR SIMPLE MEALS

The menu itself will provide the most specific clues to good choices. When only one wine is being served throughout a meal, the choice centers on the main course, but the traditional convention of matching the color of the wine to the color of the entrée is useful only when the meat or fish is served without either a sauce or pronounced seasoning. The best approach is to determine the dominant flavors and choose a wine to balance or enhance them. While there's no doubt that a delicate flaky fish in cream sauce will be complemented by a bright dry white on the mineral side like a sancerre or chablis, a grilled salmon with a red wine sauce will be enhanced by a red merlot.

Keep in mind that certain components of a wine's flavor such as acidity, tannin, and sweetness will offset or accentuate certain food flavors. Acidity balances fat and richness, whereas saltiness and spiciness are offset by sweetness; i.e., a fruitier wine with some residual sugar. Both protein and alkaline foods such as cheese soften the tannins in red wine—which explains why a good steak is a natural partner for cabernet sauvignon and why the French always save some of it to enjoy with their cheese course.

Exotic dishes with assertive and mixed tastes like sweet and sour, hot and sweet, and just plain spicy ask for fruitier wines or wines that are spicy as well. Zinfandels and both red and white Rhônes can hold their own with Southwestern and Indian food. German, South African, and Alsatian Rieslings complement Asian food—the first two are sweeter and the Alsatian quite dry. Sometimes an ice-cold beer is the most compatible beverage of all.

When more than one wine is being served, the conventions of going from white to red, lighter to heavier, and younger to older should in most cases be respected. Beyond that, most of the questions of food pairing come down to individual taste, and the unexpected can be a delight.

One of the easiest ways to make wine decisions is to develop your own "house wines" as restaurants often do. These are simple wines that go pretty much with everything without apology. Experiment with the Australian reds (shiraz) and whites (chardonnay), which are excellent values, as are the Chilean varietals (Cabernet sauvignon and merlot). Chilean reds have more aging before their release in the United States than French reds. The California zinfandel from Seghesio is worth trying. So is Ermitage du Pic Loup, a Languedoc red. The sauvignon blancs from the Touraine area of France also bear your scrutiny. The Vendange label from California (Sebastiani, though the label doesn't say so) is a reliable source for inexpensive wine, sometimes under five dollars a bottle.

Finally, dessert wines must be sweeter than the dessert, or the sugar will make the wine taste hard or bitter. From France, Muscat de Beaumes de Venise, Barsac, and Loupiac are good dessert wines; from Italy, try Malvasia and Vin Santo; and from California, Quady's Essensia. They are not inexpensive, but they are drunk sparingly, so you might want to start discovering how much more pleasant they can be than liqueurs.

What counts above all is your own taste and sensitivity. Keep an open mind: develop a trusting relationship with a knowledgeable wine merchant, keep tasting, and if you really *like* the wine, chances are it's a fine choice.

How much wine? Count on one bottle per guest. Since this book is all about casual dinners for good friends, you probably know who drinks only red or white and in what capacity. All you need to remember is that there are five to six glasses to a bottle of wine and that you will need aperitif as well as dinner wine. Obviously, it's better to have a bottle or two left over than to be caught short. Conversely, if you have an unlimited supply, you might still be at the dinner table for breakfast.

Consider putting yourself on the mailing list of Kermit Lynch, a California wine importer with a venerable reputation whose brochure on hand-crafted new arrivals can't be bought at your local newsstand. Shipping to the East Coast is dear, but there is a discount for case purchases, which helps to offset the shipping cost. Some states disallow such shipments across the border, but if you call (510) 524-1524 (fax: 528-0451) and ask for a brochure, it will be explained to you.

If you would like to stay current with the wide world of good wine, pick up *The Wine Spectator* or *Decanter* magazine at your bookstore newsstand. They are both interesting and reputable sources for learning more about the enjoyment of a variety of wine and how to shop for it wisely.

—LESLIE BLAKEY
  Le Caprice, Washington, D.C.

Index

*A*chiote marinade for spicy grilled Yucatán chicken
    with caramelized onions, 90
Aidells, Bruce, 135–39, 232
aiguillette, beef tenderloin, 159–60
aioli sauce, 180
Al Forno, 108
Allen, Drew, 3–7, 89
almond brittle, sliced oranges with, 105
anchovies:
    buying, 178–79
    red creamer potatoes with, 110
    sandwiches, Catalan, 178
    sandwiches, Santa Fe, 178
antipasto, 65–67
    cocktail buffet, mix-and-match menu for an, 174
appetizers and first courses:
    antipasto, 65–67
    baked ricotta and goat cheese with thyme, 116–17
    Catalan anchovy sandwiches, 178
    cold sesame noodles, 82–83
    fennel crudités with sea salt, 118
    fettunta with caviar, 209
    fresh creamy cheese with a sweet and spicy sauce, 5
    Mixtec guacamole with tortilla chips, 89
    olives scented with orange and lemon zest, 66–67
    olives with roasted cumin and paprika, 117
    pinzimonio, 10
    Provençal roasted eggplant vinaigrette, 153–54
    roasted onions, 66
    Santa Fe anchovy sandwiches, 178

    sautéed oysters with cumin and mushrooms, 158
    sesame soba noodles with tempura vegetables, 95–96
    soft-shell crabs with toasted hazelnuts, 143–45
    spicy fish steamed in lettuce parcels, 131–32
    steamed artichokes with lime and cracked pepper
        mayonnaise, 58–59
    steamed clams with chorizo, 177–78
    veal carpaccio on crostini with lemon mascarpone,
        123–24
apple:
    crisp with dried fruit, 226–27
    and Stilton Napoleons, 229
apricot(s):
    and hazelnuts, poached pears on raspberry sauce
        filled with, 125–27
    soufflé, 229
artichokes, steamed, with lime and cracked pepper
    mayonnaise, 58–59
Asian:
    crispies, 43
    watercress salad, 104
asparagus, grilled, with toasted sesame seeds and pear
    tomatoes, 78
Avarua, pork, 29–31
avocado, stuffed, 79

*B*acon:
    scallops and peas, bow tie pasta with, 154
balsamic vinaigrette, soft lettuce salad with, 161

251

bananas, coconut steamed, 228
Bartolotta, Paul, 8–11
basil:
    chilled tomato and red pepper soup with shrimp and, 189–90
    leaves, with feta, 44
    yellow split pea purée with garlic and, 61–62
basmati rice with lamb and tomato, crispy-bottomed, 60–61
bean(s):
    black, and rice, 184
    black, lemon chicken salad with corn, 232
    spreads, 43
    white, with garlic, oregano and tomato, 211
Beck, Simone, 188
beef:
    stew with sun-dried tomatoes and butternut squash, 224–25
    tenderloin aiguillette, 159–60
    tenderloin with rosemary, garlic chips and beet and potato puree, 92
beet and potato puree, 92
Bertolli, Paul, 12–18
Bettoja, Jo, 19–25, 245
bisque, red pea, flambé, 165–66
bitter greens, penne with mozzarella, toasted walnuts and, 67–68
black beans:
    lemon chicken salad with corn, 232
    and rice, 184
black olives:
    melon with, 79
    pulled parsley salad with pecorino and, 216
Blakey, Leslie, 71, 247–49
blueberries:
    with cajeta, 155
    grilled Cornish hens with wild mushrooms and, 145–48
boats:
    endive, 43
    pepper, 43
Bon Appétit, 188
Border Grill, 55
Boulevard, 136
bow tie pasta with scallops, bacon and peas, 154
braised lobster, spicy, 112–13

Brandel, Catherine, 235
bread, chile corn, 138
Brennan, Jennifer, 26–34
bright ideas:
    desserts, 228–230
    hors d'oeuvres, 43–44
    Pick Up a Chicken, 128
    starters, 78–79
broccoli, stir-fried, 85–86
brochettes for couscous chez Edmond, 73–76
brownies, dark chocolate, 24–25
Buben, Jeffrey, 35–42
buckwheat corn waffles, green chile crab on, 79
bulgur pilaf with cashews and golden raisins, 32–33
Burmese chicken curry with noodles, 132–34
buttermilk mashed potatoes, 17
butternut squash:
    beef stew with sun-dried tomatoes and, 224–25
    soup with crayfish, 234–35

Cabbage, red:
    salmon sautéed with orange and capers with, 124–25
    and sprouts with sesame dressing, 56–57
Caesar salad with chile croutons, Southwest, 47–48
Cafe Marimba, 88
cajeta:
    blueberries with, 155
    sundaes, Mexican, 91
cake:
    orange pistachio, 62–63
    raspberry shortcake, 199
    saffron noodle, 118–19
    Syrian nutmeg, 244–45
Cakebread Cellars vineyard, 46
California Cook, The (Worthington), 222
California Food, 222
capers and orange, salmon with red cabbage sautéed with, 124–25
caramelized:
    onions, for spicy grilled Yucatán chicken, 89–90
    pineapple with vanilla ice cream, 120

Carolina (restaurant), 195
carpaccio, veal, on crostini with lemon mascarpone, 123–24
Carpenter, Hugh, 45–52
carrettiera, spaghetti *alla*, 209–10
cashews:
    bulgur pilaf with golden raisins and, 32–33
    and pepitas, lime and chile roasted, 59–60
Catalan anchovy sandwiches, 178
caviar, fettunta with, 209
champagne and strawberry sorbet, minted, 186
chard, red Swiss, and dilled new potatoes, 39–40
cheese:
    baked ricotta and goat, with thyme, 116–17
    basil leaves with feta, 44
    chèvre truffles, 43
    cushions, 44
    dessert wine with, 228
    fresh creamy, with a sweet and spicy sauce, 5
    Gorgonzola with honey, 228
    haricots verts on baby greens with shaved goat cheese, 196
    penne with bitter greens, mozzarella and toasted walnuts, 67–68
    prosciutto with dried fruit and chèvre, 78
    Sicilian ricotta ice cream, 218–19
    spaghetti with feta, fresh tomato, spinach and kalamata olives, 57–58
    Stilton and apple Napoleons, 229
cheesecake, minimalist, 212
chess pie, lemon, with fresh berries and raspberry sauce, 41–42
chèvre:
    prosciutto with dried fruit and, 78
    truffles, 43
Chez Panisse, 13, 115, 176, 235
Chez Panisse Cooking (Bertolli), 13
chicken:
    baked, in a salt crust, 83–84
    curry with noodles, Burmese, 132–34
    lemon, black bean salad with corn, 232
    Pickapeppa, 240–41
    Pick Up a Chicken, 128
    spicy grilled Yucatán, with caramelized onions, 89–90
    tonno di pollo, 210–11

    warm bird salad with wild mushrooms and crisp potatoes, 235–36
Child, Julia, 55, 164
chile:
    corn bread, 138
    croutons, for Southwest Caesar salad, 47–48
    grilled corn with lime and, 91
    and lime roasted pepitas and cashews, 59–60
    roasted habañero salsa, 237–38
    spinach sautéed with, 103
chilled:
    cucumber soup, 37–38
    tomato and red pepper soup with basil and shrimp, 189–90
Chinese rice, perfect, 85
Chinois rack of lamb, grilled, 48–49
chocolate:
    brownies, dark, 24–25
    hazelnut mousse, 161–62
    Kahlúa decadence, 51–52
chorizo, steamed clams with, 177–78
chutney, fresh mint, 236–37
Cities for People (film), 65
Citrus (restaurant), 233
City (restaurant), 55
City Cuisine (Feniger and Milliken), 55
clams:
    baked fish fillets with leeks, Yukon Gold potatoes and, 10–11
    littleneck, spaghettini with, *macchiato*, 111–12
    mushrooms stuffed with, 78
    steamed, with chorizo, 177–78
Clevenger, JoAnn, 238
coconut:
    pudding with lime, Nancy's, 139
    steamed bananas, 228
cold sesame noodles, 82–83
Colwin, Laurie, 244
confit, onion raisin, for couscous chez Edmond, 76
cookie(s):
    giant almond, 245–46
    nut, 228
Cooking of South-West France (Wolfert), 215
Cooking of the Eastern Mediterranean, The (Wolfert), 215
Cooking with Carlo, 122

Cooking with the Master Chefs, 55
corn:
  bread, chile, 138
  buckwheat waffles, green chile crab on, 79
  grilled, with lime and chiles, 91
  kernels with rice, 6–7
  lemon chicken black bean salad with, 232
  muffins, 225–26
Cornish hens, grilled, with blueberries and wild mushrooms, 146–48
Coronado cajeta, 88
Costner, Kevin, 152
Costner, Susan, 79
country dinner, menu ideas for a, 213
couscous:
  chez Edmond, 73–76
  salad, Provençal, 204
Couscous and Other Good Food from Morocco (Wolfert), 215
crab:
  feast, mix-and-match menu for a, 143
  green chile, on corn buckwheat waffles, 79
  soft-shell, with toasted hazelnuts, 143–45
crayfish, butternut squash soup with, 234–35
cream sauce, onion mustard, for grilled salmon steaks au poivre, 38–39
creamy lemon vinaigrette, for haricots verts on baby greens with shaved goat cheese, 196
crispies, Asian, 43
crispy:
  -bottomed basmati rice with lamb and tomato, 60–61
  potato galette, 148–49
croutons, chile, for Southwest Caesar salad, 47–48
crudités, fennel, with sea salt, 118
Cuban roast pork with lime, 183
cucumber soup, chilled, 37–38
Cuisine of California, The (Worthington), 222
Culinary Institute of America, 36
cumin:
  and mushrooms, sautéed oysters with, 158
  roasted, olives with paprika and, 117
Curries & Bugles (Brennan), 27
curry, curried:
  chicken, with noodles, Burmese, 132–34
  ginger muffins, 97–98
cushions, cheese, 44

Dale, Charles, 234
dark chocolate brownies, 24–25
David, Elizabeth, 229
decadence, Kahlúa chocolate, 51–52
dessert:
  apple crisp with dried fruit, 226–27
  apricot soufflé, 229
  baked peaches stuffed with almonds, chocolate and brandied raisins, 11
  baked pears with ginger preserves and biscotti, 173–74
  blueberries with cajeta, 155
  bright ideas for, 228–30
  caramelized pineapple with vanilla ice cream, 120
  chocolate hazelnut mousse, 161–62
  coconut steamed bananas, 228
  dark chocolate brownies, 24–25
  dressed-up strawberries, 228
  fig kebabs with raspberry cabernet sundaes, 192–93
  filled panettone, 229–30
  frozen mango, 86
  giant almond cookie, 245–46
  gingerbread, 243–44
  ginger ice cream with rhubarb sauce, 149–50
  gorgonzola with honey, 228
  instant exotic ices, 228
  Kahlúa chocolate decadence, 51–52
  lemon chess pie with fresh berries and raspberry sauce, 41–42
  Mexican cajeta sundaes, 91
  Midori melon sorbet and cookies, 33–34
  minimalist cheesecake, 212
  minted strawberry and champagne sorbet, 186
  modeste, 205–6
  nut cookies, 228
  orange pistachio cake, 62–63
  oranges with Grand Marnier, 24
  piña colada mousse, 168–69
  poached pears filled with apricots and hazelnuts on raspberry sauce, 125–27
  pomegranates with orange flower water, 229
  raspberry shortcake, 199
  raspberry tart, 17–18

Sicilian ricotta ice cream, 218–19
sliced oranges with almond brittle, 105–6
sliced peaches with fruited red wine, 98
soused peaches with mascarpone amaretti, 113
Stilton and apple Napoleons, 229
strawberries and oranges with red wine sauce, 76–77
sweet potato and fresh pineapple pudding, 7
Syrian nutmeg cake, 244–45
tropical fruit salsa sundaes, 91–92
vanilla ice cream with crumbled panforte, 68–69
Venetian lemon sorbet aperitif, 229
wine with cheese, 228
dill, lemon rice with, 192
dilled new potatoes and red Swiss chard, 39–40
Dim Sum (restaurant), 130
dim sum, mix-and-match menu for, 99
dipping sauce, soy-ginger, for chicken baked in a salt crust, 85
dressed-up strawberries, 228
dressing, onion, for ginger shrimp salad, 28–29
dried fruit:
    with prosciutto and chèvre, 78
    stuffed, 43–44
duck:
    smoked, with lavender and lime honey glaze, 197–98
    warm bird salad with wild mushrooms and crisp potatoes, 235–36

*E*damame, 56
eggplant vinaigrette, Provençal roasted, 153–54
endive boats, 43
Entertaining Light (Shulman), 171

*F*eniger, Susan, 53–63
fennel:
    baked lingcod with leeks, peppers and, 14–15
    crudités with sea salt, 118
    seeds, tuna and, 241–42
feta:
    basil leaves with, 44

spaghetti with fresh tomato, spinach, Kalamata olives and, 57–58
fettunta with caviar, 209
Field, Carol, 64–69
Field, John, 65
field greens salad with Vidalia onion vinaigrette, 40–41
fig kebabs with raspberry cabernet sundaes, 192–93
filled panettone, 229–30
fillet of white fish with mixed nuts and raisins, 217–18
fish and seafood:
    baked fish fillets with clams, leeks and Yukon gold potatoes, 10–11
    baked lingcod with leeks, fennel and peppers, 14–15
    baked salmon with spinach and leeks, 190–91
    couscous chez Edmond, 73–76
    fillet of white fish with mixed nuts and raisins, 217–18
    Fish but Not Fishy, mix-and-match menu, 206
    fish Shehadi with tahini and pecans, 102–3
    ginger shrimp salad, 28–29
    grilled salmon steaks au poivre, 38–39
    New Orleans shrimp rémoulade on fried green tomatoes, 238–40
    salmon with red cabbage sautéed with orange and capers, 124–25
    sautéed oysters with cumin and mushrooms, 158
    scallop seviche, 78
    seared swordfish with a tomato and Kalamata vinaigrette, 96–97
    shrimp Jamaica, 167–68
    shrimp sautéed in hoja santa sauce, 6
    soft-shell crabs with toasted hazelnuts, 143–45
    spaghettini with littleneck clams *macchiato*, 111–12
    spicy braised lobster, 112–13
    spicy fish steamed in lettuce parcels, 131–32
    steamed clams with chorizo, 177–78
    tuna and fennel seeds, 241–42
Foltzenlogel, Edmond, 70–77
Foltzenlogel, Henri, 71
fresh:
    creamy cheese with a sweet and spicy sauce, 5
    mint chutney, 236–37

Frog and the Redneck, The, 78
frozen mango, the, 86
fruit, fruited:
    dried, apple crisp with, 226–27
    dried stuffed, 43–44
    red wine, sliced peaches with, 98
    salsa sundaes, tropical, 91–92
frying, 219–20
fusilli with red and yellow tomato vinaigrette,
    172–73
Fusion Food Cookbook (Carpenter), 46

*G*alette, crispy potato, 148–49
garden tomato salad, 145–46
garlic:
    mayonnaise, 15
    white beans with oregano, tomato and, 211
    yellow split pea puree with basil and, 61–62
Germon, George, 107–113
giant almond cookie, 245–46
ginger:
    curried muffins, 97–98
    ice cream with rhubarb sauce, 149–50
    preserves and biscotti, baked pears with, 173–74
    shrimp salad, 28–29
    -soy dipping sauce, for chicken baked in a salt crust,
      85
gingerbread, 243–44
goat cheese:
    and ricotta with thyme, baked, 116–17
    shaved, haricots verts on baby greens with, 196
    see also chèvre
Good & Plenty to Go, 195
Gorgonzola with honey, 228
Grand Marnier, oranges with, 24
green beans, hot sesame with sweet red pepper, 32
green chile crab, on corn buckwheat waffles, 79
Green Gulch Farm, 115
green olives, marinated, 178
greens:
    baby, haricots verts with shaved goat cheese on,
      196
    bitter, penne, mozzarella and toasted walnuts with,
      67–68

    field, with Vidalia onion vinaigrette, 40–41
    mixed, with smoked salmon, 78
Greens (restaurant), 115
Greens Cookbook, The (Madison), 115
grilled:
    asparagus with toasted sesame seeds and pear toma-
      toes, 78
    Chinois rack of lamb, 48–49
    Cornish hens with blueberries and wild mushrooms,
      146–48
    corn with lime and chiles, 91
    lamb chops, 15–16
    potatoes with thyme, 160
    quail with sherry-shallot vinaigrette, 202–3
    salmon steaks au poivre, 38–39
    Yucatán chicken with caramelized onions, spicy,
      89–90
guacamole with tortilla chips, Mixtec, 89

*H*abañero salsa, roasted, 237–38
Hamlin, Suzanne, 80–86
haricots verts on baby greens with shaved goat cheese,
    196
Harry's Bar, 122
hazelnut(s):
    chocolate mousse, 161–62
    toasted, soft-shell crabs with, 143–45
Hearon, Reed, 87–92, 237
Hearon, Shelby, 88
herb salad with roasted walnuts, 119
hoja santa sauce, for sautéed shrimp, 6
honey:
    Gorgonzola with, 228
    lavender and lime glaze, for smoked duck, 197
Hoppin' John's Lowcountry Cooking (Taylor), 182
hors d'oeuvres:
    Asian crispies, 43
    basil leaves with feta, 44
    bean spreads, 43
    cheese cushions, 44
    chèvre truffles, 43
    crayfish tails, 44
    endive boats, 43
    lime and chile roasted pepitas and cashews, 59–60

oyster shooters, 44
pepper boats, 43
popcorn shrimp, 44
rosemary walnuts, 43
sesame green beans with sweet red pepper, 32
smoked trout sushi, 44
stuffed dried fruit, 43–44
see also appetizers and first courses; starters
Hot Wok (Carpenter), 46

*I*ce cream:
ginger, with rhubarb sauce, 149–50
Sicilian ricotta, 218–19
vanilla, with crumbled panforte, 68–69
iced yellow tomato soup, 79
ices, instant exotic, 228
Inn at Little Washington, The, 142
instant exotic ices, 228
International Herald Tribune, 201
Italian Cooking in the Grand Tradition (Bettoja), 20

*J*ohnnycakes, 166–67
Johnson & Wales College of Culinary Arts, 108
Josselin, Jean-Marie, 93–98

*K*ahlúa chocolate decadence, 51–52
Kalamata:
olives, spaghetti with feta, fresh tomato, spinach and, 57–58
and tomato vinaigrette, for seared swordfish, 96–97
kebabs, fig, with raspberry cabernet sundaes, 192–93
Kennedy, Diana, 100–106, 243
Killeen, Johanne, 107–113
kitchen picnic, mix-and-match menu for a, 69

*L*amb:
chops, grilled, 15–16

couscous chez Edmond, 73–76
rack of, grilled Chinois, 48–49
and tomato, crispy-bottomed basmati rice with, 60–61
Le Caprice, 71
L'Economie, 157
leeks:
baked fish fillets with clams, Yukon Gold potatoes and, 10–11
baked lingcod with fennel, peppers and, 14–15
baked salmon with spinach and, 190–91
lemon(s):
chess pie with fresh berries and raspberry sauce, 41–42
chicken black bean salad with corn, 232
mascarpone, veal carpaccio on crostini with, 123–24
rice with dill, 192
roast pork with grapes and, 22–23
sorbet aperitif, Venetian, 229
vinaigrette, creamy, for haricots verts on baby greens with shaved goat cheese, 196
zest, olives scented with orange and, 66–67
lentil soup with prosciutto, 233–34
Le Perroquet, 55
lettuce parcels, spicy fish steamed in, 131–32
L'Express, 201
Liberty Bar, 4
lime:
and chile roasted pepitas and cashews, 59–60
and cracked pepper mayonnaise, for steamed artichokes, 58–59
Cuban roast pork with, 183
grilled corn with chiles and, 91
and lavender honey glaze, for smoked duck, 197
Nancy's coconut pudding with, 139
lime oil, Boyajian, 32
lingcod, baked, with leeks, fennel and peppers, 14–15
lobster, spicy braised, 112–13
Lulu, 88
Lynch, Reinhardt, 142

*M*adison, Deborah, 114–120, 176
Ma Maison, 55

mango:
  the frozen, 86
  relish, 185
Marimba Products, 88
marinade, achiote, for spicy grilled Yucatán chicken
      with caramelized onions, 90
marinated green olives, 178
Martinique (restaurant), 157
mascarpone:
  amaretti, soused peaches with, 113
  lemon, veal carpaccio on crostini with, 123–24
mashed potatoes, buttermilk, 17
mayonnaise:
  aioli, 180
  garlic, 15
  lime and cracked pepper, for steamed artichokes,
      58–59
meat:
  beef stew with sun-dried tomatoes and butternut
      squash, 224–25
  beef tenderloin aiguillette, 159–60
  couscous chez Edmond, 73–76
  crispy-bottomed basmati rice with lamb and tomato,
      60–61
  Cuban roast pork with lime, 183
  grilled Chinois rack of lamb, 48–49
  grilled lamb chops, 15–16
  pork Avarua, 29–31
  roast pork with lemons and grapes, 22–23
  tenderloin with rosemary, garlic chips, and beet and
      potato puree, 92
  veal carpaccio on crostini with lemon mascarpone,
      123–24
Mediterranean Cooking (Wolfert), 215
Mediterranean Light (Shulman), 171
melon:
  with black olives, 79
  Midori sorbet and cookies, 33–34
Mesa Mexicana (Feniger and Milliken), 55
Mexican cajeta sundaes, 91
Middione, Carlo, 121, 241
Middione, Lisa, 122
Midori melon sorbet and cookies, 33–34
Milliken, Mary Sue, 53–63
minimalist cheesecake, 212
Min Khin, Christine, 130

Min Khin, Michael, 129–134
mint, minted:
  chutney, fresh, 236–37
  strawberry and champagne sorbet, 186
  yogurt, for crispy-bottomed basmati rice with lamb
      and tomato, 60–61
mix-and-match menus:
  An Antipasto Cocktail Buffet, 174
  A Crab Feast, 143
  Dim Sum, 99
  Fish but Not Fishy, 206
  A Kitchen Picnic, 69
  A Sicilian Feast—Almost, 18
  Simply Southwest, 52
  A Sultry-Evening Supper, 42
  Super Soup, 246
  A Taste of India, 34
  A Tex-Mex Do-It-Yourself Buffet, 140
  Upscale Steak and Potatoes, 92
mixed green salad with smoked salmon, 78
Mixtec guacamole with tortilla chips, 89
modeste, 205–6
mousse:
  chocolate hazelnut, 161–62
  piña colada, 168–69
  smoked trout, 223
mozzarella, penne with bitter greens, toasted walnuts
      and, 67–68
muffins:
  corn, 225–26
  curried ginger, 97–98
Murphy, Rosalea, 43
mushrooms:
  and cumin, sautéed oysters with, 158
  stuffed with clams, 78
  wild, grilled cornish hens with blueberries, 146–48
  wild, warm bird salad with crisp potatoes and,
      235–36
Mutrux, Michelle, 236

Nancy's coconut pudding with lime, 139
Napoleons, Stilton and apple, 229
New Orleans shrimp rémoulade on fried green tomatoes,
      238–40

New Southern Cook, The (Taylor), 182
New York Daily News, 81
New York Times, 81
noodle(s):
    cake, saffron, 118–19
    chicken curry with, Burmese, 132–34
    cold sesame, 82–83
Norma (restaurant), 164, 240
Norma at the Wharfhouse, 164, 240
Norma's on the Beach, 164
Nouvelle Jamaica, 164
nut cookies, 228
nutmeg cake, Syrian, 244–45

Oakes, Nancy, 135–39
O'Connell, Patrick, 141–150
olives:
    black, melon with, 79
    black, pulled parsley salad with pecorino and, 216
    Kalamata, spaghetti with feta, fresh tomato, spinach and, 57–58
    Kalamata and tomato vinaigrette, for seared swordfish, 96–97
    marinated green, 178
    with roasted cumin and paprika, 117
    scented with orange and lemon zest, 66–67
Oliveto, 13
onion(s):
    caramelized, for spicy grilled Yucatán chicken, 89–90
    dressing, for ginger shrimp salad, 28–29
    mustard cream sauce, for grilled salmon steaks au poivre, 38–39
    raisin confit, for couscous chez Edmond, 76
    roasted, 66
    vinaigrette, Vidalia, for field greens salad, 41
orange(s):
    and capers, salmon with red cabbage sautéed with, 124–25
    with Grand Marnier, 24
    pistachio cake, 62–63
    sliced, with almond brittle, 105–6
    and strawberries with red wine sauce, 76–77
    zest, olives scented with lemon and, 66–67

orange flower water, pomegranates with, 229
oregano, white beans with garlic, tomato and, 211
oyster(s):
    sautéed, with cumin and mushrooms, 158
    shooters, 44

Paella, vegetable, 179–80
Palladin, Jean-Louis, 78
panettone, filled, 229–30
panforte, vanilla ice cream with crumbled, 68–69
parsley salad, pulled, with black olives and pecorino, 216
pasta:
    bow tie with scallops, bacon and peas, 154
    cold sesame noodles, 82–83
    fusilli with red and yellow tomato vinaigrette, 172–73
    penne with bitter greens, mozzarella and toasted walnuts, 67–68
    saffron noodle cake, 118–19
    spaghetti *alla carrettiera*, 209–10
    spaghettini with littleneck clams *macchiato*, 111–12
    spaghetti with feta, fresh tomato, spinach and Kalamata olives, 57–58
    Toti's pennette with zucchini, 21–22
Paula Wolfert's World of Food (Wolfert), 215
peaches:
    sliced, with fruited red wine, 98
    soused, with mascarpone amaretti, 113
    stuffed with almonds, chocolate and brandied raisins, baked, 11
    white, in white wine, 109
pears:
    baked, with ginger preserves and biscotti, 173–74
    poached, filled with apricots and hazelnuts on raspberry sauce, 125–27
peas, bow tie pasta with scallops, bacon and, 154
pecans and tahini, fish Shehadi with, 102–3
pecorino, pulled parsley salad with black olives and, 216
pennette with zucchini, Toti's, 21–22
penne with bitter greens, mozzarella and toasted walnuts, 67–68
pepitas and cashews, lime and chile roasted, 59–60
pepper boats, 43

perfect Chinese rice, 85
Pickapeppa chicken, 240–41
pie:
    lemon chess, with fresh berries and raspberry sauce,
        41–42
    Southwest turkey and sausage, 137–38
pilaf:
    bulgur, with cashews and golden raisins, 32–33
    Thai rice, 50–51
piña colada mousse, 168–69
pineapple:
    caramelized, with vanilla ice cream, 120
    and sweet potato pudding, fresh, 7
Pink Adobe Cookbook, The (Murphy), 43
pinzimonio, 10
pistachio orange cake, 62–63
poached pears filled with apricots and hazelnuts on
    raspberry sauce, 125–27
pomegranates with orange flower water, 229
pork:
    Avarua, 29–31
    with lime, Cuban roast, 183
    roast with lemons and grapes, 22–23
Porro, Carlos, 182
potatoes:
    baked in sea salt, 242–43
    and beet puree, 92
    buttermilk mashed, 17
    crisp, warm bird salad with wild mushrooms and,
        235–36
    dilled new, and red Swiss chard, 39–40
    galette, crispy, 148–49
    red creamer, with anchovies, 110
    with thyme, grilled, 160
    Yukon Gold, baked fish fillets with clams, leeks and,
        10–11
poultry:
    baked chicken in a salt crust, 83–84
    Burmese chicken curry with noodles, 132–34
    grilled Cornish hens with blueberries and wild
        mushrooms, 146–48
    Pickapeppa chicken, 240–41
    Pick Up a Chicken, 128
    smoked duck with lavender and lime honey glaze,
        197–98
    Southwest turkey and sausage pie, 137–38

spiced grilled Yucatán chicken with caramelized
    onions, 89–90
tonno di pollo, 210–11
warm bird salad with wild mushrooms and crisp
    potatoes, 235–36
prosciutto:
    with dried fruit and chèvre, 78
    lentil soup with, 233–34
Provençal:
    couscous salad, 204
    roasted eggplant vinaigrette, 153–54
Provençal Light (Shulman), 171
Puck, Wolfgang, 55
pudding:
    Nancy's coconut, with lime, 139
    sweet potatoes and fresh pineapple, 7
pulled parsley salad with black olives and pecorino,
    216
puree:
    beet and potato, 92
    yellow split pea, with garlic and basil, 61–62

Quail, grilled, with sherry-shallot vinaigrette, 202–3

Rack of lamb, grilled Chinois, 48–49
raisin(s):
    golden, bulgur pilaf with cashews and, 32–33
    onion confit, for couscous chez Edmond, 76
raspberry:
    cabernet sundaes, with fig kebabs, 192–93
    sauce, for lemon chess pie, 41–42
    shortcake, 199
    tart, 17–18
red cabbage:
    salmon sautéed with orange and capers with,
        124–25
    and sprouts with sesame dressing, 56–57
red creamer potatoes with anchovies, 110
red pea bisque flambé, 165–66
red pepper:
    soup, sweet, 78
    sweet, hot sesame green beans with, 32

and tomato soup with basil and shrimp, chilled, 189–90
red Swiss chard and dilled new potatoes, 39–40
red wine:
    fruited, sliced peaches with, 98
    pairing with food, 247–49
    sauce for strawberries and oranges, 76–77
relish, mango, 185
rémoulade, New Orleans shrimp, on fried green tomatoes, 238–40
Renaissance, 234
Rhode Island School of Design, 108
rhubarb sauce for ginger ice cream, 148–50
rice:
    black beans and, 184
    with corn kernels, 6–7
    crispy-bottomed basmati, with lamb and tomato, 60–61
    with dill, lemon, 192
    fried, with nutmeg, 218
    perfect Chinese, 85
    pilaf, Thai, 50–51
Richard, Michel, 233
ricotta:
    and goat cheese with thyme, baked, 116–17
    ice cream, Sicilian, 218–19
    minimalist cheesecake, 212
roast, roasted:
    eggplant vinaigrette, Provençal, 153–54
    habañero salsa, 237–38
    onions, 66
    pork with lemons and grapes, 22–23
    pork with lime, Cuban, 183
Roberts, Michael, 151–55
romaine lettuce with sherry vinaigrette, mint and garlic croustades, 72
rosemary walnuts, 43

Saffron noodle cake, 118–19
salad:
    Asian watercress, 104
    field greens, with Vidalia onion vinaigrette, 40–41
    garden tomato, 145–46
    ginger shrimp, 28–29

haricots verts on baby greens with shaved goat cheese, 196
herb, with roasted walnuts, 119
lemon chicken black bean, with corn, 232
mixed green, with smoked salmon, 78
Provençal couscous, 204
pulled parsley, with black olives and pecorino, 216
romaine lettuce with sherry vinaigrette, mint and garlic croustades, 72–73
soft lettuce, with balsamic vinaigrette, 161
Southwest Caesar, with chile croutons, 47–48
warm bird, with wild mushrooms and crisp potatoes, 235–36
salmon:
    baked, with spinach and leeks, 190–91
    with red cabbage, sautéed with orange and capers, 124–25
    smoked, mixed green salad with, 78
    steaks au poivre, grilled, 38–39
salsa:
    roasted habañero, 237–38
    tropical fruit, for sundaes, 91–92
salt:
    crust, chicken baked in a, 83–84
    sea, potatoes baked in, 242–43
Sandison, Teri, 46
San Domenico, 9
Sandot, Hubert, 156–62
sandwiches:
    Catalan anchovy, 178
    Santa Fe anchovy, 178
Santa Fe anchovy sandwiches, 178
sauces and dressings:
    aioli, 180
    creamy lemon vinaigrette, for haricots verts on baby greens with shaved goat cheese, 196
    garlic mayonnaise, 15
    hoja santa, for sautéed shrimp, 6
    lemon vinaigrette dressing for Southwest Caesar salad with chile croutons, 47–48
    lime and cracked pepper mayonnaise, for steamed artichokes, 58–59
    minted yogurt, for crispy-bottomed basmati rice with lamb and tomato, 60–61
    onion dressing, for ginger shrimp salad, 28–29

sauces and dressings (*cont.*)
  onion mustard cream, for grilled salmon steaks au
    poivre, 38–39
  raspberry, for lemon chess pie, 41–42
  red wine, for strawberries and oranges, 76–77
  rhubarb, for ginger ice cream, 148–50
  sesame dressing, for red cabbage and sprouts, 57
  sherry-shallot vinaigrette, for grilled quail, 202–3
  sherry vinaigrette, for romaine lettuce with mint and
    garlic croustades, 72–73
  soy-ginger dipping, for chicken baked in a salt crust,
    85
  tomato and Kalamata vinaigrette, for seared sword-
    fish, 96–97
  Vidalia onion vinaigrette, for field greens salad, 41
sausage:
  brochettes, for couscous chez Edmond, 73–76
  lemon chicken black bean salad with corn, 232
  steamed clams with chorizo, 177–78
  and turkey pie, Southwest, 137–38
sautéed:
  oysters with cumin and mushrooms, 158
  spinach with chiles, 103–4
Savory Way, The (Madison), 115
scallop(s):
  bow tie pasta with bacon, peas and, 154
  seviche, 78
Schweitzer, Josh, 56
seared swordfish with a tomato and Kalamata vinai-
    grette, 96–97
sea salt, potatoes baked in, 242–43
Secret Ingredients (Roberts), 152
sesame:
  green beans with sweet red pepper, hot, 32
  noodles, cold, 82–83
  seeds, toasted, grilled asparagus with pear tomatoes
    and, 78
  soba noodles with tempura vegetables, 95–96
seviche, scallop, 78
Shehadi, Norma, 102
sherry:
  -shallot vinaigrette, for grilled quail, 202–3
  vinaigrette for romaine lettuce with mint and garlic
    croustades, 72–73
Shirley, Norma, 163–69, 240
shooters, oyster, 44

shortcake, raspberry, 199
shrimp:
  chilled tomato and red pepper soup with basil and,
    189–90
  Jamaica, 167–68
  rémoulade on fried green tomatoes, New Orleans,
    238–40
  salad, ginger, 28–29
  sautéed in a hoja santa sauce, 6
  vodka, 79
Shulman, Martha Rose, 170–74
Sicilian:
  feast, almost, mix-and-match menu for a, 81
  ricotta ice cream, 218–19
side dishes:
  black beans and rice, 184
  bulgur pilaf with cashews and golden raisins, 32–33
  buttermilk mashed potatoes, 17
  fried rice with nutmeg, 218
  hot sesame green beans with sweet red pepper, 32
  lemon rice with dill, 192
  potatoes baked in sea salt, 242–43
  red creamer potatoes with anchovies, 110
  red Swiss chard and dilled new potatoes, 39–40
  rice with corn kernels, 6–7
  saffron noodle cake, 118–19
  slow-cooked tomatoes, 16
  spinach sautéed with chiles, 103–4
  steamed artichokes with lime and cracked pepper
    mayonnaise, 58–59
  Thai rice pilaf, 50–51
  white beans with garlic, oregano and tomato, 211
  yellow split pea puree with garlic and basil, 61–62
Silver Palate, the, 195
Simply Southwest, mix-and-match menu, 52
slow-cooked tomatoes, 16
smoked:
  duck with lavender and lime honey glaze, 197–98
  salmon, mixed green salad with, 78
  trout, 79
  trout mousse, 223
  trout sushi, 44
Sneed, Jimmy, 78
soba noodles with tempura vegetables, sesame, 95–96
soft lettuce salad with balsamic vinaigrette, 161
soft-shell crabs with toasted hazelnuts, 143–45

sorbet:
    Midori melon, and cookies, 33–34
    minted strawberry and champagne, 186
    Venetian lemon aperitif, 229
soufflé, apricot, 229
soup:
    butternut squash, with crayfish, 234–35
    chilled cucumber, 37–38
    chilled tomato and red pepper, with basil and shrimp, 189–90
    iced yellow tomato, 79
    lentil, with prosciutto, 233–34
    red pea bisque flambé, 165–66
    sweet red pepper, 78
soused peaches with mascarpone amaretti, 113
Southern Italian Cooking (Bettoja), 20
Southwest:
    Caesar salad with chile croutons, 47–48
    turkey and sausage pie, 137–38
soy-ginger dipping sauce, for chicken baked in a salt crust, 85
spaghetti:
    alla carrettiera, 209–10
    with feta, fresh tomato, spinach and Kalamata olives, 57–58
spaghettini with littleneck clams *macchiato*, 111
Spiaggia, 9
spicy:
    braised lobster, 112–13
    fish steamed in lettuce parcels, 131–32
    grilled Yucatán chicken with caramelized onions, 89–90
spinach:
    baked salmon with leeks and, 190–91
    flat-leaf, 58
    sautéed with chiles, 103–4
    spaghetti with feta, fresh tomato, Kalamata olives and, 57–58
split pea puree with garlic and basil, yellow, 61–62
spread, bean, 43
sprouts and red cabbage with sesame dressing, 56–57
starters:
    green chile crab on corn buckwheat waffles, 79
    grilled asparagus with toasted sesame seeds and pear tomatoes, 78
    iced yellow tomato soup, 79
    melon with black olives, 79
    mixed green salad with smoked salmon, 78
    mushrooms stuffed with clams, 78
    prosciutto with dried fruit and chèvre, 78
    scallop seviche, 78
    smoked trout, 79
    stuffed avocado, 79
    sweet red pepper soup, 78
    vodka shrimp, 79
    see also appetizers and first courses; hors d'oeuvres
steamed:
    artichokes with lime and cracked pepper mayonnaise, 58–59
    clams with chorizo, 177–78
    coconut bananas, 228
stew, beef, with sun-dried tomatoes and butternut squash, 224–25
Stilton and apple Napoleons, 229
stir-fried, broccoli, 85–86
strawberry(ies):
    and champagne sorbet, minted, 186
    dressed-up, 228
    and oranges with red wine sauce, 76–77
stuffed:
    avocado, 79
    baked peaches with almonds, chocolate and brandied raisins, 11
    dried fruit, 43–44
Sultry-Evening Supper, mix-and-match menu for a, 42
sundae(s):
    Mexican cajeta, 91
    raspberry cabernet, with fig kebabs, 192–93
    tropical fruit salsa, 91–92
Super Soup, mix-and-match menu for, 246
sushi, smoked trout, 44
sweet potato and fresh pineapple pudding, 7
Swiss chard and dilled new potatoes, red, 39–40
swordfish, seared, with a tomato and Kalamata vinaigrette, 96–97
Syrian nutmeg cake, 244–45

Tahini and pecans, fish Shehadi with, 102–3
Tanis, David, 175–80
tapas, 177–79

tart, raspberry, 17–18
Taste of Hawaii, A (Josselin), 94
Taste of India, mix-and-match menu for a, 34
Taylor, John, 181–86
tempura vegetables, sesame soba noodles with, 95–96
tenderloin:
    of beef aiguillette, 159–60
    with rosemary, garlic chips, and beet and potato puree, 92
Tex-Mex Do-It-Yourself Buffet, mix-and-match menu for a, 140
Thai rice pilaf, 50–51
thyme, grilled potatoes with, 160
tomato(es):
    fresh, spaghetti with feta, spinach, Kalamata olives and, 57–58
    fried green, New Orleans shrimp rémoulade on, 238–40
    and Kalamata vinaigrette, for seared swordfish, 96–97
    and lamb, crispy-bottomed basmati rice with, 60–61
    pear, grilled asparagus with toasted sesame seeds and, 78
    and red pepper soup with basil and shrimp, chilled, 189–90
    salad, garden, 145–46
    slow-cooked, 16
    soup, iced yellow, 79
    sun-dried, beef stew with butternut squash and, 224–25
    vinaigrette, red and yellow fusilli with, 172–73
    white beans with garlic, oregano and, 211
Toti's pennette with zucchini, 21–22
Troisgros, Jean, 188
tropical fruit salsa sundaes, 91–92
trout, smoked, 79
truffles, chèvre, 43
Trumps, 152
tuna and fennel seeds, 241–42
turkey and sausage pie, Southwest, 137–38
Twin Palms, 152

Umeshu, 33
Upperline, 238

Upscale Steak and Potatoes, mix-and-match menu for, 92

*Vanilla ice cream with crumbled panforte, 68–69
veal carpaccio on crostini with lemon mascarpone, 123–24
vegetable(s):
    in broth, for couscous chez Edmond, 74–75
    paella, 179–80
    tempura, sesame soba noodles with, 95–96
Vegetarian Feast, The (Shulman), 171
Venetian lemon sorbet aperitif, 229
Vergé, Roger, 188
Vidalia (restaurant), 36
Vidalia onion vinaigrette, for field greens salad, 41
vinaigrette:
    balsamic, for soft lettuce salad, 161
    creamy lemon, for haricots verts on baby greens with shaved goat cheese, 196
    red and yellow tomato, fusilli with, 172–73
    sherry, for romaine lettuce with mint and garlic croustades, 72–73
    sherry-shallot, for grilled quail, 202–3
    tomato and Kalamata, for seared swordfish, 96–97
Vivande Porta Via, 122
Vivande Ristorante, 122
vodka shrimp, 79

*Waffles, corn buckwheat, green chile crab on, 79
walnuts:
    roasted, herb salad with, 119
    rosemary, 43
    toasted, penne with bitter greens, mozzarella and, 67–68
Wappo Bar and Bistro, 236
warm bird salad with wild mushrooms and crisp potatoes, 235–36
watercress salad, Asian, 104
Weimer, Jan, 187–93
Weinberg, Eileen, 194–99

Wells, Patricia, 200–206
Wells, Walter, 201
white beans with garlic, oregano and tomato, 211
white peaches in white wine, 109
white wine, white peaches in, 109
Willinger, Faith Heller, 207–12
wines, simple, for simple meals, 247–49
Wolfert, Paula, 214–19, 243

Word of Mouth, 195
Worthington, Diane Rossen, 221–27

Yellow split pea puree with garlic and basil, 61–62
yogurt, minted, for crispy-bottomed basmati rice with
    lamb and tomatoes, 60–61

FRANCES MCCULLOUGH is a well-known editor who specializes in cookbooks and literary works. She was the editor of *Sylvia Plath's Journals* and *Holiday Home Cooking,* an anthology of recipes from Book-of-the-Month Club members. She was the first recipient of the Roger Klein Award for Creative Editing.

BARBARA WITT is a food writer and restaurant consultant specializing in concepts, interiors, and recipe and menu development. She is well known in Washington, D.C., and Baltimore as the former owner and operator of the nationally acclaimed Big Cheese restaurants.

THE authors' first book, *Great Food Without Fuss,* a collection of simple but extraordinary recipes from famous cooks, won a James Beard award.